Rebuilding Relationships in Recovery

How to Connect with Family and Close Friends After Active Alcoholism and Addiction

Janice V. Johnson Dowd, LMSW

Foreword by Emily Dickinson, MEd, LPC

North Atlantic Books
Huichin, unceded Ohlone land
Berkeley, California

Published by
North Atlantic Books
Huichin, unceded Ohlone land
Berkeley, California

Cover art © Vasyl Yurlov via Shutterstock
Cover design by Jason Arias
Book design by Happenstance Type-O-Rama

Printed in the United States of America

Rebuilding Relationships in Recovery: How to Connect with Family and Close Friends After Active Alcoholism and Addiction is sponsored and published by North Atlantic Books, an educational nonprofit based in the unceded Ohlone land Huichin (Berkeley, CA) that collaborates with partners to develop cross-cultural perspectives; nurture holistic views of art, science, the humanities, and healing; and seed personal and global transformation by publishing work on the relationship of body, spirit, and nature.

North Atlantic Books's publications are distributed to the US trade and internationally by Penguin Random House Publisher Services. For further information, visit our website at www.northatlanticbooks.com.

DISCLAIMER: The following information is intended for general information purposes only. Any application of the material set forth in the following pages is at the reader's discretion and is their sole responsibility. This book does not intend to be diagnostic in any way and is not a substitute for a thorough clinical assessment and professional treatment. If you are at medical risk of withdrawal or in a serious psychiatric emergency, you are encouraged to present for medical attention immediately.

Library of Congress Cataloging-in-Publication Data

Names: Dowd, Janice Johnson, author.
Title: Rebuilding relationships in recovery : how to connect with family
   and close friends after active alcoholism and addiction / Janice Johnson Dowd.
Description: Berkeley, California : North Atlantic Books, [2025] | Includes
   bibliographical references and index. | Summary: "A guide for recovering
   addicts and alcoholics on how to heal and enhance their relationships
   after active addiction and balance the demands of sobriety with the need
   for family connection"-- Provided by publisher.
Identifiers: LCCN 2024026096 (print) | LCCN 2024026097 (ebook) | ISBN
   9798889841852 (trade paperback) | ISBN 9798889841869 (ebook)
Subjects: LCSH: Alcoholics--Family relationships. | Recovering
   alcoholics--Family relationships. | Addicts--Family relationships. |
   Recovering addicts--Family relationships.
Classification: LCC HV5132 .D69 2025 (print) | LCC HV5132 (ebook) | DDC
   362.29/13--dc23/eng/20240726
LC record available at https://lccn.loc.gov/2024026096
LC ebook record available at https://lccn.loc.gov/2024026097

1 2 3 4 5 6 7 8 9 KPC 30 29 28 27 26 25

I dedicate this book to my children—
Dennis, Katie, Matthew, and Michael—
who gave me the ultimate gift for a recovering parent:
their love and forgiveness. Being your mother
has enabled me to give and experience
unconditional love and has encouraged me to
strive to be the best version of myself.

CONTENTS

FOREWORD

I met Janice in May of 2013 when she was referred to me for counseling. At the time, she was transitioning into a sober-living facility following twelve weeks of intensive inpatient treatment for her alcoholism. Janice said that she was "sick and tired" of hurting, and of hurting those she most loved. She came to me eager to learn how to live a life that heals rather than hurts both herself and the people who are important to her. Janice's tendency is to look at both sides of a subject and ask questions, but this can lead to overthinking and sometimes made her feel overwhelmed and panicked. But as she continued her journey, the results of working the twelve steps became increasingly evident in her. Her recovery was no longer based in her thinking alone; she realized that group work presented a powerful solution to loneliness and isolation and provided a safe space to discuss challenges and celebrate successes. As her insight grew in recovery, her contributions increased. She was unknowingly transitioning from the needy to the needed. The wisdom she shares in this book can only come from having lived the problem and struggled through to a solution.

Throughout the book, Janice speaks candidly of her own fears, challenges, and grief while working to restore the broken relationships in her family. She also brings professional competence as evidenced by her credentials and work experience. Janice earned her master of science in social work from the University of Texas at Austin in 1985, and her master's thesis focused on the effects of posttraumatic stress syndrome and alcoholism in Vietnam War veterans. She worked for ten years in the drug and alcohol field, and she later added medical social work to her resume. An active member of Alcoholics Anonymous, she has shared her story in AA meetings and conferences and is a sought-after speaker on related podcasts. Eleven years sober, she still participates in biweekly group therapy, where she maintains her focus on looking at herself and striving for personal growth. She has a healthy understanding of who she is and an earnest desire to become all she can be.

This book is a deep dive for the recovering alcoholic whose goal is not only to stay sober but also to grow and heal. Steps four through seven of the twelve steps of Alcoholics Anonymous are the soul-searching steps; they challenge the alcoholic to look at how their addiction has affected themselves as well as others and to honestly examine their behavior, intent, and character. After owning the character defects they find in themselves, the alcoholic will confirm their commitment to removing those defects with the help of their higher power. Steps eight and nine introduce the amends process, where the alcoholic will ask those they've injured how they can right the wrong and if there are areas of injury that haven't been addressed. Often the response is "just stay sober." That is known as a "living amends" and requires committed and sustained action focused on improving and healing relationships.

This book provides instructional information, current research, and specific suggestions that can help the reader navigate the amends process, especially within family relationships. Janice's suggestions are direct and easy to understand, although she emphasizes that the work is difficult, and she warns against half measures. She realistically asserts that there may be too much damage for some relationships to be restored and gives recommendations on how to proceed in these cases. Additionally, she provides excellent guidelines for assessing the alcoholic's readiness and motivation as well as the family's readiness, and she outlines techniques for identifying and addressing the true problems. Chapter 5 includes an extensive list of tools with instructions on how to use them successfully, and chapter 7 discusses how to use outside resources and determine which ones are best for a particular situation.

Several times while reading this book, I realized Janice was the teacher and I was the student. I wholeheartedly recommend *Rebuilding Relationships in Recovery* to those who are resolved to undertake the hard work of healing family relationships and who want to avail themselves of some practical, proven, and proactive processes for turning a daunting problem into a life-changing solution.

—EMILY DICKINSON, MEd, LPC

Emily Dickinson, MEd, LPC, has over forty years of experience in community, residential, and private practice settings. Her primary focus has been in addictions, including family of origin, trauma, and grief. She initially worked with adolescents and their families, and she currently works with clients ranging in age from fifteen to ninety-one.

ACKNOWLEDGMENTS

This book would not have been possible if I had not had the unwavering support and encouragement of Barbara Koerschner Hagey, Katie Vanorden de Assis, Emily Dickinson, and Becky Robillard Lazzari.

I will be forever grateful to Becky and Barbara, to whom I first entrusted my dream of writing a book. Katie has been a friend since my first day at college, although it seems more like we have shared many lifetimes. She and Emily have provided me with support and guidance in my personal journey of addressing my wounds, healing my inner child, and gaining understanding and acceptance of who I was and who I am now.

I am also deeply grateful to my sponsors—Gail Rosenbloom, Jana Capello, and Tippi H.—who guided me through the twelve steps, told me what I needed to hear rather than what I wanted to hear, and instilled in me hope that I could obtain and maintain my sobriety.

I owe the foundation of my sobriety to the warrior women and staff of Cottages One and Two, who provided me with the support and tough love that I needed in the beginning of my journey.

Thanks to Lisa Hagen, my literary agent, who took a leap of faith and accepted me as a client. Our connection was literally birthed in my dreams, and I am deeply appreciative of her wisdom, guidance, and friendship.

My sincere appreciation to all of the staff at North Atlantic Books, but especially to Jasmine Respess (acquisitions editor) and Brent Winter (copy editor), who brought clarity and beauty to my writing, and Janelle Ludowise (senior production editor), who provided guidance and much patience with my limited technical skills.

I would be remiss if I didn't mention my two brothers, Gary and Larry Johnson, and my parents, Doris and Dwight Johnson, all of whom wanted nothing but the best for myself and our family.

Lastly, I'd like to express my gratitude to Gay Sava and Jeanette Chase, two women who were like lighthouses to me in my teenage years, providing light and guidance through stormy waters.

1

Introduction:
I'm Sober, but My Family
Is Destroyed. Now What?

This chapter title perfectly reflects what my family life felt like in early sobriety and what it continued to be like for a long time—*when it didn't have to be that way*. I had no "family life" in early sobriety. I was physically and emotionally removed from all my family and friends. Some of this was by circumstance; my treatment center was located two hundred miles away from my home. But some of it was self-imposed isolation fueled by my inept and ineffective attempts to reach out to my family. I had entered a treatment facility thinking I would be an inpatient for twenty-eight days. However, a twenty-eight-day treatment program turned into twelve weeks of inpatient care. This was followed by a four-month stay at a halfway house and a yearlong commitment to a "sober living home." I was physically distant from family because of the rules and restrictions required by the treatment environments. In addition, I was emotionally distant from them because of my shame, fear of rejection, and unrealistic expectations.

One of the things I had lost in my active addiction and wanted more than anything was love, support, and forgiveness from my immediate family, especially my children. I wanted them to be a part of my sobriety. Unfortunately, I foolishly thought I would win back their love and forgiveness if I just *stayed sober.* I had to accept that you cannot charm, force, or manipulate your family members to forgive you.

Everyone acknowledges that having a supportive family in recovery, whether you're recovering from alcohol, drugs, or mental illness, is essential. Most rehab facilities offer programs for families as well. In addition, twelve-step groups like Al-Anon and Nar-Anon are available to family members for their support and growth. However, specific programs and instruction on how and what the addict or alcoholic can do to nurture and heal family relationships are very limited.

When I got sober, I could not find many resources on how to rebuild relationships with my children and family. Much of what I found was superficial; it only discussed things like "how to get your family member into treatment," "how to practice tough love," or "how to understand the disease concept of addiction." There was no step-by-step guide to navigate the difficult journey ahead of me. And because I was full of fear and reluctant to ask for help, I made many mistakes in my relationships with the ones I loved the most. My intentions were good, and I thought I was making sincere efforts; but I often did more to create damage in my familial relationships than to foster healing.

On top of that, an alcoholic fog still clouded my judgment and thinking for the first year of my sobriety. There is an increasing amount of literature about the damage addiction does to the brain and the length of time it takes for the brain to heal. Depending on the type and length of addiction, this healing can take weeks, months, and even years. Some effects may even be permanent. For myself, it was a long time before the effects of my alcohol use stopped interfering with my decision-making and my ability to think conceptually. As a result, I was quick to react, slow to think, and slow to consider the consequences of my actions and words. I often failed to seek the advice and wisdom of my sponsor or therapist before acting. Thus, I often made poor choices in early recovery that continued to hurt my relationships with family and friends.

Today, most of my relationships are better than I could have ever hoped—but not without a lot of struggle, and a lot of learning, along the way. Now I want to share the knowledge I've gained with you. This book comes from experience, strength, and hope. It is written for anyone struggling to regain the love, respect, and trust of their friends and family members while in recovery. The book will address not only repairing the damage you've done during active alcoholism, addiction, or mental illness, but also *how to avoid creating more damage in recovery*. In writing this book I've expanded upon my training as a social worker, reviewed the latest research and information on addiction and recovery, and consulted with other addiction professionals. I'll also share my experiences, what I know from my work with twelve-step programs and therapy, the knowledge I've gained from my sponsors and peers in the program, and the feedback I've received from my children, family, and friends. I will tell you about the many things I did wrong in early sobriety, the pain I caused, and the regrets I have in hopes that you will not repeat the same mistakes I made.

My Story in Brief

I was raised in a home with an alcoholic father. As a young woman, I swore that I would never become an alcoholic or addict; I would never do to my children what had been done to me. I thought that by becoming a social worker, going to therapy, and working on myself, I (on my own) could break the cycle of family dysfunction. My children were aged thirteen, fifteen, twenty, and twenty-one when I entered treatment. I had been married for twenty-four years. I had caused my family much pain and suffering during my active addiction, and I was ashamed that I had allowed drinking to take hold of my life. I hoped my family's love and support would help me recover. However, the rehab program I entered stressed that I had to prioritize learning to be and stay sober. Their emphasis was on the alcoholic/addict. Family programs were offered to the families, but patients were not involved in those programs. My family had very little involvement in my treatment. (Note that some rehab programs do include the patients in family programs, and many offer preliminary family therapy. Regardless, these programs are just an initial start. Rebuilding relationships takes time and effort.)

I knew I would have to apologize to my family and friends and make up for what I had done. But honestly, I had many naive beliefs about how much damage I had created during my active addiction. I didn't recognize how aware they had been of my drinking, and I thought I had hidden some of the worst parts of my drinking from them. By the time I finished treatment, I had examined some of this damage as part of my first step, but I still didn't understand the depth and extent of the harm I had inflicted upon my loved ones. I didn't realize what type of effort I would have to expend in order for them to want to spend time with me, much less to trust me with their feelings. I was willing to admit that I was powerless over alcohol and that my life had become unmanageable; but I still didn't see how my unmanageability had affected those around me.

Surviving Early Sobriety Is Hard Enough

Early recovery is a confusing and challenging time for most of us. We are learning to manage life without our primary coping mechanism: substances. We are told to change people, places, and things that trigger our drinking or using. We are encouraged to attend ninety meetings in ninety days, read and study our literature, pray and meditate, help others, and do service work. We are encouraged to put our recovery above all else. Some of us are told that no child's sporting event, family event, holiday celebration, or social event should be put before our meetings and recovery activities. These practices may help us stay sober, but they can distance us from family and friends. I embraced working the program, but in doing so, I allowed my family life to be eclipsed by my efforts to stay sober. I did not explain to my family why these new behaviors took time away from them. While I was doing everything I could to stay sober, I unintentionally alienated myself from my children and family. My actions and lack of involvement in their daily lives continued to hurt them.

As I was adding up time, earning chips, making new friendships, and building confidence in my sobriety, my family still felt distanced from me. I didn't understand why they couldn't see all the positive changes I was making. I didn't know why they didn't trust me or my sobriety. I had forgotten about all the promises I had broken in the past. I had forgotten all the times I said I was never going to drink again. I expected them to believe that things would be different this time.

When I spoke, I used a lot of recovery jargon that sounded more like a cliché than a sincere effort to stay sober. I sometimes took advice too literally and used "the program" (meaning my new healthy and constructive behaviors) to excuse or diminish certain other past or present behaviors. I expected them to understand the program, when they couldn't. I forgot that I had had twelve weeks of intensive treatment, and they were only having a few hours of therapy weekly. I forgot that, as a *family*, we were dysfunctional. Each of us had our own issues that needed to be addressed, and I didn't give them the same grace and forgiveness for their issues that I expected them to extend to me. For example, I expected them to understand why I didn't want to go to Uncle Donald's Sunday brunch, where there would be lots of drinking and alcohol; but I didn't understand why they didn't want to come with me to see me receive my chip for spending a certain length of time in sobriety. I didn't understand that the changes I was making were difficult and stressful for them. I didn't recognize that they saw these new behaviors—living in a halfway house, going to daily meetings, making long phone calls to sponsors and peers in the program, making new friends—as more of the same old confusing and unpredictable behaviors I had exhibited in active addiction. From their point of view, I was as distant and selfish as I had ever been, and I mistakenly did not take the time to explain or involve them in these new activities.

Priorities and Balance

Before moving further into this book, I must emphasize the need for you to establish priorities and maintain a healthy recovery plan. Your recovery and your sobriety must be your *first* priority. You cannot authentically improve your relationships unless you're sober. You may think, "No, I have to apologize right away, make up for lost time, attend every school event and work party I've missed." But there is a danger in this approach. First you must establish a solid foundation of recovery—one that can withstand the ups and downs of everyday life and the occasional crisis. Some family members will misinterpret your new behaviors and commitment to sobriety; they may see it as behavior akin to what you've always done: putting yourself and whatever interests you ahead of everybody else.

Spiritual, Physical, Emotional, Social, and Family Needs

You must have a *balanced* recovery plan that includes attention to your spiritual, physical, emotional, and social needs. Improving one's family relationships is essential to this balanced recovery plan. All of this requires devoting time and paying attention to:

- Proper diet and exercise
- Prayer or meditation

- Rest and sleep
- Social experiences, time for play, and fun
- "Working the program": service work, helping others, healing, rebuilding your life, making amends, and "cleaning up the wreckage of your past"
- Relapse prevention by identifying triggers

Family issues are often huge triggers and threats to your sobriety. They are often delicate and usually emotionally charged. Therefore, it only makes sense to begin to address these issues early in your sobriety. However, these initial efforts will need to be simple and uncomplicated. You may be tempted to procrastinate or delay this work for a better time; I urge you to begin immediately, but with the smallest of steps.

Responsibilties to Your Family

First, you must ensure your family has food, shelter, and safety. Some of us behaved destructively in our active addiction. We screamed, threatened, or worse, we were abusive. In these cases, progress cannot be made until the environment you share with your family is safe. This may mean supervised visits or family therapy, among other things. You cannot make progress in a relationship where someone is afraid of you. (We'll discuss this topic further in a later chapter.) The next priority is to let your family members know that they are on your mind and that you care about them and their feelings. Help them begin to understand that although these new recovery behaviors may appear to be entirely self-serving, they're also meant for the family's benefit. You may have to tell them you don't know how to be there for them or communicate effectively, but you are willing to learn. For instance, when was the last time you told your child or a family member that you love them? That they are good enough? That you accept them the way they are?

First Step: Information Is Power

In my experience, I have found that gathering information and being well-informed is an excellent starting point for defining your problems and developing a plan for resolving them. This also serves as an essential tool for reducing fear, doubt, and worry. When my mother was diagnosed with lung cancer in 2000, I made it my mission to gather as much information as possible about her type of cancer, learn about both conventional and unconventional treatments, and find out where the best care was available. I found that the more information we had, the better able we were to cope with all aspects of her battle with cancer. As a result, we made better decisions and had less fear. Along similar lines, this book will serve as a jumping-off point for you. I will provide a small amount of information about family dynamics, dysfunctional families, optional treatment, and available resources. Since much of my personal recovery is based on the practices and principles of Alcoholics Anonymous (AA), Adult Children of Alcoholics, and Al-Anon, I will provide a basic understanding of twelve-step recovery programs and how they are beneficial. I am going to warn you of some of the obstacles you might encounter, common mistakes you might make, and myths to avoid. I want to give you tools as well as hope and encouragement to find the balance that recovery and family unity require.

How to Use This Book

Most of the language in this book is directed toward an alcoholic or addict in recovery. Still, it can be used by anyone who wants to reengage or rebuild relationships with their family members or friends after struggling with any addiction, mental illness, or traumatic or difficult life experience. I am going to use the terms *sobriety* and *recovery* interchangeably. Some would define being sober or being clean as different from being in recovery. The argument is that recovery is an ongoing way of life; it's about changing our behaviors and thinking, improving ourselves in all aspects of our lives, and it never ends. Sobriety, on the other hand, is merely about changing our drinking or using habits. But in this book, I will use both terms to describe a state of being wherein:

- You no longer use drugs, alcohol, or dysfunctional behaviors to cope with the daily struggles of life.
- You engage in a process of personal growth, seeking a better, healthier way of life.

- You are attempting to correct your wrongs and make amends to those you have hurt.
- You continue to create a better life for yourself and those around you through service to others and your community.

If you want to, you can skim through the early portions of this book and go straight to chapter 3, "Assessment and Preparation," and chapter 5, "New Skills and Tools for Building Relationships." Still, I encourage you to read every chapter in this book and to return to it as often as you need. You will learn something new each time you read it, and more things will make sense to you as your insight and understanding grow. Your efforts will create better results and improve your relationships. Then, with more time and stability in your sobriety, you can address more painful and delicate family issues and wounds. I also encourage you to continue to seek additional information from other resources. An abundance of information is available now from books, podcasts, YouTube, lectures, and support groups. I subscribe to the belief that group support is invaluable. Working with other people at various levels of recovery helps us survive and walk through our most challenging times. It lets us know that we are not alone and that others have been where we are now. It also allows us to help others, which is an essential part of rebuilding our self-esteem and confidence, reminding us from whence we came and keeping us humble.

Is Your Sobriety Strong Enough to Handle the Ups and Downs of the Path Ahead?

It helps to have a solid foundation of at least the first three steps of AA or Narcotics Anonymous (NA), or to agree with the following three propositions:

- You have a problem, whether it's with alcohol, drugs, trauma, mental illness, or something else.
- There is someone out there who can help you.
- You are willing to accept this help.

One of the most challenging things you must do is look at how you have hurt your loved ones. You will have to acknowledge their wounds, be accountable for your actions, and take responsibility for what you've done, whether you did it under the influence of drugs or alcohol or not. It is vital to tread this part of your path very slowly and cautiously, with the aid of a sponsor or therapist. There may be triggers or threats to your sobriety. Are you willing to accept this challenge? Do you have the staying power and the commitment to continue toward your goal, especially in times when you see little return for your efforts?

The skills and tools provided in this book are meant to help you improve your work and social relationships, as well as your personal view of yourself. However, this is still going to be an arduous and uncertain journey. You are going to have triumphs. You are also going to make mistakes. There will be trial-and-error periods. It will take practice and repetition. What works with one person will not necessarily work with another. You will encounter loved ones who do not want to do any of this work with you. But you must proceed anyway. You can always make changes within yourself and practice healthier relationship skills with friends, neighbors, or members of your support groups. No matter how grim things feel, someone in your life will probably let you in and be open to creating a new relationship with you. These actions will, in turn, benefit your loved ones, and with time, you may be able to open doors that once were closed to you.

My Path to Healing My Relationships with Friends and Family

I happily admit that my efforts to improve my relationships with my loved ones continue today. Most of my relationships are healthier and better than they have ever been. Others still require time and healing. My path to this point has included many roadblocks, and the most difficult ones came from within me. In early sobriety, my initial reaction to family healing—I call it a "reaction" because, in all honesty, I cannot call it an effort—was denial and minimization. I avoided looking *honestly* at the damage I had done. Instead, I compared my actions to the actions of others and looked for the differences, rather than the similarities. I sought to diminish the pain I had caused by thinking, "What I did was not as bad as what *they* did." This is a common experience among recovering individuals. It's our attempt to try to reduce the amount of guilt and shame we are burdened with. Ironically, it's the recognition and admission of our actions that frees us of our shame.

When I realized that my children's pain or wounds could not be compared to anyone else's and that I had inflicted the worst emotional pain on them that they had ever experienced, my next reactions were self-loathing and self-pity. I wanted to hide from the pain I had inflicted. I could not admit to myself the severity of the damage I had caused. I quickly slipped into playing the victim. I sought to explain my behavior by blaming it on sleeplessness, my dysfunctional family of origin, stress at work, or financial problems. But this only made the situation worse. Eventually, I began to act rather than react in response to family problems. I saw that through my alcoholism, I had done different types and amounts of damage to my various family members, giving them vastly different experiences. They each had varying levels of anger, fear, hurt, and pain. Each of them had a different level of willingness to repair our relationship. They each put up different types of resistance to my efforts. They each built different walls to protect themselves from me and my behaviors. I had to understand and recognize all this as I began my efforts to heal these relationships.

Your family members' reactions may vary from forgiveness to hopeful anticipation of your return to the family unit; or their anger may be so fierce that they have disowned you. In my experience, I encountered one family member who was in denial about my addiction, one who was full of rage and anger, one who was embarrassed by my behavior, and another who withdrew from me. My mother was confused and wondered aloud about where she had gone wrong, and she said things like, "I did not bring you up to become an alcoholic." On the other hand, my employer was purely professional and allowed the human resources team to manage my situation. Friends' reactions varied from relief to skepticism.

It took various lengths of time for me to improve these relationships. Some relationships improved quickly; some took years. For my family, therapy was a valuable tool. Also, twelve-step groups were helpful then and are still important to our healing. In all of these relationships, there have been moments of regression, incidents that triggered old wounds, and issues that have had to be rehashed and readdressed. It has taken time, patience, and commitment. And in truth, the process never really ends.

My relationship with one of my children took more than four years to show any significant signs of improvement. This was very hard on both of us. To cope with this, I had to stay sober, have faith in the wisdom of my peers, strive to be consistent in my behaviors and reactions, and trust my higher power. I had to surrender to the idea that I could not force or manipulate my family members to forgive me. Instead, I learned to acknowledge and embrace all minor improvements in our relationship. I never gave up, and I sought to create an atmosphere where our relationship could grow and heal.

Hope Is the Key

Psychologist Abraham Maslow (1908–1970) created a psychological model—known as "Maslow's hierarchy of needs"—that says we all have an instinctual desire for acknowledgment, love, and belonging. We are biologically designed to strive to fulfill these needs once our basic physical and safety needs are met.[1]

This means that when we reach out to our family and friends, we're not starting with a blank slate. We *all* have the drive to feel connected. Your loved ones and family members need to feel safe, secure, and loved just as much as you do. They may set walls, limits, or boundaries for you, or they may immediately welcome you with open arms. Your job is to prepare yourself to be there for them when they reach out to you.

2

The Disease Concept
of Addiction

I am an alcoholic. My alcoholism is a disease, and I was genetically predisposed to have this disease because of a long family history of alcoholism. I did not drink for many years, and my alcoholism did not become problematic until I was in my forties. It took me a few years to progress from social drinking to problem drinking to full-blown alcoholism. I fooled myself all along the way, thinking I was too educated and smart to become an alcoholic. I drank despite knowing I would likely develop this illness because of my family history. I ignored the early warning signs. I did not stop drinking until I hit bottom in my illness. With accountability, I have been sober and in recovery since 2013.

Even after I got sober, some family members still would not believe I have a disease. They do not believe in the disease concept of addiction. Instead, they would insist it was a bad habit I had overcome. That didn't mean they took my sobriety for granted, and it didn't limit the work I had to do to make amends with them; but their attitude felt diminishing. Regardless, I had to stay sober, for me and for them. You will encounter friends and family members with various opinions about addiction and the disease concept of addiction. Thus, it is wise to review the basic arguments about the disease concept and how our addiction and mental illness affect our family and closest friends. This chapter is essential because it also addresses the science of addiction, the longer-term brain damage caused by addictive behaviors, and how these factors affect an addict's likelihood of relapsing in early sobriety.

The Debate over the Disease Concept

The current debate over whether addiction is a disease, an illness, a disorder, or a weakness of an individual's character has been going on for most of the twentieth century. Before this time, most people perceived addiction and alcoholism as a weakness in a person's character or a lack of willpower. There was little understanding about why someone couldn't just quit drinking or using drugs, despite suffering negative consequences of their substance abuse. Over the course of human history, public reaction to drug use or drunkenness has ranged from disdain and ridicule to imprisonment, torture, and execution, depending on the culture and the era.

Archaeological evidence shows that humans were taking opium and psychedelic mushrooms as far back as nine thousand years ago.[1] The manufacture of alcohol began in an organized fashion about 7000 BC when a fermented drink was produced from rice, honey, fruit, and water.[2] It is believed that by 6000 BC, grapes were being cultivated to make wine.[3] Classical Greek and Roman literature contains many warnings of the dangers of abusing alcohol.[4] There have also been periods in history when efforts were made to criminalize the use of alcohol and mood-altering drugs. For example, anybody smoking hashish in fourteenth-century Egypt might be punished by having their teeth pulled out,[5] and smoking of tobacco and opium was punishable by beheading in the Ottoman Empire in 1633.[6]

In 1600, during the reign of King James I of England, writers of the time described widespread intoxication among all classes of the nation's people. In 1606 the English parliament passed the Act to Repress the Odious and Loathsome Sin of Drunkenness.[7] In the United States, the American Temperance Society and similar antidrinking organizations grew in popularity in the 1800s. The spread of this ideology eventually resulted in the passage of the Eighteenth Amendment to the Constitution, in which the production, importation, transportation, and sale of alcoholic beverages were prohibited.[8] This amendment was repealed in 1933 by the Twenty-First Amendment.

In more recent history, the "War on Drugs" began when President Richard Nixon declared drug abuse to be "public enemy number one" and increased federal funding for drug control agencies. In 1973, the Drug Enforcement Agency was formed to consolidate federal efforts to control drug abuse. President Ronald Reagan expanded this program and emphasized criminal punishment instead of providing treatment to individuals, which led to a dramatic increase in incarcerations for nonviolent drug offenses. In 1984, Nancy Reagan launched the "Just Say No" campaign to provide drug-abuse prevention and education to school-age children.[9] Today, more than fifty years since the War on Drugs began, there are varying opinions about the efficacy of these programs.[10]

Origins of the Disease Concept

The modern-day argument for addiction being a disease may have begun in the late 1700s with politician Benjamin Rush (1745–1813), a signer of the United States Declaration of Independence, a civic leader in Philadelphia, and a social reformer who was one of the first who wrote and spoke to argue that alcoholism was a disease and that it should be treated as such. He is credited with introducing a therapeutic approach to addiction and mental illness, which included group support and occupational therapy. Rush believed that the alcoholic or addict *loses control* over their ability to stop drinking. He developed the concept of alcoholism as a form of medical disease and proposed that alcoholics be weaned from alcohol with other, less potent substances.[11]

AA has referred to alcoholism as an illness or disease ever since Bill Wilson and Dr. Bob Smith founded the organization in 1935. The book *Alcoholics Anonymous*, also known as "the Big Book"—AA's manual presenting guidelines for getting and staying sober—references alcoholism as an illness.[12] Page 18 of the Big Book says, "We have come to believe it an illness—it involves those about us in a way that no other human sickness can." Later literature approved by the AA organization continues to call alcoholism an illness and also uses the term *disease*. By 1956, the American Medical Association had declared alcoholism a disease,[13] and this idea grew more widespread in 1960 with the publication of the book *The Disease Concept of Alcoholism* by E. M. Jellinek.[14]

Over the past fifty years, other professional medical organizations have followed the American Medical Association's path. Today there are three primary approaches to alcoholism and addiction treatment: the disease concept, the twelve-step process, and the Minnesota model of treatment. All of these approaches offer addicts and alcoholics a chance for long-term recovery. The disease model refers to addiction as a medical, pathological, or physical condition that can be chronic and that involves a disruption in the brain's reward, motivation, and memory processes, while causing additional physical damage to the body. This model postulates that medical and pharmacological intervention is the preferred treatment for the disease of addiction. Treatment can be provided in either an inpatient or outpatient setting. The twelve-step model also considers addiction to be a disease, but the primary treatment consists of the addict participating in a voluntary outpatient program of behavioral change through group support. The alcoholic or addict is guided through an established set of steps to help them understand their powerlessness over alcohol, gain insight into their addiction and understand it better, make amends to those they've harmed, repair any damage they've done, and stay sober by helping other addicts. The Minnesota model is an approach that blends inpatient treatment with a twelve-step approach to counseling and therapy. Many of the staff or professionals in this model will likely be in recovery, and services may include a variety of treatment modalities, such as cognitive-behavioral therapy, biofeedback, mindfulness, and stress management, among others.

Benefits of Using the Term *Disease*

The argument for addiction being a disease often describes alcoholism as a chronic, progressive, and fatal disease if left untreated. Alcoholism is likened to other diseases like diabetes or high cholesterol because, like other diseases, alcoholism has an onset and a progression of symptoms; it can lead to death if untreated; and it can be treated and managed. Insurance coverage for treating alcoholism and addiction is one of the primary benefits of calling addiction a disease. Many insurance plans now offer reimbursement for inpatient and outpatient addiction treatment. The term *disease* may also reduce the illness's stigma and may help people acknowledge that they have a substance use disorder, which could help them seek help earlier. This does not mean addicts get to minimize or dismiss the actions and behaviors associated with their alcohol or drug use. The disease concept is presented here to help you accept your illness and to help reduce the shame you may feel. As scientific study advances, we are beginning to see alcoholism and addiction more as diseases than as choices. Each year, studies are presented revealing that addiction often evolves from a behavioral condition into a neurological disorder that can be treated with medical and behavioral interventions. Modern medicine now has many different definitions and classifications of alcoholism and addiction, and yet much still has to be learned about addiction as a disease and how to treat it.

The American Medical Association (AMA) classified alcoholism as a disease in 1956, and the organization classified addiction as a disease in 1987. In 2011, the American Society of Addiction Medicine (ASAM) joined the AMA, defining addiction as a chronic brain disorder. The ASAM further defines addiction as a "treatable, chronic medical disease involving complex interactions among brain circuits, genetics, the environment, and an individual's life experiences. People with addiction use substances or engage in compulsive behaviors and often continue despite harmful consequences. Prevention efforts and treatment approaches for addiction are generally as successful as those for other chronic diseases."[15] The National Institute on Alcohol and Alcohol Abuse currently states that "alcohol use disorder (AUD) is a medical condition characterized by an impaired ability to stop or control alcohol use despite adverse social, occupational, or health consequences. It encompasses the conditions that some people refer to as alcohol abuse, alcohol dependence, alcohol addiction, and the colloquial term, alcoholism. Considered a brain disorder, AUD can be mild, moderate, or severe. Lasting changes in the brain caused by alcohol misuse perpetuate AUD and make individuals vulnerable to relapse."[16]

The American Psychiatric Association continues to modify its description with each new edition of the *Diagnostic and Statistical Manual of Mental Disorders*, a guidebook used by health care and mental health care professionals worldwide to diagnose mental disorders. The newest edition of the manual, *DSM-5-TR*,[17] addresses substance use disorders, alcohol use disorders, and addictive disorders. It defines each disorder with specific criteria that must be present to make a diagnosis. The severity of the illness (mild, moderate, or severe) is based on the number of criteria met.

In summary, all these professional organizations have their own definitions of addiction. Although these definitions vary, they all seem to agree that addiction is a serious problem, a chronic, relapsing disease that is characterized by compulsive substance-seeking behavior despite adverse consequences. They also agree that addiction involves physical changes to the brain and body that can be treated medically, and, to varying degrees, socially and spiritually.

Your friends and family may have opinions that differ from those of medical professionals. They are entitled to their beliefs about whether alcoholism and addiction are diseases or not, but it's helpful to know what each of your family members believes about the disease concept. This will allow you to know some of the obstacles you're encountering and how this affects their reaction to your addiction. It might help if they see you as afflicted with an illness, but when an addict tries to convey this information, it's often interpreted as a manipulative tactic to avoid responsibility for their actions.

Ultimately, you cannot control other people's opinions and beliefs. Regardless, you must do the work to heal the relationship no matter what they believe. Your family and friends ultimately want to know *what you will do* about your alcoholism or addiction. They will be more interested in learning how you will maintain your recovery than in your opinion on how your problem is defined.

The Argument for Why Addiction Is Not a Disease

Those who argue against the disease concept point out that a disease should be measurable and testable. Currently, there is no one standard test for addiction, and the signs and symptoms vary tremendously from one addict to another. This view points out that it may be dangerous to call addiction a disease because that could enable the addicted individual to deny responsibility for their drinking or using. Those who do not subscribe to the disease concept think it could lead to addicts excusing their behavior and believing they have no agency regarding their addiction. Many who argue against the disease concept also point out that even if there is a genetic predisposition to developing this illness, not all who have it will become alcoholics; therefore, individuals still make a voluntary choice to drink or use drugs in the first place.

Those who argue against the disease concept may also support their claim by pointing to the thousands of people who have given up drinking and drug use without medical or psychological interventions. Some people have stopped using their drug of choice purely through the sufficient motivation to change. My father was one of those people. When he learned that his drinking was likely to increase his chance of developing Alzheimer's disease, he became sufficiently fearful and stopped drinking. Witnessing his mother's and brother's Alzheimer's disease progression was enough to scare him into sobriety.

Early Treatments for Alcoholism and Addiction

Today there are a variety of treatment resources available for addiction. Still, it may be beneficial to look at the types of treatment that have been successfully or unsuccessfully used throughout history. In North America, the earliest social therapies likely came from Native American tribes in the mid-1700s. These interventions involved abstinence-based mutual aid societies that included Native healing practices as ways to treat alcoholism.[18]

In the 1800s, organized peer-support groups began to become available. The Washingtonian movement, a precursor to AA, was a temperance fellowship founded by six alcoholics—William Mitchell, David Hoss, Charles Anderson, George Steer, Bill McCurdy, and Tom Campbell—on Thursday, April 2, 1840, at Chase's Tavern on Liberty Street in Baltimore, Maryland. Total abstinence was their goal. Their idea was that by relying on each other, sharing their alcoholic experiences, and creating an atmosphere of support, they could keep each other sober.[19]

Also around this time, "inebriate homes" or "retreat centers" arose based on the ideas of the Washingtonian movement. These homes offered nonmedical detox, rest, and removal of the addict's drug of choice. Soon, more formalized treatment facilities opened to provide medical interventions for alcoholism and addiction. The New York State Inebriate Asylum opened in 1864 under the direction of Dr. Joseph Edward Turner. It was the first medically monitored addiction treatment center in the United States and is considered to be one of the first alcohol rehabilitation centers.

Alongside these developments, treatment methodologies in North America and Europe began to use medications to treat alcoholism. These efforts met with some success as well as a great deal of cynicism. In 1879 Dr. Leslie Keeley created the "Keeley cure" or "Gold Cure" for alcoholism, and he opened more than 120 Keeley Institutes in North America and Europe.[20] These treatment centers offered an open, informal atmosphere that allowed patients to drink as much alcohol as they cared to upon admission. Each day, patients were administered tonics and "medications," such as bottled "double chloride of Gold Cures for drunkenness," and the patients were required to reduce the amount of alcohol they consumed over four weeks.[21] Dr. Keeley was criticized for keeping the ingredients of the Gold Cure a secret, but his rivals revealed the contents to include willow bark, ginger, hops, strychnine, and apomorphine.[22]

Charles Towns, in collaboration with Dr. Alexander Lambert, opened the Charles B. Towns Substance Hospital in 1901. This facility treated affluent alcoholics with its famous belladonna elixir, which was made of belladonna (deadly nightshade) mixed with fluid extract of zanthoxylum (prickly ash) and *Hyoscyamus* (henbane). This concoction could bring on hallucinations that were referred to as "a spiritual awakening." Bill Wilson, the founder of AA, was a patient at Charles B. Towns Hospital four times. The cost of treatment was $350 a day, which is equivalent to $5,610 today.[23]

Gradually, psychotherapeutic interventions were introduced into treatment programs. The Emmanuel Clinic (also known as the Emmanuel Movement), which opened in Boston in 1906, provided a church-based form of psychotherapy with a combination of spirituality and psychological interventions as part of their treatment of alcoholism.[24]

Other treatment modalities offered by hospitals or sanitariums provided detoxification, rest, and treatments such as electroconvulsive therapy, hydrotherapy, bromide sleep therapy, and large doses of insulin. Often, these treatments failed to produce long-term sobriety, leading to a belief that alcoholics and addicts were a lost cause. Carl Gustav Jung, the famous Swiss psychiatrist and psychotherapist credited with founding the school of analytical psychology, has been quoted in the the Big Book of AA in response to an alcoholic who was wondering if he could ever be cured of his alcoholism: "Exceptions to cases such as yours have been occurring since early times, here and there, once in a while. Alcoholics have had what are called vital spiritual experiences. To me, these occurrences are phenomena. They appear to be in the nature of huge emotional displacements and arrangements. Ideas, emotions, and attitudes, which were once the guiding forces of the lives of these men, were suddenly cast to one side, and a completely new set of motivations and conceptions began to dominate them."[25]

The modern twelve-step treatment and recovery model began when Bill Wilson and Dr. Bob Smith met in 1935. They were both alcoholics and were unable to achieve sustained abstinence despite their efforts to medically detox at the Towns Hospital. They founded AA based on their mutual support, faith, and Bill's experiences with the Oxford Group, a Christian organization founded in 1921 by Lutheran priest Frank Buchman. The Oxford Group had success treating alcoholics, and Bill Wilson and Dr. Bob incorporated many of the concepts from the Oxford Group into the new fellowship of Alcoholics Anonymous. They encouraged men to make a thorough self-examination, acknowledge their character defects, make resitituion for harm done, and work with others.[26]

Like the Oxford Group, AA emphasized social support and recovery to heal the mind, body, and spirit. However, Bill W. and Dr. Bob decided to take AA in a different direction from the Oxford Group, allowing it to be more welcoming to all alcoholics and avoiding the Oxford movement's strict evangelizing and formal organizational structure. They stipulated a totally sober social culture and held regular meetings that were open to all faiths, and they developed a program that focused on working through a twelve-step recovery process. In addition, Bill Wilson believed that doing service work with other alcoholics is one of the main tools that help alcoholics maintain their sobriety. They developed a program that focused on working through twelve steps. AA experienced a significant increase in growth after the Second World War. Soldiers were coming home from the war with emotional trauma, a condition commonly known as "shell shock." These soldiers often self-medicated with alcohol and drugs, and AA became a primary treatment source for them.[27]

The Hazelden Foundation is credited with introducing the next significant step forward in alcoholism treatment when they opened a "guest house"—a residential home for alcoholic men—in Center City, Minnesota. The home could host seven patients and three staff members, and it offered a behavioral health approach to treatment combined with the AA philosophy of self-help, abstinence, and behavioral change. In 2014, Hazelden merged with the Betty Ford Foundation, and now Hazelden Betty Ford is widely known and respected for its advocacy, publications, and work with addiction, including treatment of addicts.

Medication and Treatment Today

Several medications that were developed in the late 1940s and 1950s to treat alcoholism and addiction are still in use today. These medications are intended to be used in conjunction with other types of counseling and therapy. For example, disulfiram, also known by the brand name Antabuse, was introduced in the United States as a supplemental treatment for alcoholism. It produces an acute sensitivity to alcohol use, often resulting in nausea, vomiting, dizziness, extreme tiredness, fainting, and shortness of breath. The experience is so unpleasant that you do not want to drink while taking this medication. The effects of Antabuse can last up to fourteen days, enabling the alcoholic to resist the impulse to use alcohol.[28]

Methadone, introduced in 1964, is a synthetic analgesic similar to morphine and heroin in its effects. However, methadone doesn't activate opioid receptors in the brain, and it lasts much longer in the body without providing the same euphoria as heroin or morphine.[29] It is used as a substitute for these drugs because it prevents withdrawal symptoms, reduces drug cravings, and blunts or blocks the effect of opioids.[30]

The US Food and Drug Administration (FDA) approved naloxone in 1971. Better known by its brand name Narcan, this drug counters or reverses opioid overdose effects. It is credited with saving many lives and is now carried by police and EMTs.[31] The effects of Narcan may wear off after forty-five to ninety minutes, and medical attention is still required to help the individual detox from opioids safely. Naltrexone (brand names: ReVia, Vivitrol, Depade) was approved in late 1994.[32] It is nonaddictive and it blocks opioid receptors in the brain, preventing the pleasurable effects or high of alcohol or drug use. In 2006, the FDA approved an injection form of Vivitrol to treat alcohol dependence and opioid dependence. It is given as an injection once a month.[33]

In 2002, the FDA approved buprenorphine (brand name Suboxone), a medication-assisted treatment for opioid addiction. It works by tightly binding to the same receptors in the brain as other opiates. By doing so, it blunts intoxication from these other drugs, prevents cravings, and can allow people to transition back from a life of addiction to a life of relative normalcy and safety.[34,35]

Along with advances in treatment and medication came political and legal changes that enabled individuals to seek help with less fear of financial consequences such as job loss and better access to insurance coverage for the treatment of addiction. In 2008, the US Congress passed the Mental Health Parity and Addiction Equity Act (MHPAEA), which required insurance companies and group health plans to provide benefits for mental health and substance use treatment and services that are similar to the benefits they provide for other types of medical care.[36] In 2010 the Affordable Care Act expanded coverage for addiction treatment.[37] This law built upon the MHPAEA's criteria by ensuring that insurance plans offered through state health insurance marketplaces included behavioral health services, including substance abuse treatment.[38]

Treatment options today offer a variety of different models and often include multiple types of treatment modalities. These treatments may include medical detoxification, medication-assisted treatment, twelve-step programs, cognitive behavioral therapy, biofeedback, stress management, physical and occupational therapy, and holistic or natural treatment like acupuncture, yoga, and meditation. Medication-assisted treatment involves the use of medications combined with behavioral and counseling therapies to assist in the treatment of addictions. The benefits of this approach include safer withdrawal, increased retention in treatment programs, decreased illegal drug use, and reduced risk of relapse. Treatment settings may include hospitals, psychiatric facilities, inpatient and outpatient visits, halfway houses, three-quarter houses, retreats, and intensives.

Physiological Effects on the Mind and Body during Detox and Early Recovery

There is a great deal of research being conducted on the damage that alcohol and drug use cause to one's body and brain. It is common knowledge that in the short term, alcohol use impairs thinking and decision-making, slurs speech, impairs balance and coordination, and may cause respiratory depression, coma, or death by overdose. Long-term use can also damage the heart, liver, and pancreas. The use of certain other drugs causes similar side effects as alcohol. Some drugs with stimulating effects may put a user at risk for a heart attack, anxiety, agitation, stroke, or overdose.

Immediate Side Effects of Detox

Once an individual stops using alcohol and drugs, the side effects and damage to the brain and body do not immediately dissipate.[39] Instead, it takes time and healing for our brains and bodies to recover from this use and abuse. We commonly call this *withdrawal* or *detox*. Some of the most common side effects felt during alcohol detox include nausea, vomiting, stomach cramps, tremors, headache, hallucinations, sweating, chills, and lack of appetite. The most common drug-withdrawal symptoms are insomnia, nausea, muscle pain, anxiety, fever, panic attacks, and muscle weakness. Depending on the drug type and consumption duration, these symptoms can last for days.

Postacute withdrawal syndrome (PAWS) is a collection of symptoms that can include nausea and vomiting, insomnia, irritability, aggression, hostility, anxiety or panic attacks, fatigue, mental confusion, poor impulse control, and severe high and low mood swings. PAWS can occur days, weeks, or even months after the typical withdrawal period has ended.[40,41]

Damage to the Brain

The consistent use of alcohol or drugs can have a significant negative impact on our brains. It is common to experience sleep disturbances, anxiety, depression, impaired concentration, lack of enthusiasm or motivation, apathy, fatigue or low energy, poor memory, poor impulse control, and increased sensitivity to stress, among other cognitive symptoms. It is crucial to understand that your thinking, feeling, and reasoning are impaired in early sobriety, which may affect your ability to make good decisions. Your cognitive deficits make you more vulnerable to your triggers, resulting in a greater risk of relapse.[42]

Research is increasingly demonstrating that recovering alcoholics and addicts can experience substantial thinking deficits for the first two weeks of recovery, including increased confusion, increased irritability, distractibility, a decreased ability to attend and concentrate, slower reaction times, a decreased ability to use abstract verbal reasoning, decreased verbal short-term memory, impaired verbal learning abilities, and decreased nonverbal short-term memory.[43] Many people refer to this condition as *brain fog*. Examples may include feeling like you are thinking in slow motion, not being able to retain information for more than a few moments, feeling like your thinking is clouded, struggling with a sense of timing, not being able to focus your attention on any one thing for more than a few moments or minutes, and struggling with schoolwork, homework, or tasks at your job.[44]

By sixty days into recovery, distractibility, confusion, and irritability will have likely diminished, and you can expect to feel slightly calmer and more clear-headed. However, you will still suffer from significant impulsivity, difficulty with reasoning, and decision-making deficits. Problems with memory, concentration, learning, and abstract reasoning often remain for up to twelve to twenty-four months. During this period, *you are more vulnerable to relapse.*[45,46]

Thus, this is a critical time to learn and practice the basic coping strategies so often that they become new habits and begin to replace your old reactions with better and new ones. Many people refer to this as reprogramming or rewiring your brain. For the first two months to five years of abstinence, some may still experience cognitive deficits, but the good news is that bodies and minds can heal from these effects. Healing is facilitated by time, learning new tools, developing new habits, experience, and practice.[47,48]

The Science of Addiction

I am introducing this topic because I believe understanding the biological and physiological mechanisms in the brain that underlie addiction can help us understand what is happening to our body, brain, and thought processes. I want to stress the importance of consistently practicing the fundamental recovery skills you use to stay clean or sober. I also believe we can recognize and treat our addictions more effectively. I am presenting this information concisely, but I encourage you to do additional research to understand addiction science, especially as new research constantly reveals more. Addiction affects many areas of the brain, but I will primarily address the prefrontal cortex, the limbic system, and the hormones that are most often associated with mood and feelings of well-being.

The Prefrontal Cortex

The prefrontal cortex, often called the brain's "executive center," is located in the frontmost part of the brain. Its primary functions are decision-making, logic, impulse control, focusing, organizing, reasoning, and judgment. It is the last part of your brain to fully mature, which happens in your early twenties.

This part of the brain helps you keep your emotions under control and aids you in decision-making, as well as understanding whether a behavior or action is risky or not. Early alcohol and drug use can impair the development of this part of the brain, which is why many professionals will state that an individual's emotional growth stops when they begin abusing substances or engaging in addictive behaviors. For example, if a thirty-year-old male began using alcohol at age fourteen and continued from that time forward, his emotional development and intelligence would be halted at whatever level he had reached by age fourteen.[49]

The Limbic System

The limbic system, also known as the reward pathway, consists of the hippocampus (important for memory), the amygdala (responsible for emotions), the nucleus accumbens (processes reward stimuli), the hypothalamus (releases hormones in response to stress), the thalamus (passes along information), and dopamine (a neurotransmitter that sends signals of pleasure). Glutamate, serotonin, and basal ganglia are also parts of the reward pathway.

The primary function of the limbic system is to aid us in survival. It provides pleasure, arousal, and the regulation of hormones and circadian rhythms, i.e., your sleep/wake cycle. It enables us to recognize and remember favorable events so we will want to repeat them. These activities might include our instincts for reproduction, caring for our children, stimulating our curiosity and the desire to learn, and enjoying adrenaline-raising behaviors. The limbic system also aids us in regulating our emotions, behavior, and motivations, and it affects long-term memory.[50,51]

Hormones

In brief, hormones are your body's chemical messengers, and as such, they play a big part in your daily life's activities. They regulate how your body functions and maintains equilibrium, affecting your emotions, mood, blood sugar, blood pressure, sleep cycles, metabolism, growth, fertility, and sex drive. Scientists have identified over fifty different hormones in the human body. Imbalances in our hormone levels can be caused by many things: stress, menstrual cycles, aging, pregnancy, sleep deprivation, certain foods, medications, and, of course, our use of alcohol or drugs, or other mood-altering behaviors. We will examine the following hormones: dopamine, oxytocin, serotonin, endorphin, and epinephrine.

Dopamine

Dopamine, sometimes known as the "reward hormone," enables learning, the retention of information, motivation, and the production of feelings of pleasure. Dopamine also acts as a neurotransmitter, which is a type of chemical that passes signals and information between nerve cells (neurons). In this capacity, dopamine controls our pleasure and reward centers in the brain and is the chief neurotransmitter affected by addiction. Natural dopamine is biosynthesized inside two areas of the brain: the ventral tegmental area and the substantia nigra in the midbrain. Dopamine's other hormonal functions affect many of our daily tasks by modulating physiological functions such as memory, motor movement, sleep, cognition, libido, and addiction. It also contributes to regulating mood, pleasure, and the reward cycle. Deficiency in this hormone can result in procrastination, lack of motivation, low energy, an inability to focus, difficulty in learning new skills, and increased depression or feelings of hopelessness. Therefore, it is vital to maintain adequate levels of dopamine throughout life.

Certain everyday behaviors and activities aid in maintaining a moderate level of dopamine. These include going out in the sunshine, engaging in light exercise such as walking or bicycling, listening to music, dancing, meditating, drinking green tea, taking cold showers, chatting with friends or family, getting sufficient rest and sleep, volunteering, teaching, or learning a new activity. Our bodies and brains can manage these natural highs and lows in our dopamine levels. But when we engage in certain activities or ingest certain substances, like alcohol, drugs, nicotine, sex, sugar, or gambling, an overload of dopamine is introduced to our system. When this happens, the body attempts to regulate the amount of dopamine by shutting down the body's natural dopamine-producing ability, which may be why you may feel like you need to nap after eating a hefty lunch or sweet dessert.[52]

Unfortunately, for most people, dopamine levels also decrease with age. People with low dopamine may exhibit depression, hopelessness, defeat, fatigue, anger, mood swings, low libido, poor outlook, and lack of motivation. More than 70 percent of US residents are estimated to have suboptimal dopamine levels.[53] Some ways to increase your dopamine naturally include:

- practicing meditation or mindfulness activities;
- doing light exercise;
- being creative in art, music, writing, or dance;
- creating and working on a daily to-do list or setting and achieving small goals;
- spending time in nature or getting daily sunshine;
- eating sufficient amounts of protein, which is vital in the production of dopamine. Eating a balanced diet with plenty of protein from foods like turkey, eggs, beef, legumes, soy, and low-fat dairy helps ensure your body has what it needs to maintain the proper dopamine levels.

Oxytocin

Oxytocin is a hormone most commonly associated with pregnancy, delivery, and birth. But it is also widely known as the "love hormone," as it increases naturally when you hug someone or have an orgasm. When oxytocin is high, the associated emotions are sometimes described as warm, fuzzy feelings, such as the emotions you feel when you hold a sleeping baby, get a hug, or receive a genuine compliment. Oxytocin is also linked to increased levels of social interaction, empathizing with others' feelings, generating positive memories of experiences, bonding with others, and overall well-being. Oxytocin is also believed to aid in reducing stress and anxiety. Low levels or lack of oxytocin may result in insomnia, mistrust, difficulty building and sustaining relationships, low energy, increased focus, and fear, especially social anxiety.[54] To increase oxytocin naturally:

- Listen to music.
- Meditate.
- Engage in safe physical touch.
- Receive or give a massage.
- Spend time with friends.
- Perform a random act of kindness.
- Care for a pet, such as a dog or a cat.

Serotonin

Serotonin regulates moods, sleep, digestion, nausea, wound healing, and sexual desire. It is thought to also play a role in learning and memory. Serotonin is sometimes called the happiness hormone or the mood stabilizer. Lack of serotonin can result in low feelings of self-worth or significance, being "overly sensitive," being more prone to anxiety attacks, social phobia, insomnia, obsessive-compulsive behaviors, mood swings, impulsive behaviors, and physical aches and pains.[55] Interestingly, about 90 percent of the serotonin in your body is in the cells lining your intestinal tract; only 10 percent is produced in the brain. This reinforces the latest research about the gut-brain axis: *You are what you eat.* To increase serotonin naturally:

- Engage in light to moderate exercise.
- Reminisce about a happy event, memory, or experience.
- Socialize with loved ones.
- Spend time in nature and in natural sunlight.
- Consume more foods and probiotics that contain tryptophan.

Endorphin

Endorphins (usually referred to in the plural) are hormones that are naturally produced in the body. They typically produce a brief euphoria to mask pain and relieve stress. They are also released when you feel pleasurable activities such as eating, massage, exercise, and sex. They are commonly known as the painkiller hormone. Lack of the ability to produce endorphins may result in anxiety, depression, mood swings, aches and pains, insomnia, and impulsive behavior.[56] To increase endorphins:

- Laugh.
- Cry.
- Eat something you enjoy, such as dark chocolate.
- Receive an acupuncture treatment.
- Exercise.
- Participate in group activities, such as sports teams or dance classes.
- Watch a film in a genre you like.

Many people confuse dopamine and endorphins because they are both hormones that are part of the brain's reward center and help you experience happiness or pleasure. The critical difference is that endorphins are released quickly and are more often associated with exercise and the body's natural response to pain. On the other hand, dopamine is released slowly and is more related to your mood or the good feelings that linger after such experiences as a bout of exercise or seeing an inspiring movie. For example, endorphins naturally soothe a runner's achy muscles, but dopamine is responsible for the "runner's high" that lingers after a workout or run.

Epinephrine

Epinephrine, also known as adrenaline, functions as a neurotransmitter that plays a role in metabolism, attention, focus, panic, and excitement. Its other hormonal functions influence different body parts and stimulate the central nervous system, and it is responsible for emotions such as fear, anger, and the fight-flight-freeze-fawn response. Abnormal epinephrine levels are linked to sleep disorders, anxiety, high blood pressure, and lowered immunity to illness.[57] To maintain a healthy level of epinephrine:

- Consume a healthy and balanced diet.
- Perform moderate exercise.
- Engage in a relaxing hobby.
- Practice meditation or other stillness exercises, which can be as simple as focusing on the rhythm of your breath or repeating a mantra, statement, or affirmation.
- Try practices such as yoga or tai chi, which incorporate elements of both exercise and meditation.
- Practice good sleep hygiene, get adequate sleep, have a regular sleep schedule, and reduce stress-inducing activities before bedtime (such as watching the news or scrolling on social media).

How All of This Works Together

When the human pleasure principle is working normally, every time you experience something positive, dopamine levels and pleasurable feelings increase.

This information is passed from one cell to another through synapses and neurotransmitters, alerting other areas of the brain that something pleasurable has been experienced. The intent is to teach the brain to remember this pleasurable experience and to encourage the individual to seek out this behavior or substance again. The duty of the prefrontal cortex (the executive center) is to make a judgment on whether or not to pursue this pleasurable experience again immediately, to wait, or to avoid it altogether. For example, you are test-driving a sports car, and upon accelerating to get on the highway, you get a rush of excitement as you feel the energy of the engine. Your reward system is triggered by this adrenaline, and you are tempted to increase your speed far past the speed limit to get another adrenaline rush. However, you also notice the car salesman sitting beside you with an expression of fear on his face, so the prefrontal cortex—the rational, decision-making part of your brain—influences you to drive responsibly. In simplest forms, the prefrontal cortex and the reward system work together to enable you to make good decisions.

When alcohol, drugs, or an addictive behavior is introduced, the prefrontal cortex and the reward system work to numb the ability of the prefrontal cortex to make good decisions, and they empower the primitive brain to influence judgment and behavior. With some behaviors and drugs, a substantial, unnatural surge in dopamine is released, resulting in euphoria. This extreme release of dopamine brings us more pleasure than any other biological activity can, and the primitive brain is compelled to want to reexperience these feelings. Unfortunately, the prefrontal cortex is not strong enough to combat the primitive brain's drive to seek out this experience again. This massive surge in dopamine also shocks receptors that are receiving the dopamine. With repetitive use, the receptors become damaged from overstimulation and have difficulty accepting the substance messages over time. The addict then requires greater amounts of the addictive substance to get the same effect. This results first in tolerance and then in dependence.

The Broken Brain and Neuroplasticity

The *broken brain* is a commonly used term to help explain the lingering damage to the brain after long-term alcohol use, drug use, or a behavioral addiction. The excessive use of alcohol or drugs or an addictive behavior figuratively takes over the brain. The active addiction begins to control emotions, motivation, and decision-making, thus affecting our behaviors and consequently explaining why the addict continues to seek out pleasurable experiences despite knowing that the consequences are disastrous. It does this by inhibiting the brain's own ability to create the hormones that bring us pleasure and damaging the neurotransmitters that normally transport these messages from one nerve cell to another.

Neuroplasticity is the brain's ability to heal and reform the synaptic connections that the overloading of dopamine has damaged in one's system. This process may take months or years, but to encourage your brain to heal:

- Switch up your routines; for instance, if you are right-handed, use your left hand to brush your teeth.
- Read books.
- Learn a new skill or hobby.
- Learn a new language.
- Interact socially.
- Exercise or play a sport.
- Travel. Go to a new location such as a museum.
- Make art or music.[58]

What Happens When You Use Alcohol?

Alcohol use has many effects that are similar to those of drug use. Still, people often ask, "Why do I feel relaxed, less stressed, and more socially comfortable when I consume alcohol?" Although alcohol is a depressant, the first drink or two may result in a euphoric feeling because alcohol releases the neurotransmitters dopamine and norepinephrine into the brain. Norepinephrine is a neurotransmitter associated with arousal, accounting for increased physical activity and excitement when someone begins drinking. Elevated levels of norepinephrine can increase impulsivity, which helps explain why we lose our inhibitions and may explain why some people do things they may not otherwise do under the influence of alcohol.[59] Alcohol can also have an anti-anxiety effect, and many people report that they drink alcohol as a way to deal with anxiety or relax after a hard day at work. This is because alcohol also blocks the transmission of anxious nerve signals through the neurotransmitter gamma-aminobutyric acid,[60] which is the major inhibitory neurotransmitter in the brain.

As you continue to drink in an attempt to increase or reexperience those first feel-good feelings that the dopamine produced, the depressant effect develops. The prefrontal cortex and the cerebellum are most affected by the increased consumption of alcohol, which is why we may act without thinking, be more prone to emotional outbursts, make poor decisions, or do or say something that we later regret. Decreased activity in the cerebellum (the part of the brain that controls motor activity) is why we struggle with balance and coordination and have difficulty driving a car or walking a straight line after we've been drinking.

Understanding Anxiety, Stress, and the Fight-or-Flight Response

Anxiety, stress, and the fight-or-flight response are all interwoven together. There is not a specific area of the brain that is entirely responsible for the emotion of anxiety. The limbic system, which we have previously identified as the reward pathway in the brain, could also be called the emotional center of the brain, and this is where anxiety and the fight-or-flight response originate. Anxiety is a prevalent mental health complaint in our society today. It has been gathering much attention in the media as public attention is drawn toward it, and many celebrities are sharing their personal experiences with anxiety. In addition, many alcoholics and addicts state that they struggle with anxiety and have tried to self-medicate with alcohol or drugs. An integral part of your recovery is understanding and learning to manage your anxiety. Your family members almost certainly have struggled with their own anxiety in response to dealing with your alcoholism or addiction. Being understanding and compassionate about how your loved ones manage their anxiety is important.

Much of our anxiety and fight-or-flight response is innate; it comes from our primitive brain. However, some of our anxiety responses are learned, and we can learn new behavioral techniques to improve our mechanisms for coping with stress, anxiety, and anxiety attacks. This will, in turn, help you improve your relationships when you're addressing your conflicts, triggers, and stressors. The main areas of the brain that are involved in fear, stress, and anxiety include the brain stem (controls heart rate and breathing), the limbic system (emotions and hormones), the prefrontal cortex (reasoning and judgment), and the motor cortex (muscle control).

The Fight-or-Flight Response

The fight-or-flight response is sometimes also called the fight-flight-freeze-fawn response. It is your body's natural response to danger; it is a type of stress response that enables you to react to a threat, like an oncoming car, a falling baby, or a vicious animal. The reaction causes instant hormonal and physiological changes. This is not a conscious decision but an automatic response, so it is difficult to control. Typically, your heart rate gets faster, which increases oxygen flow to your muscles, your pain perception drops, and your visual and hearing senses sharpen. "Fight" is the response where you seemingly react or act without thinking to save yourself or someone else. "Flight" is the response where the impulse to run or leave a situation takes over; you can run from a burning building. "Freezing" is when the flight is put on hold; it involves the same physiological change, but you remain completely still. This is another way to protect yourself. A good example of this would be when a rabbit's first response to a dog stalking it is to be entirely still, waiting to run only when the dog lunges for it. "Fawning" is a behavioral reaction in which your response includes becoming submissive to a threatening person, animal, or situation as a way to deescalate the threat. An example of this may be when an individual becomes submissive to a partner who is physically threatening them, in order to prevent the abuse from escalating.[61]

The physiological response begins in your amygdala, the part of your brain responsible for emotions, memory, and perceived fear. The amygdala responds by sending signals to the hypothalamus, which stimulates the autonomic nervous system (ANS).[62] The ANS consists of the sympathetic and parasympathetic nervous systems; the sympathetic nervous system drives the fight-or-flight response, while the parasympathetic nervous system drives freezing and fawning. How you react depends on which system dominates the response at the time. When your ANS is stimulated, your body releases adrenaline and cortisol, the stress hormones. These hormones are released very quickly, which can affect the following bodily processes and structures:

- **Heart rate.** Your heart beats faster to bring oxygen to your major muscles. During freezing, your heart rate might increase or decrease.

- **Lungs.** Your breathing speeds up to deliver more oxygen to your blood. In the freeze response, you might hold your breath or restrict breathing.

- **Eyes.** Your peripheral vision increases so you can notice your surroundings. Your pupils dilate and let in more light, which helps you see better.

- **Ears.** Your ears "perk up," and your hearing becomes sharper.

- **Blood.** Blood thickens, which increases clotting factors. This prepares your body for injury.

- **Skin.** Your skin might produce more sweat or get cold. As a result, you may look pale or have goosebumps.

- **Hands and feet.** Your hands and feet might get cold as blood flow increases to your major muscles.

- **Pain perception.** The fight-or-flight response temporarily reduces your perception of pain.

Your specific physiological reactions depend on how you typically respond to stress. Usually, your body will return to its baseline state after twenty to thirty minutes. During this time, you can use any number of techniques to deal with these uncomfortable physical changes in your body. Examples include deep breathing; telling someone about your distress; holding eye contact with them; grounding yourself by touching or feeling things around you; repeating a soothing mantra; singing or reciting the lyrics to a favorite song, poem, or nursery rhyme; or using the five, four, three, two, one countdown tool (acknowledge five things you see around you, four things you can touch, three things you can hear, two things you can smell, and one thing you can taste) to help dissipate anxious feelings in the moment.

By practicing these skills and incorporating other self-soothing activities into your regular schedule, you may be able to decrease your overall susceptibility to stress, anxiety, and panic attacks. Activities you could incorporate into the rest of your life include regular meditation, massage, yoga, listening to binaural beats, allowing your stress to bubble up in manageable amounts, and paying attention to diet and exercise.

The key is to find what works for you and to understand your body's physical reaction to stress or fear so you can determine what *can* be changed and what you have control over. It takes time, practice, and experimenting with different tools to see what works for you. This may mean making small changes and taking small steps to face your fears, and acknowledging and accepting the stressors (or things that you cannot control) in order to stop putting energy into a battle you cannot win. It will also serve you well to plan and prepare for how you will handle stressful or challenging situations before they happen. Addressing minor stressors before they become crises is also a helpful technique for changing your response to stress and danger. Setting boundaries, decluttering your environment, practicing self-compassion, and getting support from safe peers will help in multiple areas of your life, preventing relapse, unnecessary conflict, and drama, and improving your relationships.

I'm not giving you this information so you can use it as a tool to justify or rationalize your past or present behaviors or actions. Instead, I'm introducing these concepts so you can understand the need to reprogram your habits and to help you avoid crises through planning and preparation. Understanding these concepts can also help you be more empathetic and understand your friends and family's responses to stress and danger. Just as you respond counterproductively to rebuilding relationships, they may also be struggling with their fight-or-flight response to you.

The Family Disease Model of Addiction

No matter the classification or definition of addiction, we have come to recognize that the entire family is affected when one or more members have an addiction or mental illness. Family members are affected by the same stress, anxiety, and emotional turmoil that one might encounter when a loved one is diagnosed with an illness like cancer or when experiencing a particularly stressful life event like a pandemic, home fire, or hurricane. As a result, family roles shift, priorities change, sacrifices are made, and the impact on the family can be dramatic. In cases of addiction or alcoholism, the negative stigma of the illness may cause additional stress as the family tries to hide or compensate for the behaviors and actions of the addicted person. Family members can react and respond to addiction or mental illness in a family member in a variety of ways, such as

- They may have mixed feelings of guilt, responsibility, confusion, anger, resentment, and sadness.

- Mental health problems such as depression and anxiety can worsen.

- Physical health issues can result from focusing on the addicted individual instead of attending to one's own health.

- Financial issues are expected as the addict or alcoholic either no longer earns a consistent income or spends it on their addiction or treatment costs.

- Feelings of helplessness and hopelessness are common and can lead the entire family toward increased isolation.

- The essential family element of trust may be damaged or lost, especially if the addicted family member has lied to or stolen from the family.

Family members may find themselves falling into more specific roles in an attempt to distract from the central issue of addiction or mental illness. Sharon Wegscheider-Cruse[63] expanded on Virginia Satir's family roles[64] concept to identify six common roles that family members may assume in a dysfunctional family:

- The Addict, Alcoholic, or "Identified Patient."

- The Hero/Rescuer—this overachiever is probably very responsible and is trying to bring esteem to the family.

- The Mascot or Clown—this is often the youngest child, who distracts from the tension in the home by being cute, humorous, and playful.

- The Scapegoat—this individual may act out in an attempt to distract from the addiction, or they may be unjustly blamed for the problems in the family.

- The Lost Child—this person withdraws from the family and becomes figuratively invisible. They may escape by isolating themselves, reading, or playing video games.
- The Chief Enabler—this is the person who unintentionally fuels the addict's behavior by denying there is a problem or attempting to clean up the problem or cover it up.

The dynamics of a dysfunctional family can have both immediate and long-lasting effects on children and adolescents:

- They may start withdrawing from their social circle as they stop bringing friends to the house because of their shame and embarrassment.
- Feelings of helplessness and being alone or different are common. Children may not know where to turn to for help, especially if they've been asked to keep the family secrets. For example, a family member may have said to them, "Don't tell Grandma and Grandpa why Mom did not attend Thanksgiving dinner tonight."
- Family roles or boundaries may be blurred as older children have to take care of younger ones or assume the responsibilities of the absent parent.
- Children may become hyperresponsible as they take on these new roles in the family, which may involve carrying more responsibility than they should have to at their age, such as the ten-year-old child who gets the younger siblings up and ready for school in the mornings and makes their lunches.
- Problems at home often affect their grades or behavior in school and extracurricular activities. Sometimes their schoolwork declines, but sometimes they may instead excel, seeking to be the perfect child or student so as to not stress the family more.
- They may act out or become an additional family scapegoat to divert attention away from the sick parent.
- They may experience depression and anxiety.

A great deal of information about the long-term effects a dysfunctional family can have on children can be found from authors such as Claudia Black[65] and Janet G. Woititz[66] and from the twelve-step group Adult Children of Alcoholics. This support group is dedicated specifically to helping adults who were raised in addicted or dysfunctional homes. The *ACA Fellowship Text*, often called "the Big Red Book," offers extensive information about understanding the experiences and consequences of growing up in a dysfunctional family. In addition, it gives ideas for breaking these dysfunctional cycles and improving one's life. The Big Red Book identifies the most common characteristics of an adult child of an alcoholic, known as the laundry list.[67] This list includes traits such as people-pleasing, fear of authority figures, low self-esteem, and being overly responsible.

Enabling and Codependency

Enabling and codependency are two of the most common concepts addressed when looking at family members' relationships with the identified patient. The term *enabling* is often used to describe the behaviors of family members to help or harm the addict or alcoholic. These behaviors include making excuses for them, cleaning up their messes (literally and figuratively), taking over their responsibilities, yelling, fighting, appeasing, and calling in sick for them. Most of the time, these actions are performed with the misguided intention of helping the addict. But in truth, they usually only serve to protect the addict from the consequences of their behaviors, thus actually allowing the disease to progress.

> **NOTE** Just because your family member "enabled" you does not mean you can blame them for your actions, addiction, or dysfunction.

The emotional pressure from living with an alcoholic, addict, or dysfunctional relationship can become so great that the family member becomes as dysfunctional as the alcoholic or addict. This is often called *codependency* or *relationship addiction*. Codependency is not a mental illness. It may develop when the family member becomes overly concerned with the identified "sick" family member to the exclusion of taking care of themselves. They may be hyperresponsible and perfectionist, and they may take pride in caring for or rescuing others. They may detach from their feelings and emotions and be unable to set boundaries. They may even suffer secondary physical symptoms such as sluggishness, hair loss, weight fluctuations, anxiety, sleeplessness, suicidal thoughts, difficulty concentrating, and loss of interest in areas of life not connected to the addict.[68]

Some may even say that the family could be suffering like the addict and in need of therapeutic attention. It is not your job to alert your family members to their need for help or therapy. You cannot force your loved ones to seek this help; however, you may introduce the idea and encourage their participation. Regardless, while you are seeking love and support from them for your illness, you need to offer the same type of understanding and empathy to them. They will need help looking at their history within the family system and working through their part of the family dysfunction. This is a great time to consider their level of pain and suffering and offer them the same kindness, support, and patience you would offer to a new member of your support group (e.g., AA, NA, etc.). Within the twelve-step community, we believe that we have a disease that can be overcome with the group's support and through working with our community. We get sober and stay that way by getting help from others and giving help to others. This is going to be true for your family members as well; so allowing them to gain support from others and from you is in your best interest. It is common for some of us to fear their involvement in these support groups, as they're getting healthy and will be better able to assert their boundaries. But hanging onto beliefs like this is an indication that you have not truly surrendered to your powerlessness. It is important to note that this healing work is hard and painful for them. You are not responsible for their efforts to heal and care for themselves, but you can assist them in healthy ways. It is hard work for them, and it is hard work for you.

A word to the addict: did you create these problems in your loved ones? No, but you have likely contributed to their pain and suffering through your *past* dysfunctional behaviors. The best way to make amends to your friends and family is to recognize this and make an ongoing effort to break the cycle of dysfunction.

Summary

AA has been calling alcoholism an illness since its inception. Finally, science is slowly catching up to this notion. The more research is done on addiction and the brain, the more strongly we can support the belief that alcoholism is a disease. It is essential to understand the following points before you continue in this book:

- Alcoholism, addiction, and mental illness are, at the very least, illnesses that affect your physical, emotional, mental, and spiritual health.

- Addiction changes both the structure and the function of the brain, just as cardiovascular disease damages the heart and diabetes impairs the pancreas.

- We must pay attention to our brain health as part of our overall recovery plan and our efforts to improve our physical health.

- Things like diet, exercise, learning new skills, having social interactions with others, reading, fresh air, and time spent in nature all enhance neuroplasticity and the healing of the brain.

- Your family has been deeply affected by this disease, and they have their own recovery journey to pursue. Your progress will be significantly improved if you support them in their journey to healing.

- If left untreated, your illness and the family's unhealthy environment will get worse, not better.

- Information and understanding are substantial first steps in making a change.

Lastly, you are not alone; many avenues of help are available to you and your family. You can initiate family healing and break the cycle of family dysfunction, even if your friends and family are not actively participating in this journey.

3

Assessment and Preparation

Identifying and having a good assessment of the problems in your relationships are essential to solving them promptly and efficiently. This assessment process is not intended to be an opportunity to shame yourself or blame others. It is a tool to understand your problem areas better and create a starting point for doing the work. You must be fearless in your efforts to examine your actions and behaviors. This requires looking at what your part of the problem is without self-judgment. You have already taken the first step in repairing your relationships by finding this information. Never underestimate the significance of this effort. It can be difficult and painful to face one's faults; it takes courage to become willing to do this. From this starting point, we will expand upon what works well, improve areas of need, and add new skills.

All relationships, whether healthy, functional, or dysfunctional, have strengths and weaknesses. Speak to any couple who have been married for more than thirty years, and they will tell you that their marriage was not without trials, mistakes, and hardships. The most common problem areas that affect all families include communication, division of labor and authority, inability to manage conflict, anger, stress, and financial difficulties.

You cannot fix something you do not understand or are unaware of. The Johari window, developed by psychologists Joseph Luft and Harrington Ingham, is a tool that can help you become more aware of how you conduct yourself in relationships.[1]

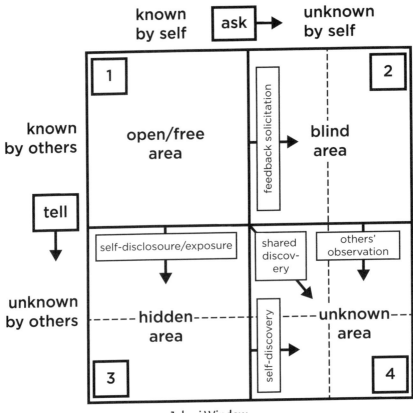

Johari Window

The Johari window divides the self in relationship into the following four areas:

Open/free area—This area represents what you know about yourself and what others know about you. This may include the skills, talents, and behaviors we are willing to share.

Blind area—This includes the things that others can see in us but that we do not see in ourselves. Examples: talking too much, interrupting another's conversations, and not taking verbal cues from others.

Hidden area—These are things that we know about ourselves but do not let others know about us. This may include our insecurities, self-doubt, and fears that we mask with other behaviors.

Unknown area—These are aspects of our life that affect our relationships despite the fact that we don't see them, nor do others know these things about us. This includes the parts of our lives that we have yet to understand or explore, such as how the unresolved issues and influences from our early childhood affect our behaviors in the present.

The goal of using the Johari window is to increase the open/free area in our communication and relationship skills, to increase our understanding of ourselves, and to share more of ourselves in our relationships.

The Filter Effect

How we view the problem areas in our relationships begins long before we have entered into the current relationship we are trying to improve. All individuals bring a past, a set of experiences that shape their approach to every relationship they are currently in or will enter. These include perceptions about relationships in general. For example, do we view being in a relationship as work or something that takes away from our free time and recreation? Or do we approach being in a relationship as a way to expand ourselves and open ourselves up to new opportunities and experiences? Do we *need* a relationship to give us a sense of belonging, to complete ourselves? Do we feel incomplete without a partner?

Most of these preconceived notions have come from our life experiences or our families of origin, but our past relationships, as well as the influence of TV, movies, and social media, also shape our opinions and expectations. Your friends and family members also bring their experiences with relationships, life, loss, sharing, and so on into their current and future relationships, including their relationship with you. It is important to identify these filters that influence your relationship's future.

> **NOTE** New information, stressors, and even positive changes are constantly being introduced into relationships, requiring the people in them to evolve and adapt to grow stronger. If you don't, changes can cause cracks and divides that can end relationships entirely.

Questions to Determine Each Relationship's Baseline

The first thing to examine is your friend or family member's attitude toward *healing the relationship with you*. Are they open to rebuilding a relationship with you at all? What boundaries are they imposing? What are their main objections, fears, and concerns? Are they overly optimistic? Psychologist Paul Ekman, a pioneer in the study of emotions, suggests we have six basic emotions: sadness, happiness, fear, anger, surprise, and disgust. Take some time to think about your relationships with these emotions. Which emotions are most prevalent in your life? Which ones are you uncomfortable with? What messages did you receive about these emotions when you were growing up? Which one is most prominent in your relationships with your loved ones?

It is important to note that your loved ones' feelings, opinions, and emotions cannot be called either right or wrong; they just are what they are. You can only control how you act in response to these emotions. You cannot control the feelings of another person. You can only work to positively affect their attitude toward rebuilding a relationship with you by staying in recovery, continuing to improve yourself, and behaving consistently. The following questions are designed to help you gain insight and understanding about the healthy or unhealthy patterns in your relationships.

> **NOTE** You may choose to write your answers to these questions down in a journal or folder.

What Is the Current Atmosphere of Your Home Life?

Is there an aura of fear or tension at home? Have your family members been walking on eggshells around you? Have family members lived in a fearful environment for a short time, or perhaps for years? Is your family home a safe place to be in? What level of violence or emotional turmoil has been present in the past? Is there a denial of the family's problems? Are they taken seriously, or are they minimized or dismissed? Is there an atmosphere of denial, sugarcoating, or overlooking the issues and conflicts within each relationship?

What Are the Communication Patterns in Your Family?

Are there some members of the family who dominate conversations? Is there an individual you consider a good or a bad listener? Does someone not talk at all? Do you interrupt each other, raise your voice, try to intimidate, or influence others by your body language? (Improving communication skills will be addressed in chapter 5.)

Problem-Solving Skills and Conflict Management

These two areas often go hand in hand. How does your family deal with everyday problems and minor issues? Are they ignored or swept under the rug until someone, or something, blows up? Does one person or group of people always defer or submit to another? Do conflicts quickly escalate to shouting or name-calling?

> **NOTE** If problems and conflicts are not resolved when they are smaller, they will become issues that require significantly more time and attention. You cannot avoid, ignore, or wish problems away.

How Are Emotions Expressed?

Are family members allowed to have and express the full range of emotions? Or are some feelings (for example, grief and sadness) not allowed to be shared? Are there family members who never show or share their feelings? How is anger expressed in the home? Does it create an unsafe environment?

What Stressors Are Present, and How Is Stress Managed?

Stressors could include finances, legal problems, children's and adolescents' behavioral challenges, and physical health problems. What stressors are particularly troublesome for your family? What are the individual stressors for each member of the family? How do you all manage stress? What healthy or unhealthy coping mechanisms do you and your family use?

Decision-Making

Who is/are the primary decision-makers in the family? Who has input into how decisions are made? Do all family members find this to be a satisfactory arrangement? How would each of the family members like decisions to be established? How can this be improved?

What Type of Discipline Is Present in the Home or Relationships?

How are rules established? Are they clear and defined? Are they consistently enforced? Are consequences reasonable? Do the children understand the rules? Do the children have any input?

Boundaries

Boundaries are the invisible lines or ground rules people set in relationships. They can be physical (do not touch me) or emotional (do not use curse words when speaking to me). Healthy boundaries are essential for cultivating good relationships, but many of us were not raised in an environment where healthy boundaries existed. A necessary part of self-care is setting and holding boundaries. It is an integral part of all relationships.

It is crucial to evaluate the boundaries in your life and determine how they either support or harm your relationships. Take time to assess the boundaries or lack thereof in the relationships you are trying to repair. Do members respect each other's personal space and privacy? Is everyone allowed to ask for what they need physically and emotionally? Are secrets honored or shared?

Deal-Breakers

Finally, what are each of your family member's deal-breakers? What are the nonnegotiable issues that, if left unresolved, will cause your loved one to walk away from the relationship? Are you all willing to learn and honor these? Have you defined your deal-breakers? Examples of typical deal-breakers would include threats of physical violence, a return to active addiction, noncompliance with treatment or aftercare, or other recommendations.

Self-Assessment: How Stable Is Your Sobriety?

Are you sober and in recovery? How much time sober do you have? It is not enough to just not drink. Your sobriety must be stable for any in-depth work. You don't necessarily have to wait until you feel stable and confident in staying sober before you begin reconciling or rebuilding your relationships; you must tailor your interactions and interventions to the strength of your sobriety. For example, if you have just left treatment and are still beginning to create a foundation for your sobriety, you may want to go no deeper than using common courtesy to your family members. Your efforts may be perceived as no more than being consistent in your behavior and actions. While this may seem superficial, it is still a step in the right direction.

Has your sobriety been tested? Do you understand your triggers? Are you removing the people and places that trigger your drinking or drug use? Is your sobriety strong enough to withstand the challenges of repairing and rebuilding relationships? Have you worked the steps? Are you still struggling to stay sober? What is your current sobriety support network? Do you have a sponsor and peers you can rely on to pick you up when you get down?

If you are working the steps of any traditional twelve-step program, I recommend completing the first three steps before you attempt to address any deep therapeutic problems in your relationships. The first three steps are about accepting your addiction or issues; being honest, open, and willing to do the work required to become sober; and becoming ready to do the challenging work of steps four through nine. Again, this does not mean that you postpone or delay any work you can do to repair these relationships; but you tailor the work to what your recovery can handle. Remember that you will carry old, dysfunctional behaviors into sobriety. Are you working on these behaviors? Are you experiencing "dry drunk" symptoms?

> **NOTE** *Dry drunk* is a term used to describe an individual who has stopped drinking, using drugs, or participating in their addictive behaviors, but who has not addressed the issues that led them to their addiction. This individual will often still be exhibiting behaviors similar to those they displayed when they were in active addiction.

What Is Your Baseline or Starting Point?

Take some time to examine the following aspects of your current behaviors, strengths, and weaknesses. This knowledge is important to have when relating to yourself and others in a healthy manner. Please consider this an objective, neutral exercise; there are no good or bad responses. Then answer the following questions about yourself. When you learn about the traits and skills revealed by these questions, you'll understand yourself better and know more about what you bring to your relationships.

What Tools and Strengths Do You Already Possess That Will Aid You in This Journey?

What have you been told you are good at? What do people like about you? Are you creative, curious, kind, understanding, and interested in learning more? Are you hardworking, diligent, persistent, and solution-oriented? Are you willing to try new things?

How Patient Are You?

Do you react impulsively? Do you have difficulty making decisions? Are you more impatient with yourself or others? Can you delay gratification and put your wants aside so you can focus on your needs? Can you postpone or set aside your desires for the sake of others' wants and needs? How can you be motivated to keep pursuing your goals even during times of difficulty?

As you identify your strengths, you will see your weaknesses, faults, and mistakes. You may be inclined to put unnecessary guilt or shame on yourself for them, but note that there may also be hidden strengths in each weakness. Instead of calling them *weaknesses*, you could try to call your challenges "growth opportunities." For example, I used to react without thinking. This sometimes got me into trouble when I did or said things I regretted later. I previously saw this characteristic as a purely bad trait. However, I have learned that this ability to react and think quickly can be an asset if harnessed correctly. I had to learn to use it in a way that helped me in a healthy way and did not hurt others. Thus, I have learned to add a momentary pause before I speak, or to take time to think about what I am hearing and how I will respond.

What Do You Value Most?

Values are what you believe are important in how you live and work. They can vary from person to person. Knowing your values will help you define your sense of self or purpose. They are a central driver of who you are, who you want to become, and how you judge others. When you live in a way that matches your values, you are more likely to be content and make the best decisions for yourself. Many of us have yet to reflect much on our values and have unquestioningly either accepted what our families taught us or fought against them.

If you cannot immediately identify your values, think back to when you were your happiest or most content without using an addictive substance. What were you doing, who were you with, and what other factors contributed to this sense of well-being? Then take some time to imagine who you want to become, what traits you want to reignite, or what traits you want to acquire. Now take some time to consider the following values and assess how they fit into your life today and where you want to grow:

- Spirituality—faith
- Loyalty—integrity, authenticity
- Consistency—reliability, dependability
- Honesty—trustworthiness
- Humility—selflessness
- Compassion—kindness, empathy, generosity
- Altruism—helping others
- Responsibility—accountability
- Being Realistic—setting goals and expectations
- Courage—toughness, fearlessness
- Contemplativeness—cautious, a dreamer
- Self-reliance—independent, resourceful
- Intelligence—education, continuing to seek intellectual or emotional growth
- Tolerance—open-minded, willing to learn new things, fairness to others

- Financial wealth—income, financial freedom
- Ambition
- Manipulation—controlling, dominating
- Perfectionism
- Overindulgence
- Pridefulness—greed, envy
- Slothfulness—laziness

Are You Willing to Learn?

Are you coachable or teachable? Can you humbly say that you don't know how to do something? Are you comfortable asking for help when you need it? This requires a willingness to look at your faults or weaknesses with objectivity. This is a tricky skill for most of us. Getting better at it takes seeking out objective opinions from others, time, self-compassion, and practice. For some, just asking for help is difficult. We fear that we are inconveniencing someone else. But it is important to remind you that the helper usually gets as much satisfaction from helping others as the receiver does from being helped.

What Are Your Physical Limitations?

Are you currently living separately from your family? Do you live in a different town than you did before starting recovery? Are you still in treatment or a therapeutic environment that limits your contact with family members? Do you have reliable transportation? Are there court orders that you must comply with? Do you have access to a phone and mail service? These may be obstacles that need to be addressed.

Do You Have Any Mental Impairment/Brain Fog?

As addicts and alcoholics, most of us have done some level of damage to our ability to process information and see things clearly, and it may take up to two years for the resultant brain fog to clear (as we discussed in chapter 2). This fog will likely interfere with your decision-making and problem-solving skills. You need to look honestly at this and acknowledge that some things that don't make sense right now will improve. Use this insight to seek second opinions from your peers, sponsor, or therapist when making any major decisions.

> **NOTE** Some memory loss can be attributed to blackouts, and some of this information may never be regained. You may not recall all your words and actions, so try to accept what your friends and family say about your past behaviors and incidents, especially how your past behaviors made them feel. It is essential to recognize and validate your family member's recall of such events. Making excuses for the past by saying you cannot remember will only damage your relationships.

Do You Have a Spiritual Life?

Who or what is your higher power? Are you confused about your religious and spiritual beliefs? Do they conflict with your loved one's beliefs, or are they the same? The goal here will not be to change your or your family members' beliefs but to understand each other better and acknowledge and accept your similarities and differences.

How Do You Express Emotions?

Do you struggle with expressing your emotions? Is it difficult for you to define how you feel? Do you have emotional walls up to protect you from the hurt and pain of the world? Do you find yourself to be dramatic, overly sensitive, and easily wounded by the slightest criticism? How do you manage your emotions? Whatever your approach is, does it work for you or against you? There are no right or wrong answers to these questions. We are only setting a starting point in hopes of being able to measure and acknowledge the growth and changes you will make.

How Well Do You Communicate with Others?

How do you express your thoughts and feelings? Are you shy and quiet? What communication skills do you possess? Do you understand the power of listening? Are you empathetic? Do you practice humility? Do you know the difference between telling the truth tactfully and hurting someone's feelings? Are you able to express feelings of love and gratitude toward others? For example, when did you last tell your family members any of the following statements:

- I love you.
- You are enough.
- I would not change you.
- I accept you the way you are.

Have you told your children that your illness, addiction, or problems are *not their fault*? It is important to let them know that nothing they said or did caused you to withdraw from them. Have you told them that you understand that you harmed them? Are you ready to hear from them about how you hurt them?

How Do You Manage Your Anger?

Anger is one of the core emotions, and it is a normal, healthy emotion. It can be used to motivate us, to get us to act, or to set boundaries. Some of us were taught never to express our anger, while others were exposed to dangerous levels of anger in their environments. The key is to learn how to manage this emotion healthily and productively. How do you manage your anger today? Do you scream and yell? Do you give people the silent treatment? Do you suffer in silence? Are you passive-aggressive? How do you deal with other people's anger when it is directed toward you? What changes would you like to make in how you manage your anger?

How Do You Manage Your Boundaries?

How do you emotionally protect yourself? Do you have any boundaries at all? If so, what boundaries do you place around yourself? Are these boundaries appropriate and helpful to you? Do you feel that people take advantage of you? To start, your boundaries must include not accepting physical, emotional, mental, or spiritual violence or abuse. Your boundaries can also be more personalized, such as an insistence that you participate in therapy or twelve-step programs.

What Are Your Stressors and Triggers?

What pressure points do you tend to react to unthinkingly, without thinking your reaction through? What trigger points or vulnerable areas will typically get you off track? This knowledge and understanding are crucial for maintaining your sobriety.

What Baggage Do You Bring to Your Relationships?

What wounds do you have from your childhood or prior relationships that adversely affect your current relationships? Do you project those issues onto existing relationships? For example, I carried unresolved issues into adulthood from my childhood experiences of growing up in a home with an alcoholic parent. I had a fear of abandonment, which fed my people-pleasing behaviors and my willingness to accept maltreatment by other people. I wasn't aware of this issue because it existed in the "unknown area" quadrant of my Johari window. I learned about it in my therapy and self-help groups.

> **NOTE** There is abundant literature addressing how our family of origin (or lack thereof) affects our lives and relationships later in life. This does not mean you can blame your family for your behaviors and actions. You are an adult; therefore, you must take responsibility and be accountable for your actions. It is helpful to acknowledge and recognize how these past experiences affect your current behaviors and life.

Do You Have Insight into What Drives Your Behavior?

Can you accurately explain your actions and motivations? For some, this isn't easy. We fear looking at ourselves; we fear what we might find. Others may be confident in their self-perception, but searching and expanding your insight can add more meaning and peace to your life. By studying yourself more closely, you may be able to come to terms with your past actions and make changes in your current life.

Vulnerability

Brené Brown, a prominent researcher and social worker, has written extensively about how being vulnerable is a strength rather than a weakness. Can you let yourself be vulnerable? Can you admit your mistakes, look at your flaws, and understand them as potential strengths rather than weaknesses?

It may be easier to address your vulnerability by asking yourself the following questions: How can I improve my ability to solve problems, resolve conflicts, and handle disagreements productively? What have I done in the past that doesn't work? Which of my behaviors and actions are working?

Tests of Readiness

The following questions are intended to challenge any remaining amount of denial or bargaining you might have about the difficult work of repairing relationships. Although this work can often be as fun and rewarding as it is difficult and painful, there are no shortcuts to family reconciliation.

- **Am I healthy enough to make good decisions?** It's a good sign if you are willing to ask yourself this question because it demonstrates a willingness to self-evaluate objectively. It also illustrates that you understand the benefit of objective support, advice, and feedback on your more challenging choices.

- **What is my motivation?** What do you hope to gain? Do you have sincere reasons? Are you doing this to get out of trouble? Are you trying to avoid losing material things? Is your motivation based on financial needs, fears, or concerns? Or is it something else?

- **What do I have to lose?** Do you believe that some of your relationships are beyond repair? If so, making an effort (however small) will not do more damage than has already been done, as long as you honor the boundaries the other person has established.

More challenging questions:

- **Am I ready to face the pain?** Are you able to handle possible rejection? Can you manage the effort that it may take? Do you have a support system and enough coping skills to prevent relapse if the pain feels overwhelming? Again, there is no right or wrong answer to this question. The important part is to be aware of where you stand and to communicate this to your support system and family members. You must maintain your sobriety. This does not mean that you get to avoid dealing with the harm that you did. It means you develop a game plan for dealing with it when you are ready to.

- **Am I ready to move out of pain?** There are two sides to this question. For some of us, all we have known is victimhood. Some of us were raised in an environment that was so chaotic or traumatic that being victimized is what we perceive as normal. Our victim mentality has been programmed into us as a coping mechanism for survival. It is natural to be reticent about wanting to address the more painful events and memories of your life. Moving out of this role can be frightening and challenging until new coping mechanisms, boundaries, and support systems are in place to keep us from relapse. But the darker side of playing the victim is that it can lead us to justify our actions, avoid taking responsibility for our behaviors, and manipulate others. Some may do this to achieve the secondary gains of obtaining sympathy and compassion in order to get their wants and needs met. The first step in breaking this pattern of behavior is to accept responsibility for your actions. Ask others to hold you accountable and give feedback when you have slipped into excusing your behaviors or blaming others.

- **Am I willing to look at what my part of the problem is?** Are you willing to do the work necessary to make changes within yourself and your relationships? Are you willing to acknowledge and make amends for your contributions to the drama and conflicts in your life? Are you ready to leave the (victim, hero, patient, problem, etc.) role? Eleanor Roosevelt once said, "It is not fair to ask of others what you are not willing to do yourself." You must learn to accept responsibility for only your actions and behaviors and to look for areas where you can improve, keeping the focus on yourself. This won't be easy, but adopting a positive attitude about this work is important.

Family Assessment

This term refers to assessing your family's demographic factors, not a clinical assessment. I approach this area with a great deal of apprehension. I do not want you to attempt to clinically assess or judge your loved ones or your family as a unit. This portion of the book is not meant to be an opportunity to place blame or point fingers. Instead, it is intended to help you identify the general readiness of your family and friends to begin the steps to healing. It is meant to identify problems and establish a starting point to measure your progress. Finally, it is intended to help you identify the strengths and talents of each of your family members in order to develop a positive foundation to work from as you move forward.

A Few Words about Healthy Families

I believe healthy families do exist, and all families fall along a continuum ranging from severely damaged and dysfunctional to flourishing and healthy. Some characteristics of healthy families include:

- Fostering and encouraging the development and growth of individuals and the family
- Establishing and maintaining boundaries that are clearly defined yet flexible
- Constructive communication
- Healthy demonstration and encouragement of the expression of a full range of feelings
- Managing conflicts while honoring rules for fair fighting
- Supporting each family member's opinions, thoughts, and feelings
- Regular practice of kindness, patience, and understanding
- Designated time for fun and relaxation
- Following reasonable, consistent rules
- Self-care practiced by all members
- Commitment to the relationship demonstrated by all members
- Allowing members to grow and change
- Involvement with the outside community, such as a place of worship, volunteer work, school, and sports

Family Reactions to Your Past Active Addiction, Your Sobriety, and the Behavioral Changes You Are Making to Support Your Recovery

Each of your loved ones will have different feelings about your active addiction, your desire to seek sobriety, and your efforts to do so. The range of emotions can vary from joy, relief, and happiness to fear, anger, and denial. Whatever their feelings are, they are valid. You must accept their feelings as they are. There is no right or wrong way for any of them to feel. It will be necessary to know how they think and affirm their feelings. I cannot stress this enough: you must try not to minimize, deny, or diminish their feelings.

Stages of Recovery

You and your family members will likely be at different stages of recovery, which will significantly affect the work and the level of reconciliation you can obtain at a given time. For example, suppose you have participated in a rehabilitation program or are attending ninety meetings in ninety days. In this case, you are likely to get more support and help for your sobriety and recovery than your friends and family members are getting for their needs, feelings, and education. This difference in your situations is significant in several ways:

- **Quantity.** You are getting intensive help for your problems; they probably are not. There are fewer resources available to your loved ones for learning how to care for themselves, their codependency, or their personal recovery needs.

- **Availability.** Support like therapy or Al-Anon meetings is much less readily available to our family members. For example, at my recovery clubhouse, we have an average of four daily meetings aimed at recovering individuals. However, there are only four weekly meetings that offer support to family members.

- **Support**. Your family members may be struggling with having little to no family support because they have either hidden your addiction from their friends or relatives, or because their friends and relatives are discouraging them from trying to heal their relationship with you.

- **Responsibilities.** If you are in a rehabilitation center, you may be removed from your responsibilities and problems, while your family has been left behind to clean up your mess, manage the house, do the chores, and handle the finances. This puts additional pressure on their time and energy.

- **Recovery.** They will likely not be as far along in their recovery as you are. Therefore, it is to your benefit to offer them the same support, compassion, patience, and forgiveness you hope to receive from them for your addiction/mental illness.

Demographic Information about the Adults in Your Familial Relationships

What are the roles, characteristics, and ages of all the adult relationships in your immediate household? This includes any stepchildren or in-laws living with you. You will interact most with these people, which makes them the most important people in supporting your recovery. Then identify the other people in your broader circle of relationships who play a significant role in your day-to-day life. This may include your ex-wife's new husband, the stepfather to your children, your spouse's best friend, grandparents, aunts, uncles, and others who are active in your family life. This basic information gives you an idea of the people you have affected with your active addiction or mental illness. The number of people may seem daunting, but the point is to determine which relationships require more immediate action than others. You will see that as one relationship improves, it will have a positive trickle-down effect on others. For example, investing in your relationship with your spouse will positively affect your relationship with your children, your in-laws, and your spouse's friends.

Demographic Information about Your Adult Friends

A "family" does not mean only the people you are biologically related to or were raised with. After identifying your familial relationships by biology and marriage, look outside this circle to list all the other significant people in your life who have been affected by your addiction, who hold some level of influence over you, or to whom you are accountable. This may include your best friend, your manager at work, a religious advisor, or the licensing board of your profession. It's also valuable to examine who will support or challenge your current efforts at sobriety.

Assessment of Children and Adolescents

A parent's addiction can affect children in many ways. Different reactions can surface as children try to cope and adapt to the stressors in the home. Behavioral problems in school or at home are common because children may act out the stress they're experiencing at home. On the other hand, some children may move toward perfectionism or excellence by immersing themselves in their academics, athletics, or extracurricular activities as a way to assert control or people-please. Children are likely to have feelings of confusion, shame, hurt, or anger, which they may or may not express. These feelings can develop into depression and anxiety. In addition, children in this situation may be socially awkward, shy, or withdrawn. They may be bullied or become bullies themselves. They may not want to bring friends or classmates to their homes because of the chaos and inconsistency of the home atmosphere, leading to feelings of isolation. When children try to make sense of the chaos and inconsistency at home with no success, they often blame themselves for their parents' addictions. They may think, *If I didn't cause so many problems at school or if I didn't cause my parents to fight over me, then my parents wouldn't drink so much.*

Growing up in a dysfunctional home can also have more long-lasting effects. At the very least, these children are more likely to become alcoholics and addicts themselves or to surround themselves with alcoholics and addicts throughout their lives. It is absolutely crucial to involve your children in your recovery process and to have age-appropriate, honest, and open discussions about your illness. They need to understand that your disease is not their fault; they did nothing to cause it and can do nothing to cure it.

> **NOTE** I was raised in an alcoholic home. I experienced the damage of having an alcoholic parent. I carried the wounds into my adulthood, addiction, and relationships. Even into recovery, I was haunted by the traits I possessed as the adult child of an alcoholic (as addressed in chapter 2, in the section "The Family Disease Model of Addiction.") However, I found that as I addressed these wounds, my recovery blossomed even more, and I became a better, more present, and more engaged parent to my children.

Home Life

What is the current status of your romantic life? Are you married, divorced, or separated? Are you living with a partner, or are you physically separated from your significant other temporarily or permanently? Who is living in the home with you? Is this living situation desirable for everyone involved?

What are the ages and genders of each of your children and stepchildren? Who is living at home currently? Who is away at college, or who has moved away? Are the school-aged children attending school, or are they being homeschooled? How is their current academic, social, and behavioral progress at school? Who are you financially responsible for? This is relevant because how you communicate with your six-year-old will be very different from how you communicate with your sixteen-year-old, as will be the ways you heal those relationships.

What coping mechanisms does each family member use, such as sports, music, friends, activities, isolation, or drug use? What is each family member's communication style—quiet, avoidant, friendly, aggressive, or something else? What extracurricular activities, hobbies, and interests do you share as a family? What activities do your family members participate in individually? What are the unique talents and strengths of each of your family members? What brings each family member joy? What is their love language? What do they value? What is important to them? How can you use this information to improve these relationships?

More challenging questions:

- Has there been criminal activity? Does anyone involved have a criminal record? Is there pending litigation? When will this be resolved?

- What are the clinically diagnosed physical or mental health challenges present in this dynamic?

- What behavioral problems or consequences are currently documented at work or school? How has the family responded to and dealt with these stressors?

- What are each family member's roles? Some examples include addict, sick individual, patient, caretaker, chief enabler, rescuer, hero, mascot, clown, and the scapegoat.[2]

- Have there been any reversals in family roles? Has one of the children become the "acting parent" or caretaker of the younger children? Has the active addict assumed the role of the child, even if they are not a child? Who holds a position of leadership and exercises power in their familial role?

It is perfectly all right not to know the answers to these questions, and there are no right or wrong responses. I just want you to start thinking about all the elements that affect your relationships. You have no control over some of these elements; but by knowing them, you can consider your interpersonal dynamics while making changes and improvements.

Summary

Healing your relationships begins with understanding their current statuses and strengths, and knowing the areas that offer opportunities for change. This path is not smooth, linear, or straightforward. When you have a starting point and a positive attitude, this will enable you to continue your research and do the necessary work to rebuild your relationships. In recovery, expect the unexpected. As one family member heals, others may regress.

Finally, instead of focusing on what you have lost, focus on what you have left and what you have to gain. The ultimate goal is to heal relationships and promote the health of your family. A healthy family is one that, despite having conflicts and hardships, still strives to communicate openly and support each family member in their individuality, interests, and goals. The members of a healthy family spend quality time together at meals or engaging in fun activities. They support and encourage each other; they allow each individual to express their emotions, goals, and interests. They have flexible boundaries that grow and adapt to change as family members leave for school, get married, or move away from home. Finally, they demonstrate commitment to the family as a unit and to each individual within it. The process of getting to that place may be painful, but it will be worth it. You deserve healthy relationships, and your family and loved ones deserve a healthy relationship with you.

4

Expectations, Myths, and Mistakes

was frightened and unsure when I first walked into my treatment center, but I thought I knew what to expect from this inpatient facility and what sobriety would mean for myself and my family. I was, after all, a social worker by profession. Early in my career, I worked at several prominent drug and alcohol treatment facilities. I had been a family therapist in charge of running the family programs for these treatment centers. I also worked as a therapist, counselor, and coach with children, teens, and families. I personally referred people to various types of treatment over the years. I had an excellent understanding of Al-Anon, ACA, and other twelve-step support groups because I had participated in these programs myself.

When I walked into that treatment center, I believed I would get medical attention, participate in therapy, receive education, and learn how to stop drinking. I thought my family would be invited to partake in family therapy. I also hoped they would be offered a family program to start them on their own path to healing. Finally, I imagined I would "graduate" treatment with an aftercare plan and a supportive family welcoming me back home with open arms. However, it did not take long for me to realize that I was wrong about these preconceived beliefs. My expectations only became liabilities and mistakes in my attempts at sobriety and healing my family relationships.

The Burden of Unrealistic Expectations

In AA, we are discouraged from setting expectations. There is a phrase often quoted in AA: "Expectations are premeditated resentments." I interpret this to mean, "I am setting myself up for disappointment if I make unrealistic expectations of myself or others." As a result, having expectations increases the chance of failure and thereby risks the development of resentment toward others. These resentments can threaten my happiness, peace, and sobriety.

There are differing opinions about the relationship between expectations and goal setting. Some self-help writers and motivational speakers speak about the benefits of setting expectations high to help you achieve your "full potential." They encourage you to believe in yourself and to reach for the highest possible level of success, and they support these ideas with platitudes like: "Reach for the moon; if you miss, you will land among the stars." On the other hand, other motivational speakers will warn you of setting your goals too low, stating that you must push yourself beyond your usual limits to reach your full potential. Both extremes can set you up for failure.

Types of Expectations

Expectations come in many different forms. Some can be subtle and so ingrained into our thinking that we do not even perceive them as expectations. We take them for granted as absolute truths. Family patterns are a good example. For instance, spanking your child with your hand on the bottom was once perceived as an appropriate form of punishment. But today, most educators and counselors would advise against this type of discipline. In addition, recent research shows that spanking can cause lasting trauma.[1]

Early in my recovery, I expected my family to be proud of my newfound sobriety and to be happy for me whenever I received a new chip or key tag as recognition of my accrued time in sobriety. But they found little comfort in seeing my chips and key tags, even though I wore them like badges of honor. I was proud of my efforts to maintain my sobriety, but my children were embarrassed by the AA chips and NA key tags I clipped to my purse. They were afraid that people might ask questions about them, and they were not ready for the world to know that I was an alcoholic—that their mother had alcoholism.

Some expectations can come in the form of predictions; for instance, "If I fail to call my partner when I am going to be late, they will be angry." If these predictions are based on prior experiences, then it may be safe to believe them. But if these predictions are based upon your own internalized fears, assumptions, or generalizations, you may be assuming how others will behave and react. For example, you may think, "I know my parents will never forgive me for stealing from them," but your parents may be more concerned with the issues and reasons behind your behavior.

We may also have expectations about what we think we deserve. For example, you may think, "If I work hard on this project at my job, I will surely get a raise." "If I finish this drug and alcohol treatment program, my family will take me back." "If I fail this exam, my world will end." Other expectations can come in the form of denial or magical thinking: "If I just pray hard enough," or "if I am good enough," or "if I believe strongly enough, my desires will come to pass." That can take a number of different forms, such as: "If I make ninety meetings in ninety days, I will be able to maintain my sobriety forever." "If I just detox, then I can return to normal drinking."

I am not saying that all expectations are wrong or bad; I am just stating the need to be mindful of our expectations. Unreasonable or unmet expectations can lead to disappointment and discouragement, which can result in losing motivation or becoming complacent. Setting expectations or goals too high can make them seem unlikely or impossible to achieve. Lastly, unobtained goals or expectations could lead to an increased risk of relapse.

What I know today is that as I entered treatment, I had many expectations of myself and my family:

I expected my family to support me, forgive me, and miss me while I was gone.

I thought I would quickly regain their trust and respect. I hoped they would believe in me and my intent to stay sober. I knew my family would go through hardships while I was away and that my husband would have to step up and take over some of my responsibilities with the kids and the house. But I had no idea how disruptive my departure had been. I didn't know that after they adjusted to my absence, my family found a new sense of peace without me.

I did not expect my family to enjoy their life without me.

Sometimes, families welcome the break from the chaos and uncertainty of living with an alcoholic or addict. They may even hope the alcoholic or addict does not return home. Often, alcoholics and addicts will not be active in daily family life and won't participate in family activities. Families usually find it challenging to adapt to our new sober behaviors or to renew or regain interest in a family life that includes the addict. It is also not uncommon to hear family members say, "I liked them better when they were drinking." In my family, my daughter had taken over many of my responsibilities in raising her two younger brothers. They had come to rely upon her, and she had become very protective of them. It was difficult and uncomfortable for all four of us when I attempted to take over this task. They no longer trusted my parenting skills or me.

I did not expect the pain of rejection to be so intense.

Recovery is hard, and in early recovery, we try to navigate life and its struggles without our number one coping mechanism: alcohol or drugs. Now that we are in recovery, we have to face life without this crutch. We are learning new tools, but they are not second nature to us yet. The pain we face is greater because we have fewer ways to dull it. For me, rejection and fear of abandonment are core issues from my childhood. Thus, when my family resisted my efforts to renew relationships, the pain was magnified, both because I didn't have a coping mechanism for dealing with the pain and because it stirred up unresolved pain from my childhood.

I did not expect to want *not* to leave treatment.

The treatment setting became a safe and secure environment. My access to alcohol and drugs had been removed. My peers at the facility all had experiences similar to mine, and I was not alone in my pain or struggles. However, as my discharge date grew close, I began to fear life outside the treatment setting and the temptations that would present themselves out there. I have come to realize that this is a normal and reasonable reaction to leaving the environment where I first entered recovery. Your fear is an indication that you recognize the dangers and triggers of the unstructured world.

I did not expect to experience moments of joy in treatment.
Upon entering treatment, I was full of guilt and shame. I didn't feel as though I deserved any peace or happiness. I could not imagine that I was going to have fun or experience any laughter in treatment and sobriety. So when I first found myself laughing or smiling, I felt guilty for these tiny bits of reprieve from the intensity of treatment. But it is important to have these moments of fun and comic relief. Learning to laugh at yourself is an important part of healing. This enables you to release some of the guilt and shame that fuel the feelings of hopelessness and depression. Eventually, you can share your experience, strength, and hope with others, empowering yourself while being of service.

I did not expect to have a period of deep depression in sobriety.
In one of the first few days of my treatment, I heard a young man share his battle with depression at six months of sobriety. He told how his life had taken a turn for the worse and that nothing seemed to be going right for him. Yet he had remained determined not to drink. Sadly, he slipped into deep despair. He shared these experiences, how he eventually worked through them with time, and the tools he used to survive this difficult period. I, too, experienced deep depression at about five months of sobriety when I suffered several setbacks all at once. I made it through this time because I didn't give up; I practiced the fundamental sobriety tools of the program (morning meditation, daily inventory, attending meetings, and talking to my sponsor). I also recalled what I had heard this young man share: there would be really tough times in early sobriety, there would be challenges and crises, and this was part of recovery. I had a tough time staying hopeful, but I clung to the belief that if it had worked for him, it would work for me too.

I did not expect to feel so out of control.
I felt out of control because I didn't know how to live without alcohol or how to cope with everyday stresses. At first I had to live under the rules established by the rehab facility and later a halfway house. I found it easy to follow the rules that were imposed upon me. During that time, I had all

of my choices taken from me, and to get the most out of treatment, I had to surrender my will to the will of others. Ironically, to be successful in recovery, you have to be willing to admit that you have lost control over your use of alcohol, drugs, or addictive behavior. You must surrender and become willing to try life in a new, sober manner. For many of us, this is terrifying. Many addicts have spent the last months or years of their active addiction so high, drunk, or intoxicated that they have not been thinking clearly. For most addicts, the world revolves around their drug or addictive behavior, getting high, getting a fix, figuring out how to get the next high, and keeping their addiction secret. When they enter recovery, they are thrust into a sober world and told that their efforts to maintain sobriety require surrender and letting a higher power give them direction. As a recovering adult child of an alcoholic, I had spent my entire life trying to control my external world—trying to find comfort by managing the people, places, and things around me. The sensation of admitting that I was powerless and could not control most things in my life was contradictory to my nature.

I did not expect to feel hopeless.

I thought I would learn new tools and find answers to my questions and solutions to my problems quickly. But, in truth, I experienced a hopelessness that left me wondering if I would ever find peace and happiness again or if I would ever regain admission into my family. It seemed that my efforts to get and stay sober weren't solving my family and personal problems. I wanted immediate results for my actions, and I felt hopeless when that did not occur. I did not drink to escape these feelings, but I sat in self-pity and grief until I admitted that I needed help and could not do it alone.

Here are some other expectations that many addicts have when they enter recovery:

If I can stay sober, all of my problems will disappear.

Most of your problems are still waiting for you when you enter recovery. In fact, now that you are not numbing yourself with your addiction, some of your problems will be much more painful. You do not have to tackle them all at once, but ignoring them will not make them disappear. Get help and support from your sponsor, therapist, or trusted, objective peers. Do not try to walk through these problems alone. If you can, break down the steps to resolve the issues into pieces so small that it would be impossible to fail. Let's say you know you are in debt and have a stack of bills waiting to be paid. Start by taking the most minor steps: sorting your mail, organizing your emails, and identifying all your bills. Praise yourself for taking this step. The next step may be to sort through the bills and, ultimately, to make a plan for paying them off one at a time.

Life will never be the same again.

This expectation is well-founded, but do you want your old life back? Was your drinking or drug use pleasing you? Which did it generate more of— pleasure or pain? Do an honest assessment of your relationship with your drug of choice, as discussed in chapter 3. Life will be different, but with work and hope, it can be much better than you have ever experienced before.

I will never have fun again.

You don't have to attend many AA or recovery support meetings to see smiles and hear laughter from the people in attendance. We have fun in sobriety; we celebrate special occasions, and we learn how to attend events like tailgates and concerts without using alcohol or drugs. It takes practice, planning ahead, and frank conversations with your family and friends. You may have to temporarily avoid certain people and places where the triggers to drink or use are strong. But, with time, you can attend social, family, holiday, and sporting events without using your drug of choice. Early sobriety is a good time to volunteer or to participate in sober social activities available in your recovery community. Service work is gratifying, and the self-esteem built while doing these activities will replace some of the guilt and shame you have from your past.

Because of my sobriety, I have had the opportunity to experience more joys and thrills than I could ever imagine. I have ziplined through Ecuador's rainforests, hiked to the highest point on the Appalachian Trail, and seen orcas swimming and playing in the Alaskan waters. But, most importantly, I have experienced the pure joy of having time with my children, family, and friends.

I got this! (being overly confident in one's sobriety)

I have rarely slipped into this type of thinking. I have resisted this idea because I have witnessed what has happened to my peers who did not maintain their efforts to stay sober. The consequences of continued use of addictive substances will indeed result in institutionalization, jail, or death. As I write this book, I have had many years of sobriety, and I feel reasonably confident that I will remain sober today and tomorrow. But I firmly believe this is primarily because I continue to work my program; that is, I am continuing to do the things that aid me in sobriety. For me, that is daily prayer and meditation, attending meetings as often as possible, talking to my sponsor, and doing service work. I have learned that many people relapse because they get complacent in their sobriety habits; they quit practicing good sobriety hygiene. Never take your sobriety for granted.

Family Influences on Expectations

Some families have legacies of expectations, beliefs, and values. Usually, these are so ingrained into our families' histories that we have come to accept them as normal without taking the time to acknowledge that these legacies often contain messages that are counterproductive in today's culture and damaging to our mental health, and that can have long-lasting impacts.

For example, my parents were children of immigrants who came to America to live the American dream. They each built farms on which to make their living. These farms required never-ending work. Children were often considered free farm labor and were expected to contribute to the workforce. It was essential to respect your parents without question, to be an excellent example of the family name in public, and to be loyal to the family above all else. Little time was devoted to sharing emotions and dealing with feelings after suffering a misfortune or loss.

Both sets of my grandparents had good intentions. They imparted their beliefs and values to my parents, who passed them on to my brothers and me. These included practicing a religion, believing in a higher power, valuing an education, and being of service to others. But many of the values they passed down are counterproductive in today's world, such as:

- Work first; play later.

- Plan for the worst outcome.

- Don't get your hopes up.

- The glass is half empty, not half full.

- Do not share the family business with others; protect the family's honor at all costs.

- There is always more work and a better way to do it.

- Nothing short of perfection is good enough.

- You can accomplish anything in life if you work hard enough.

- Most people are untrustworthy, so they will take advantage of you if you let them.

- Boys have more value than girls.

In summary, unrealistic expectations can lead to setbacks and disappointments, but realistic expectations are essential to individual and family recovery. They can help you anticipate and prepare for the obstacles you could encounter. It is essential to have positive long-term goals. Approach your goals with flexibility and be willing to modify them. Be mindful of your inner dialogue. Write and repeat your positive affirmations multiple times a day. Set yourself up for success.

Common Mistakes

Mistakes in early sobriety are to be expected. Some will happen due to habitual behaviors that occur almost instinctually after addiction. Some mistakes will be made because you have not yet learned a better way of doing things. Others will be made due to pride, fear, or an inability to ask for help. You will make mistakes. You will repeat mistakes. The goal is to make an effort to understand where these patterns come from and break your destructive cycles. As you gain time in sobriety, you will gain new insight into and understanding of your behaviors. The first objective is to become more aware of your mistakes; then you can catch yourself while making them and correct the behavior. Then you will practice using new, healthier tools. Over time, your ineffectual behaviors will fade away, and new ones will replace them.

If you are working a twelve-step program, you will eventually complete the fourth and fifth steps: making a searching and fearless moral inventory of yourself, and admitting to God, to yourself, and to another human being the exact nature of your wrongs. During this activity, you will gain greater awareness and understanding of these mistakes and additional weaknesses that have contributed to your disease and the destruction of your relationships. You can use this information to help you strengthen your recovery program.

In the next section we'll discuss some common mistakes that addicts make during recovery, and some new, healthy skills you can practice instead.

Mistake: Selfishness; Forgetting That the Family Is Also in a Crisis

Selfishness is not a character trait that anyone likes to claim. But as an alcoholic or addict, you have likely been highly selfish in your behaviors during active illness. Early sobriety, especially if you are isolated in a treatment facility, can foster continued self-centeredness. The primary focus is directed toward the treatment of the alcoholic or addict in crisis. They are the center of attention, and the family and significant others are often overlooked. But it is important to remember that your family is also in crisis. You have probably left them to clean up the messes you left behind. Your family has to pay the bills and run the household without you. They may feel the need to explain your absence to extended family, friends, and neighbors. They will likely have feelings of embarrassment about your actions. They may also feel ashamed at being relieved that you are no longer in the home, or they may feel even more unsettled because they don't know how you are doing in treatment. Your family will be wondering what life might be like when you return home. Regardless, early recovery requires self-centeredness for you to maintain sobriety. This means prioritizing recovery behaviors—going to meetings, daily meditation, and talking to a sponsor or trusted individual—over other family activities or social events. Simply put, you will not be able to be there for your loved ones consistently, even after beginning recovery. You will have to make difficult decisions about how and where you spend your time. Finding this balance is one of the fundamental principles of this book.

Healthy skills: While your sobriety tools usually have to come first, take time to explain your goals and values, and be open to discussion about how to balance your needs with your family's needs. Make efforts to become aware of your significant other's needs too. Ask them for patience, and use active listening skills to demonstrate that you have heard what they are saying. This includes not talking when someone else is speaking, maintaining eye contact, demonstrating an understanding of their needs, repeating the information they shared, asking for clarification, and acknowledging that you have received what they said.

Mistake: Diminishing or Minimizing Your Actions by Comparing Them to Others

It is easy to look at the actions of others and compare your mistakes to theirs to reduce your guilt and shame. For instance, you may want to compare a behavior like passing out at your son's band performance to another addict who got into a fight at their child's science fair. By comparing your behavior to another addict's and saying "it could have been worse," you are downplaying your family's pain and embarrassment and minimizing your responsibility. You must own how you have inflicted pain upon your loved ones, because you have violated their sense of safety and trust.

Healthy skills: Acknowledge to yourself that you have harmed your family and friends, and do not compare your or their experiences and emotional pain to others. When the opportunity arises, or while completing the eighth step of making amends, reach out to each individual you have harmed and validate their feelings and experiences as their truth.

Mistake: Not Taking Ownership of Your Feelings ("You made me so mad when . . .")

This is a common mistake in communication. It is important to acknowledge your feelings and take ownership of them. It is important to understand that *feelings are reactions to emotions.* Emotions are typically instinctual and hormonal. It is difficult to block an emotion as it is triggered. But you are in charge of how you *react* to these emotions and how you define your feelings. No one *makes* you feel any particular way.

For instance, I can choose how to respond to a driver who has cut me off in traffic. I can yell and honk at them and allow this incident to ruin my day, or

I can give the driver the benefit of the doubt and assume they were in a hurry and it was an honest mistake. This way, I give the driver grace and preserve my peace of mind.

Healthy skills: Practice naming and verbalizing your emotions. Fear, sadness, joy, anger, disgust, and surprise are all fundamental emotions. Contemplate how you typically react to these emotions. Which feeling words come up when you experience them? Think about how you can change the way you react to the feeling. Take time to explore new ways to respond.

Mistake: Taking Advice from People Who Only Tell You What You Want to Hear

There is a slogan in AA: "Stick with the winners." This means you should listen to and seek out the wisdom of the old-timers and others you respect. There are various levels of experience and recovery in the sobriety community. There are even some individuals with a great deal of sober time who still have habits you do not want to emulate. Finding someone who will tell you what you want to hear is easy. You can always find someone to help you justify or rationalize your actions or thoughts. For example, I had a friend who did not like some of the rules of the halfway house where we lived. She constantly complained about them and struggled against them. She even got her temporary sponsor to agree with her. The two commiserated about everything wrong with the halfway house. Unfortunately, this did not serve either of them well; it only fueled their frustration and wasted time on something neither of them could change. She could have used this experience to practice patience, give up control, and accept authority—all things that people in treatment are asked to do. Instead, she allied with someone willing to enable her unproductive behavior.

Healthy skills: Seek the advice of multiple peers and look for varying opinions. If you're in AA, request a topic at a discussion meeting to get multiple points of view on an issue. When I had difficulty remaining positive about my relationships with my children, I asked people to share their experiences around rebuilding their relationships with their own children. I asked younger group members what they would like to see in their relationships with their parents and family. What worked for them, and what didn't? I sought out and received much hope, advice, and encouragement.

Mistake: Not Explaining or Clarifying Recovery-Oriented Slogans or Activities

To the outside observer, some of the slogans, therapeutic terms, and activities of the newly recovered individual may look odd. The new habits can seem cult-like or just as dysfunctional as those you displayed during active addiction.

Healthy skills: Communicate to the best of your ability. Take time to explain the recommendations of your therapists and sponsors to your loved ones. This includes the rules of your treatment center, the deeper meaning of slogans, and explanations of program work.

As you listen to their concerns and complaints, respond to what they say, and reassure them. Be careful not to misuse the practices and principles of the program to justify or excuse your behaviors. In my social work practice, family members often complain to me that their recovering loved one is absent both emotionally and physically, just as they were during active addiction. The intensity of your participation in these sobriety-focused activities will reduce with time. Your loved ones need to know that you will eventually find a balance between your sobriety activities and your family roles.

Mistake: Being Superficial in Words or Deeds

While I was in a treatment center, I mistakenly thought that if I was making an effort with my kids, the quality of the effort did not matter. I wrote letters each week to each of my children. I was surprised to find most of them unopened when I returned home. Later, I learned that they perceived my letters as superficial and self-centered. Essentially, my letters created more damage than healing. I wrote the letters because I was afraid to make phone calls. I wrote the same things weekly, addressed what was happening to me, and I did not ask many questions about them and their lives. These letters were not sincere because I was scared. On the occasions when my family visited, I directed conversations toward the weather, TV, and the news—nothing of consequence. I never shared meaningful thoughts or demonstrated significant guilt, so I did not appear sincere. They wanted to know the answers to important questions: Was I sorry? When was I coming home? What was going to happen to our family?

Healthy skills: Walk through the fear. Have real conversations and be honest about your fears and feelings. Be vulnerable. Take an active interest in your loved ones' activities and feelings. Practice saying, "Tell me more about that," or "How did that make you feel?" This may be awkward at first, but it is worth it.

Mistake: Letting Ego and Arrogance Sabotage Your Recovery

At the opposite end of guilt and shame are ego and arrogance. In early recovery, some people can experience a "pink cloud," or positive and uplifting feelings of hope for a better future. A pink cloud can occur when we overcome some of our more basic obstacles. It is great to feel accomplished, but you must be careful not to allow your ego to be overinflated. Ultimately, your self-worth is boosted by your number of clean and sober days, so seek out support from fellow alcoholics and addicts, and be realistic, honest, and humble in recovery.

Healthy skills: You should be proud of your clean time. Nonetheless, be sure to remain aware of how you portray yourself to your loved ones. As you share your successes and joyful feelings with them, make sure you let them know that you are still working on your weaknesses and building up your strengths. Remember where you came from, and be optimistically realistic.

Mistake: Avoidance and Procrastination

There are many reasons why people procrastinate, including fear, dislike of completing unpleasant tasks, lack of clear goals, indecisiveness, anger, lack of ability to focus, or feeling overwhelmed.

Healthy skills: Break tasks into small steps, making them easier to complete. Life coach Katie Vanorden de Assis recommends, "If you're feeling stuck, make your steps so small they feel too easy *not* to do. If a step seems ridiculously tiny, good! A tiny step taken is greater than a larger one that isn't. The mind tends to minimize our efforts, so be kind with yourself, and celebrate your efforts!"[2] Keep a journal of your activities, and reward yourself for good work. Share your short-term goals with another person. Ask people to hold you accountable, and schedule time to take action. Focus on success, not failure.

Mistake: Perfectionism

Let's begin with the fact that there is no one way to get clean or sober. Nor is there any one way to repair relationships. These paths are not linear and will have ups and downs, highs and lows. There is no such thing as a perfect relationship or perfect recovery. My sponsor often reminds me that my perfectionism is another way I procrastinate. I often get so wrapped up in doing something perfectly that the task never comes to completion. Perfectionism can also be another way of imposing negative self-talk on yourself by setting your standards too high to be achievable.

Healthy skills: Stop comparing yourself to other people. Give yourself and others grace and forgiveness. Allow yourself to make mistakes, and learn to take pride in your ability to rebound from setbacks. Document and acknowledge your positive efforts to make changes, no matter the outcome.

Mistake: Overthinking, Overanalyzing, or Indecision

This can be a form of procrastination and self-deprecation. Many people overthink to try to gain control or mastery over a skill or situation. This can lead to becoming stuck on thoughts about the past, the future, fears, or potential outcomes of decisions, resulting in inaction.

Healthy skills: Write out your thoughts. This will allow you to slow down your repetitive thoughts. Then you can better understand the ineffectiveness of your ruminations. I encourage my clients to let themselves "shelve" issues so they can put a particular subject away, up on a shelf, to be addressed at a later time. This is different from avoidance, since you have a concrete plan to take the issue or topic off the shelf and address it. You should commit to revisiting the issue or problem at a particular time. You can also use this skill to manage communication problems with friends and family. In a later section I will share some problem-solving skills that can be used in conjunction with this practice.

Mistake: People-Pleasing and Seeking the Approval of Others

While you need to consider the needs of your loved ones, do not deny your own needs or stretch yourself too thin. People-pleasing can manifest in many ways. One common way is putting others' needs before your own and having difficulty saying no. It may also look like trying to help everyone who asks for your time or resources, telling people what they want to hear, or making promises you cannot fulfill.

Healthy skills: Learn to pause and give yourself more time to respond to requests for your time, efforts, and resources. You can do this by saying, "Let me think about that," or "I need more time to consider that before I respond." Then assess the request and get feedback from an objective individual, sponsor, or therapist.

Mistake: Overcompensating with Compliments, Generosity, or Gift-Giving

This may seem an easy way to try to make up for the past, but gift-giving is typically a short-term fix and is often viewed as an insincere effort to fix problems.

Healthy skill: Be genuine, give what you can at appropriate times, and do not overextend yourself. It is important to accept your limits. Stay in the present. Verbalize your desire to be more selfless, as well as the need to set healthy limits and boundaries.

Mistake: Overreacting or Underreacting

Many of us instinctually fall back into our fight-flight-freeze-fawn mode in response to fear, danger, or conflict. This reaction can be good or bad, depending on the situation. Unfortunately, others may misunderstand your behaviors as either combativeness or apathy.

Healthy skills: Take time to examine, learn about, and understand your reaction to fear, danger, and conflict. Determine what works for you, and change what does not. Take time to learn new ways of coping in high-stress situations. Practice pausing. Give yourself time to put new behaviors and reactions into practice. If you tend to freeze and do nothing, try to implement asking for more time, admitting that you have become tongue-tied, or stating that you don't know what to do next. Let the other person know that you haven't fallen into apathy or disinterest; instead, you are experiencing an emotional overload response to this stressor.

Mistake: Talking to Your Children as if They Are Adults, or to Adults as if They Are Children

Age-appropriate communication is crucial. When you interact with adults, don't baby them or talk down to them. By the same token, don't expect younger children to understand adult matters—but don't dismiss their perceptions and awareness, either. Typically, younger children have a sense of the health of the dynamics in a home. However, they are not mature enough to cope with adult stressors. Do not seek advice from your children. I remember the fear and confusion I felt when I was seven years old and awoke to my mother throwing my father's clothes out of the house. My father was drunk and crying, seeking my thirteen-year-old brother's help in resolving his fight with my mother in the middle of the night. To add to my confusion, the next day my parents acted as if nothing had happened.

Healthy skill: Educate yourself, learn communication skills, and speak to others with age-appropriate language. Improve your communication skills, and ask questions. Practice your listening skills.

Mistake: Not Providing Closure for Shelved Topics, Conflicts, or Disagreements

It is essential that you revisit shelved conflicts. My family never discussed the argument of that night. As I recall, we all had breakfast the following day and got ready for church. We acted like nothing had ever happened. As a child, I did not know if it had been a bad dream, if I had imagined it, or if it would happen again.

Healthy skills: Do whatever it takes to return to shelved topics, even if only to let the other person know you haven't forgotten about the issue or conflict. Make an appointment with yourself or the other person involved. Be consistent with your actions.

Mistake: Becoming Complacent, Comfortable, or Bored with Your Recovery

It is important to take time for recreation and rest, but not to the exclusion of continuing to do the recovery work you have begun. New skills have yet to become habits, and slipping backward or falling prey to unexpected triggers is easy. This is not to say that you must always be working on your sobriety, but you must always prioritize your recovery.

Healthy skills: Find a healthy balance between play and work. Continue to reinforce the foundational skills necessary for you to maintain your sobriety and improve your relationships. Set small, attainable goals, finding new ways to challenge yourself or continue to grow. These can be simple tasks like complimenting your partner for their patience with you, helping your child with their homework, or making the coffee for your twelve-step meeting.

It may be helpful to keep a journal or calendar of your activities or commitments to sobriety, family, and work. This will give you a visual reminder of how you spend your time, thus enabling you to recognize when your efforts are weighted too heavily in one area or another.

Mistake: Making Assumptions, or "Mind-Reading"

No matter how long you have known your loved ones or how well you think you know them, do not assume you can successfully predict their answers or responses. Instead, take the time to ask your loved ones what they want, think, or believe.

Healthy skills: Remember that you are asking your loved ones to accept your *new* ways of thinking and living. Give them time to develop new reactions, thoughts, and beliefs.

Mistake: Wasting Time Sitting in Self-Pity, Making Excuses, or Complaining

Some people may use self-pity to avoid responsibility for their actions. They may put themselves in the victim role to hide or deflect from their part of the problem, or they may choose to stay in the victim role and not take action. Nothing constructive can come from sitting in self-pity. This does not mean you deny or minimize your aches and pains; instead, express them, vent them if necessary, and then let them go.

Healthy skills: Reframe self-talk, and consciously decide to choose joy over pity. Try to surround yourself with positive people. Distance yourself from the negative influences in your life. For example, do not say self-deprecating things. Focus on how far you have come instead of how far you still have to go.

Mistake: Making Significant Life Changes in the First Year of Sobriety

The first year of sobriety is stressful enough without adding other major changes to it. Staying sober requires a great deal of time, attention, and energy. Moving, changing a job, beginning a new relationship, and ending a marriage are additional stressors that pose distractions from your number one priority: your recovery.

Healthy skills: Consider this a time to heal. Allow any bit of lingering brain fog to pass. Take time to improve your decision-making skills. Keep your life as consistent as you can, so you can handle the inevitable challenges life will throw at you.

Mistake: Replacing an Old Relationship with a New One

The danger of entering into a new relationship too quickly is that it can be a distraction that disrupts the foundation of your recovery. New love may give you a high that replaces the feeling you once got from alcohol or drugs. However, new relationships often have emotional lows as well as highs, and early in recovery you are probably not ready to use your newfound mental clarity in a romantic relationship.

Healthy skills: Keep it simple. Take time to get healthy and learn from your mistakes in your close relationships, especially if you have children. If your loved ones have stayed with you through these challenging times, they are more likely to stay with you in sobriety.

Mistake: Trying to Do the Work of Recovery Alone

Recovery from addiction and mental illness isn't easy. It takes time and work, and there are no shortcuts. Having a support group of individuals with similar problems can provide you with information, education, emotional comfort, friendship, wisdom, and hope. In addition, it keeps you accountable and offers you the opportunity to gain self-esteem by giving back and doing service work for others.

Healthy skills: It may take a bit of research or asking for referrals to find the right support group for you. Thankfully, support groups come in all shapes and sizes. There are in-person meetings, Zoom meetings, and even phone conference meetings. In-person meetings are also held in various settings, such as churches, clubhouses, schools, hospitals, and rehab facilities. Do not be discouraged if you have to try several different meetings before you find a place where you feel comfortable.

Myths vs. Facts

Usually, myths about sobriety are addressed and debunked early in treatment or when attending twelve-step groups. Some of these myths go as follows: "You will never have fun again." "You have to hit rock bottom before you can get sober." "You can never be around alcohol again." Such myths have arisen out of misinformation and fear. Sometimes they have been created simply by misconceptions and gossip. Myths can prevent us from getting the help we need or keep us stuck in negative patterns. There are also many myths about family recovery that can impede our efforts to heal these relationships.

Here are some of the more common myths about addiction, recovery, and family relationships:

Myth: Addiction Is a Choice

We may have chosen to take that first drink, but most people do not choose to become addicted to any substance or activity. The reality is that the addict or alcoholic has lost the ability to stop drinking or using once the addiction has been triggered.

Myth: The Only Thing You Can Get Addicted to Is Alcohol or Drugs

Food, gambling, shopping, attention, sex, and love are a few of the many things one can become addicted to. Neuroscience research continues to evolve and is beginning to demonstrate that behavioral addictions are accompanied by changes in brain activity that are similar to the changes seen due to substance addiction.

Myth: If You Aren't Moving Forward, You're Moving Backward

This is a commonly used phrase in some twelve-step groups. However, its validity varies from one individual to the next. Maintaining sobriety skills is essential; it's like building muscle. If you don't continue to do at least a minimal amount of work, the muscle begins to atrophy. But you do not always have to be building greater and greater muscle to be healthy. Plateauing and enjoying the peace you have found are necessary parts of recovery. Rest and play are as important as hard work.

Myth: Family Recovery Is All Work and No Play

Family bonding and recreation are as important as the work you do in recovery. Play can strengthen the bonds among family members, and it creates an environment for trust to develop. It can improve interactions and reduce stress. The truth is that family healing takes place in small and big ways, and having fun and socializing together by going to the park or playing a board game can be an entertaining and essential part of healing.

Myth: Family Therapy Is the Best Way to Get Help

There is no one magical cure or best way for families to heal their collective wounds. There are many helpful resources available for individuals and families, and each family member will have different needs and responses to family therapy. There are also alternate resources such as twelve-step groups, religious and spiritual organizations, self-help books, YouTube videos, and speaker series. Often, a combination of these resources will be the best foundation for recovery.

It is important to note that family therapy does not have to be a long-term process and that therapists will not place blame on a single person or familial element for the problems that the family is exhibiting. The therapist is there to observe and evaluate difficulties within the family. Their role is to educate family members, guide them through crises, and help them resolve ongoing issues. Therapists help families replace dysfunctional behaviors with healthier ones. The goal is for the family to become a healthy environment that fosters individual and group growth.

Myth: The Ideal Family Life Is Free of Worry or Conflict

Healthy families do have conflicts, but they also have tools for managing conflicts. Conflict-management skills help families address minor issues and misunderstandings before they escalate into unmanageable problems. Learning how to resolve disputes can encourage trust among family members, and it allows people to be vulnerable and true to themselves.

Myth: All Your Problems Will Go Away Once You Become Sober/Get Clean/Overcome Your Depression or Anxiety/Develop New Tools . . .

The truth is that a lot of your problems will still be waiting for you. Some will seem more painful or intense now that you are not medicating your feelings with your addiction. The best course of action is to accept this, approach your problems with a plan, set your priorities, and maintain sobriety.

Myth: There Are No Winners or Losers

The truth is any given relationship, one person often gives more than another. Sometimes the division is fifty-fifty; sometimes one person offers 95 percent and the other only offers 5 percent. Sometimes there is a winner, and it is not you. During the times when you are the one giving 95 percent, remember that while you were in active addiction, you probably took more from your loved ones than you gave to them. You now have the opportunity to demonstrate your ability to give back. Do this with no expectation of gaining anything in return. Do not keep a scorecard; this will only build resentment. However, do not become a doormat, either; instead, seek to establish and maintain healthy boundaries. Try performing random acts of kindness for strangers. It is a good practice, and it makes it easier to do the same for your loved ones.

Myth: Life Will Never Be the Same

The goal of recovery is improvement. Life is going to change, and there will be losses. All your family members' lives are going to be different. The important part is accepting and welcoming the changes, learning from the painful ones, and welcoming the positive ones. Ultimately, these changes will improve your quality of life.

Myth: It's Time to Forget the Past; Forgive and Forget

Forgiveness can come without having to forget the past. Our painful pasts can become a tool or motivation to help us maintain positive momentum in our recovery. Your willingness to remember and share some of those more painful events may prove helpful to others. Acknowledging the differences between denial and choosing to forgive and forget are important. Denial implies that you have not accepted or taken responsibility for your actions, which means it won't make the hurt go away. On the contrary, denial often prolongs and worsens the problem. Choosing to forgive and forget does not mean the issue will never be addressed again; the individual on the receiving end accepts your apology and becomes willing to move forward.

Sometimes it is all right to shelve (meaning to postpone, not to forget) problems, issues, or feelings in order to gain perspective or move out of an emotionally charged event, or when you need to wait until you have the support of a therapist or peer who can help mediate the conflict. But this only means that the issue is on a temporary hold and will be addressed later.

Myth: You Now Have a Clean Slate to Work From

There is no clean slate. Your past is always your past. The ninth step of AA makes a number of promises to recovering alcoholics, including this one: "We will not forget the past or wish to shut the door on it." Your past can be a strength; it can propel you forward and help others. Hopefully, you will begin to create new, positive memories that will fill the minds of your loved ones to replace the pain of the old memories.

Myth: You Can Make Up for Lost Time

It is a hard fact that you have missed out on special occasions such as births, deaths, holidays, and celebrations due to your addiction. These occasions and events are gone and will not come back. This may be a painful reality that you have to face. In this case, take time to grieve the time you have lost, learn from it, and move on. Don't waste more time dwelling on the lost time now. Try putting your energy and effort into the present moment. You can create new experiences and memories that you and your family will come to cherish.

Myth: Time Heals All Wounds

My experience is that untreated wounds leave scars at best; at worst, they fester and become infected, and they can even kill you. Time can ease the pain, but unresolved and unprocessed pain and grief build on themselves and accumulate. I recommend addressing each loss, change, and wound as it arises so the feelings do not become overwhelming or insurmountable. If the pain is too great and keeps you from moving forward, seek additional help through your support network or from a professional.

Myth: You Can Wait It Out

You cannot ride out conflict by doing nothing. Sometimes you can see things more clearly by putting distance between you and the conflict, but you cannot pretend it did not happen. It would be best if you took responsibility for your actions and addressed the fallout head-on. Our loved ones often need time and space to trust us again. They may need to see actions instead of words before trusting you and allowing you back into their lives.

Myth: You Can Buy Your Way Back into the Hearts of Your Family and Friends

Gifts only offer a short-term fix, and they set a precedent that takes time, effort, and resources to keep up. You cannot buy your way into an authentic relationship. Your family wants *time* with you; they want your consistent, sober behavior more than shiny, new gifts and toys.

Myth: We Should All Strive to Love Unconditionally

Many people think we should love our spouse, parent, or child unconditionally. It is a myth that this type of love never breaks down because of the actions of another. True "unconditional love" is about loving someone else with reasonable boundaries. This love can be flexible and can adapt as a relationship changes or evolves. Believing that you must love another without any limits sets standards that are impossible to maintain in any relationship. A relationship does not have to have unconditional love to be good. You do not have to accept everything your loved one does to have a strong relationship.

Myth: If You Don't Cry, That Means Your Apologies and Regrets Aren't Genuine

I do not cry easily in times of conflict, anger, great stress, or tenderness. As a result, I may not seem genuine when apologizing or making amends. This does not mean I am not remorseful for my actions. I just have difficulty crying; it is not a matter of hiding my vulnerability or being insincere. There are other ways to express regret and remorse. Try using your actions to demonstrate that real change is occurring. Learn and practice listening and empathy skills so you can show people how you feel.

Other Behaviors to Avoid

Do Not Make Promises

You probably cannot list, much less remember, all the promises you have broken in your active addiction. Until you prove your trustworthiness, your promises hold no weight with your loved ones. When you make a promise, you set up an expectation that may be hard to fulfill. Instead, express authentically what your intentions are; then follow through with your actions. Start small. For example, tell your loved ones, "I will call you when the meeting is over," or let them know what time they can expect you home.

Never Say "I Know How You Feel"

No, you do not know how they feel. No one really knows how another person thinks or feels. Even when you say this in earnest, it can seem insincere at best; at worst, it makes you appear insensitive, uncaring, and dismissive. It is better to say, "I can't imagine what that felt like" or "That must have been awful," or to ask, "Is there anything I can say or do to help you?"

Do Not Try to Justify, Minimize, or Rationalize Your Actions

Do not tell a loved one that what you did or said was "not that bad" or "not as bad as what so-and-so did" or "it could have been worse." These are all forms of making excuses and not taking ownership or responsibility for your actions. If you do this when your family member asks for an explanation of a particular situation, you will appear inauthentic. Instead, pause and ask them precisely what they want to know; then answer that question as concisely as possible.

Never Reply to Another's Statement with "Yes, but . . ."

When you do this in conversation, you negate everything the other person just said, even if your intent was good. You miss the opportunity to demonstrate that you have understood what the other person has said. Saying "Yes, but . . ." confirms that you were not listening to the other person's point of view; you were only waiting to respond with your own perspective.

Do Not Compare Your Loved One to Someone Else

For instance, don't say things like, "Why can't you be like John's wife? She forgave him for such-and-such." This can be seen as disrespectful, and it's a sure way to create hostility or to deflect from the conversation at hand. Recognize that each person is unique and is on their own path. The people in your life will adapt to your new recovery in their own time and in their own way. This situation is hard for them as well. Please give them the compassion and understanding you would hope to receive.

Do Not Ask Questions That Have No Specific Answers

For example, don't ask, "What do you think I am trying to do?" or "Who do you think you are?" These types of questions are counterproductive. They are confusing and may be seen as deflection or avoidance.

Never Question or Invalidate Your Loved One's Memory or Impression of Past Events

Don't say, "No, that's not how I remember it." Their reality is their reality. They are allowed to have their opinion or memory of an event. Do not tell them they are wrong. Doing so will not nurture healing in your relationship.

Do Not Negate or Deny Your Loved Ones' Feelings

I cannot stress this enough: your friends and family members have unique reactions to and feelings about your active addiction and recovery. A more helpful response to their feelings could be, "I accept that you are angry with me. You have every right to your feelings," or "I will try to understand where you are coming from."

Summary

The truth is that the journey of reconciling with your family will have its ups and downs. However, through becoming aware of the dangers of unrealistic expectations and learning common mistakes that others have made during their process of healing their families, you can avoid some of these experiences. Progress comes in small steps as well as large ones. Sometimes you reach a plateau where it might seem you cannot gain any more ground no matter what you do. All of this is normal.

It's also dangerous to have high expectations of others. The best expectation you can have here is to know it will take work, just like your sobriety does. But the results are worth it. My relationships with my children, family, and close friends today are far better than I could have imagined at the start of my recovery. Our relationships are not perfect; we all make mistakes, but I try to acknowledge and correct mine quickly while encouraging open communication. Old hurts, issues, and wounds still arise and must be addressed. Sometimes this happens at inconvenient times, but we do our best to talk about them in the moment. If I cannot immediately address them, I will acknowledge them and follow through by returning to them at a later time.

Although this chapter has been framed from a black-and-white, right-versus-wrong perspective, I acknowledge that there are often nuances in family conflicts and issues. This chapter is meant to help you become aware of potential mistakes and prevent you from continuing to commit errors that could sabotage your efforts to reconnect with your close relations. You can achieve the results you seek through action, time, authenticity, vulnerability, accepting help, and maintaining hope. Taking small steps, letting go of expectations, and finding something to be grateful for all advance your efforts to reunify with your family and friends in a healthy way.

5

New Skills and Tools for Building Relationships

I was once where you likely are now: isolated from family and most close friends. I had a difficult time believing that things would ever get better, and I thought my relationships could not get much worse. But thinking like this didn't help; it only kept me in the problem. I was not moving toward a solution. In time, and with a lot of effort, I eventually gained the support and trust of most of my family members and close friends. In each of these relationships, growth came at different paces. In some relationships, the road was easy, and forgiveness was granted without much pain or struggle. With others, it took many years and a lot of work for me to demonstrate that I could reciprocate their time and love again. But the good news is that according to Maslow's hierarchy of needs, it is a basic human instinct to want to be loved, to feel like you're a part of something, and to have a sense of belonging. While you're working toward love, your family is likely reaching for the same goal, and they will probably reach for what is familiar: you. The key is to be available to them, to be willing to compromise, and to be ready when they take your hand after you have extended it.

The information in this chapter culminates research, work, practical experience, and wisdom from professionals and recovering individuals who have successfully worked through their family problems. Let's begin with an approach that embraces a positive attitude and the most essential tool of all: hope.

Relieve the Suffering and Increase Hope

You are here; you are seeking a way to repair your relationships. This is a huge first step. Embrace this motivation, embrace your willingness, pat yourself on the back, and know *you are never alone* (YANA for short), or you never *have* to be alone on this challenging journey. You can choose to lean on a higher power, a guardian angel watching over you, or you can rely upon the guidance of your therapist, support groups, and peers. Also, know that there is an endless amount of knowledge and wisdom available to you, so continue educating yourself on how to rebuild your relationships. If one path does not prove fruitful, you can seek out and follow another; you must keep trying and not give up. We will start by strengthening your foundation and creating a place to begin your path. This chapter will help you recognize your strengths and show you the essential tools needed to build a sturdy foundation so you can move on to new relational skills. As you read this chapter, ask yourself: "What am I learning? How can I use this? And when can I apply it?" Thinking about how this information applies to you will help you break the old patterns of thinking and behaving that no longer serve you.

Getting Started: Seek and Find Joy

It may seem simple, but I recommend you begin each day with gratitude, positivity, and hopeful expectations. You will attract good things by starting your morning routine and ending your day with a positive self-examination. Reflect on what is working, what has brought you joy, and what you can improve upon. When I wake up, I use a statement like "I can't wait to see what today brings me" as opposed to "What will happen to me today?" or "How could it get any worse?" In time, making this subtle change will become second nature.

Come Prepared and Well Rested

It is essential to ensure that you address the needs represented by the acronym HALT: are you hungry, angry, lonely, or tired? I am not saying you must wait until you are satiated and rested before you begin this work, but be aware that your ability to create and maintain change is affected by HALT. Good results do not come with hope and prayer alone. Good results come from preparation, planning, practice, and effort. A phrase commonly used in twelve-step groups is "Do the work and leave the results to God" (God as you understand them). This is wise advice, as it sometimes takes weeks or months for results to appear from an intervention or a sincere effort to change. Be willing to be patient, and in the meantime keep learning.

Acknowledge and Praise Your Current Skills

Examine yourself by taking an emotional inventory every morning and evening. Praise yourself for what you are doing right, and acknowledge where you can still improve. Avoid dichotomous thinking—looking at your actions as black or white, right or wrong. With practice, you will develop insight into your behaviors and learn to accept what works and where you can improve. Remember that information is power. The more you understand, the better you know how to work with it. For example, most of us like to be well prepared for a job interview. We research the company before the interview and find out what the employers are looking for in a future employee. You will be better able to present yourself as a candidate for the job if you understand your strengths and weaknesses and how you could help the company achieve its goals. Why not do the same research when preparing to rebuild relationships? What change do your family and friends hope to see? What do they want? What are their needs? How can you meet these needs? What do you hope to see? What do you want? What are your needs, and how can they be met?

Educate Yourself in Multiple Formats

This book provides one source of information and education; there are many other information and education resources, such as books, blogs, and social media. I recommend consistently reviewing new information and seeking advice and wisdom from healthy peers, sponsors, and therapists. Ask others what has worked for them, always strive to improve, and keep learning more. Read up and fill your mind and your playbook with new skills and tools.

Manage Expectations; Set Realistic Goals

It is easy to set your goals too high or too low. Take time to ask yourself whether you have unrealistic expectations. Are you willing to challenge these thoughts? Having expectations that are too high for your sobriety and your ability to reconnect with your family members can cause delays and frustrations. It is important to have realistic goals for your relationships. Observe and note where these relationships are now. What is your starting point with each connection that you hope to improve? Some individuals may be open to rebuilding relationships with you, but be prepared for others to stay angry with you, keep their walls up, and resist your efforts. There may be some who will never let you in. For these relationships, you may have to grieve and learn from this experience. But this does not mean you still can't plant a seed in hopes that, with time and patience, a relationship could grow. Don't expect a response of rejection and pain; just be emotionally prepared to handle disappointment. Rejection is a *feeling*, a *reaction* to pain and sadness. It can be managed. Please do not attempt to predict or make assumptions about any individual's response to your efforts. Their reaction may indeed be anger or fear of being hurt again.

Do not set limits, ultimatums, or timetables for how long reconciliation will take. In my experience, my children were at different ages and developmental stages when my drinking became unmanageable and when I found recovery. Thus, I harmed them in different ways. I did not see significant improvement in my relationships with my children for quite some time. It took over a year before I could see any measurable progress. The most challenging relationship to mend took over four years to change. Even today, there is room for improvement in each of these relationships, and from time to time, old wounds have to be addressed and new amends have to be made. The key is to establish small goals to work toward.

Be Coachable

Even the most talented athletes use coaches to improve their skills. There is always something new to learn and more information to gather. Unfortunately, many of us have difficulty admitting that we need help and asking for help. Some of us think we already know everything or can find the information ourselves. There is great strength in recognizing that you do not know what you do not know. For example, some of us don't know what a healthy family is. No one ever taught us how to be a good spouse or parent. Some of us have habits that we perceive as normal but that truly are dysfunctional. We may not even realize that we are products of dysfunctional families. Our perception of a "normal" family is based on our experience. In my family, my parents rarely had major conflicts or fights at home, and they rarely raised their voices at each other. Instead, conflicts were addressed behind closed doors or through passive-aggressive behaviors, complaints, and sarcasm. I never learned to use healthy conflict-resolution skills to manage everyday issues. I thought avoiding conflict and never expressing your feelings were normal behaviors in marriage.

Be Authentic and Practice Humility

Authenticity and *humility* are terms that you hear a lot in recovery. For clarity, I will define these as simply as I can. I see humility as freedom from pride or arrogance. This does not mean you cannot be proud of yourself, your talents, or your accomplishments. Instead, it means that you share them in moderation, with modesty, giving credit to others when appropriate.

I define authenticity as allowing yourself to demonstrate to others who you are. To be genuine, you do not present a false facade of yourself. Rather, you allow yourself to be vulnerable and to admit and accept your flaws and weaknesses. For example, when I have a problem with my car, I have no hesitation in taking it to a mechanic. I look to someone with expertise who has more knowledge than I do. Although we can't hire someone to improve our relationships, we can seek assistance to guide us through this journey.

Be Consistent and Develop Routines

This will reinforce your credibility and demonstrate that you can be held accountable. Your family and friends will take comfort in seeing a consistent behavioral pattern. This indicates that you are committed to this process. Remember that they have probably seen you "stop drinking" or "turn over a new leaf" many times. Most likely, you have consistently failed in these attempts to stick to sobriety. Developing and committing to new routines—even smaller and simpler acts, such as ensuring you are home to eat dinner with your family every weeknight—will help them build trust in you.

Become Willing to Give or Change without Expectation of Compensation, Acknowledgment, or Reciprocity

In all your close relationships, be willing to make an effort, perform acts of service, be kind, forgive, and change yourself without expecting anything in return. This attitude is constructive when trying to heal the wounds of your loved ones. However, it requires clear and honest motivation and may take practice. I recommend starting with random acts of kindness or service to strangers, acquaintances, and friends. Compliment the cashier checking you out at the grocery store; let someone cut a line in front of you; be a more patient driver. At home, make an effort to do chores around the house—make the bed, empty the dishwasher—with no expectation that the act will be reciprocated or even acknowledged. A more complex example of this might be making an effort to listen silently during a conversation and maintain eye contact, with no expectation that the other person will do the same for you.

However, this attitude does not require you to become a doormat and let people walk all over you. Instead, I ask you to make positive changes and take positive steps without expecting the same treatment in return. Changes on the part of your loved ones will come with time.

Respect Your Loved Ones' Feelings and Where They Are Emotionally and Mentally

I cannot emphasize this enough: when listening, take time to validate and empathize with the speaker's feelings. Make sure they believe that you heard what they said. You do not have to agree with them, but you cannot tell them that they shouldn't feel that way, that it wasn't that bad, or that they are wrong. *Their feelings are valid.* Their version of reality *is their truth, their reality.* The more you try to tell someone their version of the story is wrong, the more you distance yourself from them. Your goal is to validate their feelings and their experiences. Honoring their feelings and memories makes them more likely to take their walls down, and they may be more open to trusting you with their feelings.

Seek Connection, Not Control

As discussed earlier, we come to relationships with ideas and perceptions of what we can give to and receive from another person. Unfortunately, our history, fear, and weaknesses often influence what we want or believe we should have in our relationships. I urge you to release your past expectations and definitions of a healthy relationship and instead seek a connection with your loved ones. This entails:

- Looking for the commonalities in your relationship, not the differences
- Accepting what you do not have in common, and considering how each person's talents can enhance the other person's life
- Accepting the other person, despite their weaknesses and flaws, and accepting your own
- Lovingly exchanging talents, services, and support for each other
- Not trying to change the other person

Tools for building self-awareness of your controlling communication behaviors:

- How often do you find yourself teaching, preaching, or lecturing to your loved ones?
- Take note of the tone of your voice as you speak.
- Do you have a tendency to ramble? Might you need to be more concise and get straight to the point of what you are trying to say? It is better to be as brief as possible until more information or an explanation is requested.
- Do you raise your voice, yell, or assume an intimidating posture or tone of voice? Once you raise your voice, you will put the other person into a defensive or self-protective mode.
- Do you use phrases like "Because I said so"?

Tools for building connection:

- Slow down your speech. Keep your voice as calm and controlled as possible.

- Listen with the *intent to understand and learn* something from the other person, instead of trying to win an argument or make them understand your point.

- Look for similarities in opinions, thoughts, and ideas. Acknowledge these as the conversation continues.

- Express gratitude for the other person's time and effort, regardless of whether or not you achieve a resolution.

- Learn what their "love language" is, acknowledge it, and be receptive to it.

- Perform a random act of kindness without expecting to receive anything in return.

- Compliment and praise your loved ones in front of other people.

Specific Skills for Improving Relationships

You now have an excellent foundation of information about yourself, your substance use disorder, and your strengths and weaknesses. Hopefully you have healed some of your guilt and shame and have acquired sufficient hope to help you move into learning and using more specific skills for improving your relationships.

Improve Your Levels of Emotional Intelligence, Empathy, and Sympathy

Emotional intelligence is the ability to control and manage your emotions while being aware of your situation and considerate of those around you.[1]

Empathy is understanding or being aware of another's feelings from their perspective.

Sympathy is when you feel emotion toward someone for their feelings or experiences. For example, you feel sorry for the person who has experienced the death of a parent. You understand some or part of their pain, so as a result, you can support and validate their feelings.

NOTE Emotions and feelings are two different things. *Emotions* are physical states that arise from instinctual responses generated by the limbic system in the brain and the hormones it releases. Primary emotions include anger, sadness, fear, surprise, disgust, and joy. *Feelings* are the mental associations and reactions that we connect to our emotions. We often label our feelings as happy, confident, stressed, playful, calm, aggravated, and so on.

NOTE Some people were raised in families with high emotional intelligence. In addition, some are born with a more substantial capacity for emotional intelligence, while others must learn it. Improving your emotional intelligence includes reducing negative behaviors associated with painful emotions, staying calm while in distress, being assertive when necessary, and staying proactive rather than reactive in crises or difficult situations.

Strategies for improving your emotional intelligence include:

- Begin with recognizing your own emotions. Be observant of your feelings and how you react to the basic emotions of anger, sadness, fear, surprise, and joy.
- Start with small, less intense or painful emotions.
- Observe how others respond to similar situations, and reflect on similar problems in the past and present.
- Incorporate the skills that you find healthy and effective.
- Practice labeling your emotions and feelings. Ask yourself if your responses to triggers are reasonable. Ask for and get feedback from professionals, sponsors, and trusted friends. Become aware of how you behave while experiencing triggering emotions.
- Begin to use your thoughts and feelings to manage these emotions (to control impulses and delay reactions).
- Take responsibility for your feelings and actions.

- Recognize and become aware of others' emotions, and demonstrate empathy (i.e., understand, hear, and respond to another person's feelings).
- Recognize how your own emotions differ from the emotions of those around you.
- Ask yourself: *how can I do this better?*
- Be kind and forgiving to yourself. This skill takes time and practice to develop.

As you work on your emotional intelligence, you can also practice skills of sympathy and empathy. All start with a similar foundation of abilities. Here are some ways to improve your capacity for sympathy through active listening to another.

Tools:

- Come with a willing attitude.
- Do not speak or interrupt.
- Before you respond, allow the speaker to pause and collect their thoughts to ensure they have made their point or expressed their opinion.
- Remove outside distractions.
- Don't stop to look at your phone, computer, or television.
- Maintain eye contact.
- Stay in the present moment. Do not bring up the past.
- Acknowledge their feelings.
- Seek objectivity. Remove your judgment or bias, and ask yourself, "How would I respond to a friend or coworker who presented this information to me? Would I be able to be more objective and less judmental?"
- Monitor your body language and facial expressions. Avoid showing pity, disagreement, or disinterest.
- Ask what you can do to help.
- Ask what you can do to better understand the other person's feelings and emotions.

Being empathetic to another person uses all these tools and expands upon them, which requires more self-awareness. To improve your empathy skills:

- Become aware of your preconceived ideas and biases.
- Practice empathy in relationships that are less significant to you. Observe the vocal tone and body language of public speakers, news reporters, and television characters as they communicate. When listening to another person, give them your uninterrupted attention.
- Focus on the individual and the words they are presently saying, not what they have said in the past.
- Only offer advice if it is requested.
- Do not give the other person your opinion unless they request it.
- Do not try to solve or fix their problems.
- Do not create a rebuttal or response to what they have said.
- Seek clarification and understanding of what they said. This may sound like, "I think I heard you say that you are feeling angry (sad, disappointed, etc.). Is that correct?"
- Remember, this is about *validating* their emotions and feelings, rather than trying to change their feelings, influence their opinions, or change their mind.

Learn about and Understand What Your Loved One Values Most

This begins with good listening skills and understanding the other person's needs and wants without taking this information personally. Ask them for what they *need* right now. Is it safety, space, time, or a hug? Then, find out what they *want* and what they are hoping for. The goal is to understand what is most important *to them*. Once you have done this, you can take practical actions to reassure your loved ones that you are attempting to understand and empathize with their feelings and thoughts by honoring boundaries and supporting them.

Tools:

- Ask them what their priorities and essential needs are. Their answer may be as simple as taking out the trash or as complex as accompanying them to their family functions. Initially, no task is too small to demonstrate that you are making an effort.

- Be patient; don't rush them. They may be used to *reacting* to tense situations, people, and places when they are unsure of what they want or need.

- Be flexible; their interests and desires will likely change and evolve. Some of their more restrictive wants and needs will likely diminish. For example, they may initially want to know where you're going and what you're doing daily. Providing your schedule will enable them to build trust in you, and their scrutiny should decrease over time.

- Don't make assumptions. Regardless of your history with them, you can't assume you know how they feel, what they believe, or what they need.

- Understand that different people have different needs.

- Seek to understand them, and refrain from attempting to tell them what they need or want.

Each of your loved ones will have different priorities. The needs and preferences of your six-year-old will differ vastly from those of your twelve-year-old, your adult child, and your spouse. Demonstrate to them that you understand the differences.

Remember to *talk less and listen more*. Listen to each of your loved ones and affirm that you have heard them or are trying to understand what they are saying. Let them know that you understand, and then respond.

Learn to Pause before Reacting or Talking

This is a tricky area for many of us because of the fight-flight-freeze-fawn response. We are hardwired to react, but this is an instinct that you must overcome where your close relationships are concerned. The goal is to be able to sit back and observe without reacting. Only some things need immediate action or a solution to a problem.

Tools:

- Practice in nonthreatening, unexcited, or unemotional situations. For instance, any time anyone asks you a question, respond with "Let me think about that for a moment."

- Practice stalling for time by taking a deep breath, counting to ten, and saying a prayer or mantra. Practicing this in everyday conversations will help you develop habits that will carry over into situations where you feel frightened, vulnerable, or defensive.

- Make sure you respond out of love and strength, not out of pain and defensiveness.

After Taking an Action, Learn to Detach and Release Obsessive Thoughts

In many twelve-step groups, you will hear people say, "Do the work and leave the results to God." Similarly, you must do the work to repair your relationships without expecting immediate results. The fruits of our labor often take days, weeks, or months to manifest in a positive outcome.

Tools:

- Observe and acknowledge your obsessive thought, feeling, or desire to act.

- Examine the thought/feeling. How powerful is it?

- Ask yourself: Is this true? Is it valid? Are you catastrophizing or being impatient?

- Be kind to yourself as you examine your responses.

- Remember that psychological pain is normal. The goal is to remove the *unnecessary* pain, not to become numb to all feelings.

- Recognize you have *choices*; you are not powerless. You can choose how you are going to respond to every situation. For example, are you going to act on this thought or feeling? Are you going to obsess over the idea? Are you going to sit in self-pity? Are you going to be kind to yourself and work through it?

- Acknowledge that repetitive actions and thoughts can be counterproductive.

- Stay in the present moment. Focus on what is in front of you.

- Practice self-acceptance and kindness toward yourself.

- Use functional behaviors or actions to distract from obsessive thoughts, e.g., keep yourself busy; replace thoughts about outcomes with thoughts about the present moment; practice self-care; engage in a hobby; perform some kind of physical activity; or meditate.

- Get support from others, and become accountable to another person.

- Think creatively, and look for alternative ways of handling situations.

- Look for success, focus on improvement, and trust in the process.

Therapeutic Options

Suppose your struggles with obsessive and compulsive thoughts do not respond to these efforts. In this case, you may be interested in therapy or help from a professional specializing in obsessive-compulsive disorder (OCD). They may use the therapeutic techniques of cognitive behavioral therapy (CBT) and acceptance and commitment therapy (ACT). Both of these modalities have proven track records of successful treatment for obsessive thoughts.

CBT is a treatment that focuses on identifying how your unhealthy thinking affects your learned behaviors and patterns. Its techniques are typically specific, structured, and goal-oriented. The therapist will help you identify inaccurate or negative thinking and self-talk and then aid you in understanding how this affects your behaviors. Afterward, you will learn healthier ways to think and respond to life's challenges.

ACT practitioners help individuals recognize how their attempts to suppress, manage, and control emotional experiences create psychological pain and challenges. By acknowledging and addressing these challenges, individuals can better manage their discomfort. ACT is based on relational frame theory (RFT), a school of thought focusing on human language and cognition. RFT suggests that the rational skills used by the human mind to solve problems may be ineffective in helping people overcome psychological pain. Based on this theory, ACT was developed to teach people that although psychological distress is uncomfortable, one can learn to live with these challenges by shifting their thoughts about unwanted emotional discomfort. This includes acceptance of things as they come without evaluating or attempting to change them. This skill is developed through mindfulness exercises in and out of therapy sessions. ACT does not attempt to directly change or stop unwanted thoughts or feelings, as CBT does, but instead encourages people to develop a new and compassionate relationship with those experiences.

Practice Patience with Your Loved Ones

I am asking you to be patient not only with yourself but also with your loved ones. While making changes within yourself and improving your relationships, your loved ones may respond slower than you would like or hope for. Your efforts to enhance relationships may not produce results for months or years. You may be frustrated and tempted to give up when you do not see results from changes within yourself. It is important to continue pushing forward and doing the work regardless of the immediate outcome. Your past behaviors may have been unpredictable and unreliable. Your loved ones will likely need to see a consistent change in your behaviors and actions before they can change their reactions to you.

It takes patience and perseverance to continue to do the right thing when your loved ones are not responding or reacting positively to the changes you are making. This type of perseverance does not mean you sit complacently on the sidelines, waiting for results; instead, you let go of the expectation for immediate results. You look for and acknowledge any positive reaction, no matter how small.

Tools:

- Make behavioral changes within yourself without expecting others to react positively.

- Make every effort not to repeat negative behaviors, once you identify them.

- Reassure the other person that their perceived experiences are valid and that you acknowledge their hurt.

- Allow time for the other person to process their feelings and experiences; do not expect an immediate change in their behaviors.

- Acknowledge your efforts to be patient with them. Look for positive feedback from objective resources—such as your sponsor, a healthy peer, or a therapist—when you do not receive it from your partner.

- Ask for what you need. Be as specific as possible, and make it as simple as possible. For example: "I would appreciate it if you would say thank you to me when I help with the dishes after dinner."
- Take time to step back and reflect on how far you and/or the relationship have come.
- Create new, happy, peaceful experiences with your loved ones.

Demonstrate Commitment and Staying Power

Be prepared for your friends and family members to remain angry with you for a long time. Also, offer patience and understanding when old issues resurface after periods of calm. You may be tested and feel this is unfair, but standing up to these challenges will build trust in these relationships.

Tools:

- Understand that new habits take time to become ingrained into our everyday behavioral routines; hence, the recommendation to attend ninety meetings in ninety days. This is true for our loved ones as well.
- Practice your new habits, skills, or behaviors.
- Find an accountability partner: someone to report to who will give you positive feedback for your efforts. It is best if this is someone outside of your immediate family.
- Understand your "why." What is your motivation? What are your long-term goals? When feeling discouraged, focus on the potential positive outcome and the small successes you have already achieved.
- Plan for setbacks, mistakes, and obstacles. Much like cheating on a diet or taking a break from an exercise program, not all is lost if you have one bad or off-kilter day.
- Set reasonable goals, and begin with small time commitments. For example, do a new activity for ten minutes a day for one week; then increase it to twenty minutes a day for thirty days; then thirty minutes a day for sixty days; and then forty minutes a day for ninety days.

- Start with small goals. I began texting my children every other day, and my goal was for them to unblock me and then respond. After success, I moved to a phone call, and eventually, I made dates for ice cream or coffee.

- Celebrate small successes, and focus on small advancements in your relationships.

- Find balance in your commitments. What commitments do you currently have to your sobriety, family, job, and, when applicable, the court?

- Do you have regular routines? Is your life chaotic and unstable? Can you institute some order? Routines are generally reassuring for most people, and your family members will observe and adapt to your new healthy habits and routines, thus supporting your sobriety. This is an important need for your family members. They have been so used to your unpredictable or negative behaviors that seeing consistency in your actions will provide comfort and help build trust.

Apologize; Learn How to Say "I'm Sorry"

There are many ways to say you're sorry, and just because you offer an apology, that doesn't mean the recipient will accept it. The following outline for an apology is one that I have used with my children since they were little. But first you must decide if you are genuinely remorseful for your mistakes or behaviors. Some questions to ask yourself:

- Are you ready to apologize?

- Do you honestly see and understand the pain that your behavior inflicted upon them?

- Can you empathize with their pain or reaction?

- Are you willing to do the work and make the changes necessary?

Tools (my recipe for an apology):

- State the action you performed/mistake you made/injury you caused.

- Acknowledge the pain/injury inflicted upon the other person.

- Say the words "I am sorry for . . ." and fill in the blank with your misdeed (e.g., "not taking out the trash").

- Follow with your plan of action for the next time: "In the future, I will . . ." (e.g., "make a better effort to take the trash out before you have to ask me to do it").

- Wait for a response from the other person.

- Pause to demonstrate that you heard them and to avoid becoming defensive about whatever they say.

- Maintain eye contact.

- Listen. Refrain from interrupting while they are speaking.

- Repeat to them what you heard them say.

- Ask them if you have the information correct.

- Listen and empathize by responding as often as it takes for them to believe you have heard them.

- Make a sincere effort not to repeat the offending behavior.

- When you do, acknowledge it, and take responsibility for it.

- Start the process over whenever you have a new issue or incident to address.

The quicker you can apologize after an offending action, the better. This will limit the damage done and prevent resentment from growing. However, be honest when you are not ready to apologize or don't see your part of the problem because of defenses, brain fog, or other reasons. Do not make a false apology, such as saying "I am sorry that you feel that way." Instead, you can use wording like this:

- "I am working on seeing it from your side."

- "I am working on understanding why this is so painful."

- "I want to try to understand your point of view."

- "I need to think about this for a little while."

- "I would like to get feedback from my sponsor/therapist/friend to understand better what I did wrong."
- "I will get back to you on this topic."

In addition, understand that an apology is not the same as an amends; this will be addressed later.

Communication

Effective communication is one of the key characteristics we must possess to improve our relationships. Yet so many people say things like, "I don't know how to communicate." "They don't listen to me." "I'm shy; I can't speak up for myself." But we all communicate. Even if we cannot express ourselves in words, our actions and body language are always turned on and always reflect what we think and feel. For example, are you aware of what your "resting face" looks like? Are you approachable? What feedback do you get from coworkers, friends, and peers about how you express yourself? What are you good at? Where can you improve? I urge you to continue researching ways to improve your communication skills.

Tools:

- Stop talking. This is essential, yet so hard to do. You cannot learn what the other person thinks or feels if you are talking. You are not communicating if one person is doing all of the talking; this is instead a lecture or a presentation.
- Listen without interruption. Allow for some uncomfortable silence; sometimes it takes a few moments for the other person to gather their thoughts.
- Be empathetic. Affirm that you are trying to understand what they are saying and what they are feeling. Acknowledge that what they are saying is important to you.
- Pay attention to body language and visual clues, but do not make assumptions. If the person's body language does not match their words, take notice and ask for clarification.

- Remember that they ultimately want to know that you have heard and understood what they said.

- You can smile or nod to demonstrate that you are paying attention. Then, ask questions that will encourage them to expand on their thoughts. For example, "Tell me what's going on with you." "Tell me more about that." "What happened next?"

- When it is your turn to speak, be clear and concise. Get to the point as quickly as possible. Stick to the facts, and do not exaggerate, overgeneralize, raise your voice, or use offensive language. Try to "talk less to say more."

- If you ask for a change in the other person's behavior, name the specific action you seek.

- Tell the truth, and be transparent and accountable. Answer questions authentically and honestly. It is far better to tell the truth and get in trouble than to tell "white lies" or lie by omission to cover up for more significant harm. Those small white lies contribute to the person's lack of trust in you.

- Be tactful when sharing something distasteful. There are many ways to share bad news or disagree with another. For example, say "I prefer the red pants over the blue skirt," rather than "The blue skirt makes you look chubby."

- Follow your words with actions. If you say you will do something, do it immediately or as soon as possible.

- Learn age-appropriate communication. The information your six-year-old understands and needs to hear varies significantly from information appropriate for your twelve-year-old. Therefore, it is crucial to speak to them on their own level. By the same token, do not speak to your eighteen-year-old in the same manner as your twelve-year-old. Do not overshare with your child. Do not provide them with more information than is necessary.

- Do not use metaphors when talking with children. Instead, be as short and clear as possible. Reassure children that they are not responsible for your problems.

- Remember that it takes five compliments to make up for each criticism.
- Seek to continue improving your communication skills through further study.

To build a better general atmosphere for communication, try giving frequent words of support, compliments, and gratitude. Compliment your loved one often in front of others. Make sure to compliment your spouse in front of your children.

Conflict Management and Problem-Solving

The first step to improving how you deal with conflict is to understand how you manage conflict now. Observe how you approach problems. Do you make an effort to resolve them quickly? Do you need to be more active in addressing them? Are you comfortable asking for help? Are you afraid to tell others, "I don't know how to do this"? Are you a leader or a follower? Do you know how to ask for help? Are you a take-charge kind of person? Are you all talk and no action? Do you expect others to follow your actions and advice? Do you delegate? Do you shrink away from authority figures? Are you a rule follower? Or a rule breaker?

To manage a conflict, first clear your mind and focus on the conflict in front of you. The answers will not come when your mind is busy; they will come when your mind is still. Build a positive attitude, because resolving the relationship conflict begins with a good attitude and the belief that the issue can be resolved. It is crucial to be approachable and believe that each individual has a right to their thoughts and opinions and that the outcome should provide equity to all. Be in the present, and act immediately if possible. Address problems when they are small and manageable, before they grow.

Tools (my recipe for problem solving):

- Problem definition: remove the anger and the emotionally charged parts of the problem. Try to define the root of the problem, and break it down into a definition that is as clear and concise as possible. For example, rather than saying "you never listen to what I am saying," frame the problem as "please don't interrupt me when I speak."

- Brainstorm: seek many solutions to the problem. Be creative.
- Choose one solution to resolve the problem, and take action or implement the change.
- Pause and assess whether the action worked wholly or partially.
- If it was unsuccessful, return to the problem definition, or try an alternate solution to the problem.
- Repeat until resolution is achieved.
- When necessary, seek outside, objective help from a therapist, sponsor, or friend, when you have the permission of all parties involved in the conflict.

Additional skills to support problem-solving:

- Confirm with the other person whether the results are sufficient or whether adjustments are needed to achieve a better outcome.
- Ask yourself often, "Would I rather be right or happy?" "Is there room for us to agree to disagree?" "What are the costs of my having to be right?"
- Separate the behavior from the person. You can dislike the behavior of an individual but still love the person. This concept is crucial to forgiveness. Your loved ones are probably suffering just as much as you are. Give as much love and guidance to your families for their Al-Anon or codependency issues as you would give to the newcomer walking in the doors of an AA meeting.
- When I'm indecisive about how to resolve a problem, my go-to strategy is to fall back on a shortened version of a famous quote by psychologist Carl Jung: "Just do the next right thing."

Fighting Fair

This topic needs its own section, because conflict cannot be avoided entirely. You will have emotionally charged disagreements. In these cases, it is necessary to understand the essential tools of engagement. There are numerous resources on the web and in print about fighting fairly. Below I highlight some of my favorite strategies.

Tools:

- Approach with a win-win mentality, no matter what. Your goal is to understand the central conflict/disagreement and address it with an attitude of "What do I hope to do here? What do I expect to learn? What is my part? Where am I willing to compromise?"

- Schedule a time to address conflicts or problems. Pick a time when you both are at your best: rested, fed, and calm.

- Have a predetermined tagline that indicates that one person or the other needs to take a break to cool off, gather thoughts, or recompose. For example, "Can we pause for a moment?"

- Honor the other person's request for a time-out.

- Stick to the main point, and address one conflict at a time. Do not generalize. For example, the statement "You have an anger problem" is far too vague to allow the other person to understand the root of the problem. Instead, define the problem and keep it simple and short. Do not group multiple issues.

- There should be no physical contact, positively or negatively. Threatening contact is entirely counterproductive, and more intimate contact can deflect or distract from the problem.

- Only give ultimatums if you are going to carry them out.

- Resist bringing up the past.

- Don't push their buttons, hit below the belt, or pick on their weaknesses.

- Never use your children as a weapon, threat, or excuse. Leave your children out of your conflicts. If they know about the conflict, reassure them that it is between two people who will do their best to resolve it. Do not let them think you are fighting over, about, or because of them.

- No name-calling, cussing, offensive language, or yelling.

- Phrase statements as "I" statements, not "you" statements. For example, instead of saying "You made me so angry when you did not pay the electric bill," say "I am angry because the electric bill was not paid, and the power got cut off." Express your feelings with words (as few words as possible). Use common language.

- Don't build a case. Be as short and straightforward as possible; extra details will only muddy the water and dilute the main point.

- Don't interrupt. Allow each person to have time to speak. This can be done with a timer, or as we occasionally do in our family, you can use a spoon. Whoever is holding the spoon gets to speak. If you want to talk, you ask for the spoon when the speaker has finished making their point.

- Don't catastrophize or exaggerate. This will either make your argument seem silly or provide the other individual with good details for rebuttal.

- No deflecting; stick to the original point/problem.

- No gaslighting. Do not make others question their thoughts, feelings, or reality. This only builds hostility and strengthens defenses. Your partner's feelings and thoughts are always valid or true for them. You are not going to change their feelings by winning an argument. The way to resolve a problem is to listen to their thoughts and feelings.

Pay attention to your physical responses to conflict. Are you overheated or overemotional? Take time-outs when needed. Walking away from most conflicts is perfectly suitable if the discussion is unproductive. Likewise, it is all right to agree to disagree. When dealing with a hostile response or becoming heated, I encourage you to use the "agree and limit" technique to put a time-out on the conflict safely. To do this, you agree to a small part of the conflict but put a hold on further conversation. The goal is to give enough to remove yourself from the situation. On the other hand, when you find yourself at a standstill because the other person is crying, emotionally drained, or experiencing a moment of weakness, do not use this as an opportunity to win the argument. Instead, use it as an opportunity to heal, to offer compassion and understanding to the other person.

Stress Management

Information about ways to manage your stress and anxiety is readily available through various resources. Coping with stress and anxiety has become a popular topic, making it much more acceptable for those struggling with this mental health issue to ask for help. Talk shows, news programs, books, podcasts, and YouTube videos address how to build the skills to manage your stress. This section offers a preliminary insight into becoming aware of the issues surrounding stress and anxiety, preventing them from occurring when possible, and managing them when they do.

Self-Examination and Awareness

Anxiety comes in many forms; it can look like perfectionism, people-pleasing, overanalyzing, repetitive behaviors, depression, claustrophobia, insomnia, or headaches, among other things. Understanding and coping with stress begin with self-examination and awareness.

- What are your current stressors and your commitments to job, self, sobriety, family, and work?

- What physical symptoms of anxiety/stress do you have now? This may include achy muscles, breathlessness, the need to urinate often, itchiness, tics, sweating, dizziness, increased blood pressure, muscle tightness or pain, or the inability to speak or react.

- How do you currently manage stress and anxiety? Do you overeat, lose your appetite, sleep too much, or lose sleep? Do you ruminate on stressful thoughts? Do you become frozen or incapacitated by feeling overwhelmed? Are you short-tempered with others? Do you take out your frustration on your spouse, partner, kids, or pets? Do you avoid stress/anxiety through video gaming, TV, or sports?

- Habits that make anxiety worse include skipping meals, not drinking enough water, not getting exercise or going outside for fresh air, overeating sugar, or spending too much time on social media.

- How have you attempted to deal with stress in the past? What did and did not work for you?

- What self-talk or repetitive thoughts do you experience when attempting to address your stress?

- How would you like to manage stress in the future?

Prevention is an integral part of reducing your overall level of stress. Here are some elementary prevention skills:

- Practicing self-care, regular (moderate) exercise, sleep, and nutrition are fundamental to preventing stress. You are much more vulnerable to stressors when hungry, angry, lonely, or tired (HALT).

- It's helpful to understand and identify the physical indicators of your stress, such as heart rate, breathing, blood pressure, tightness in muscles, headaches, or digestive issues.

- Become aware of your time and energy commitments. You may need to be made aware of all the obligations you have taken on.

Keep in mind that anxiety is a natural bodily response to danger and stress. In moderation, it serves a purpose to help us regulate our activities. Below are some specific tools to address excessive anxiety and stress.

Tools:

- Make a list of everything and everyone to whom you have responsibilities. Sometimes we discover that we have taken on more commitments than we realize until we write them down on paper. These may include but are not limited to spouse/partner, family, work or employer, sobriety, therapist or sponsor, friends, extended family, hobbies, sports teams, extracurricular activities, volunteer positions, and family life, including bills, yardwork, and home maintenance, carpool schedules, homework, and kids' after-school activities.

- Prioritize among these commitments. Which ones are essential? Which ones can be addressed quickly and removed from the list? Which ones can you delegate to others? Which ones can you delay?

- Manage your time. Begin by setting achievable and measurable goals. Prioritize tasks based on importance. Set a time limit to complete a task or activity. Give yourself flexibility on these goals.

- Seek to balance responsibilities between work, home, recovery, and recreation.

- Delegate some of your responsibilities to others (appropriately).

- Learn to say no or "let me think about that" to new requests for your time and energy. When you eliminate some responsibilities, communicate clearly with those who will be affected.

- Take time for rest and play. Sufficient sleep is essential.

- Become aware of and limit nonproductive self-talk, generalizing, catastrophizing, and all-or-nothing thinking.

- Learn a new skill like meditation, yoga, or biofeedback to help manage your stress. Biofeedback is a mind-body technique that uses visual or auditory feedback to teach people to recognize the physical signs and symptoms of stress and anxiety.

- Keep a journal. Writing out your thoughts and feelings may help you see and understand your actions and self-talk. It will also slow down any runaway thinking that can fuel your anxious feelings.

- Engage in small acts of service or random acts of kindness. For example, compliment the cashier at your grocery store, wave hello to a neighbor, or open the door for a stranger.

- Begin or return to a hobby that brings you joy, such as gardening, puzzles, arts and crafts, or cooking.

Tools for managing the physical manifestations of stress, such as racing heartbeat, muscle tension, headaches, or runaway thoughts:

- Grounding techniques help us get out of our heads or unstuck from uncomfortable physical sensations and enable us to reconnect with the present moment. They help separate us from physical or emotional distress by returning our brains and bodies to the immediate environment.

- Practice the five-four-three-two-one grounding technique to talk yourself back into the present moment and release anxiety or physical distress. List and say aloud (if possible) five things you can see, four things you can feel, three things you can hear, two things you can smell, and one thing you can taste.

- Practice box breathing:

  1. Breathe all the way out. Hold the completed exhale for four seconds with no air in your lungs.

  2. Take a slow, full breath in over four seconds.

3. With your lungs comfortably full, hold your breath for four seconds.

4. Breathe out slowly and entirely over four seconds.

- Practice mindfulness—staying in the present moment and resisting the tendency to drift into worry and fear.

- Chant a mantra or affirmation that is particularly poignant to you. For example, "I grow stronger and wiser every day in every way." "I release the fear of speaking in front of people; I affirm that I have an important message to share."

- Release physical agitation or excitement through exercise, such as going for a walk or run, going to the gym, or mowing your lawn. You could also play a video game that requires concentrating on the game.

Anger Management

Managing your anger for yourself and your family is another essential step in rebuilding relationships. There is a great deal of information on the web and in bookstores about managing anger if it has become a problem in your life. These tools range from simple to complex. Following are some ideas to help you get started.

Taking Ownership and Responsibility

The first step in managing your anger is to take ownership of your feelings and recognize that you have a choice about how you will react and behave when you're angry; no one can "make you" feel angry. Only you can choose how you will respond to an anger-provoking stimulus. For example, a car cuts you off in traffic. You can react by swearing at the other driver, honking, and acting in a manner that increases your anxiety or anger; or you can let them in and breathe a sigh of relief that the other driver did not hit you while attempting to get ahead.

Here are some more anger-management tips:

- Release your desire to get even or get revenge. Allow karma or your higher power to pass judgment on them.

- Phrase your verbal response to the situation as an affirmation. For example, "I will release my rage over this incident and affirm that I can handle these stressors." Or "I will not allow the other driver to steal my joy (peace, contentment, etc.) over this incident."

- The next step is to become aware of your anger and study it. Observe yourself. Are you happy with how you manage your anger? Is it working well for you? Could you improve it? What lessons are you teaching your children through your current anger-management techniques? Is this how you would like them to act?

- Know your anger triggers. Write them down. Give examples of how you have responded to these triggers in the past. Look at them objectively, or have someone else look at them and determine whether your reaction was appropriate.

- Create new and more productive ways of reacting to similar situations in the future. For example, if someone cuts in front of you while you're standing in line, make a plan for how you'll handle this situation in the future.

- Work on your sense of worth and self-esteem. The more you feel confident in yourself, the less likely you will be bothered by slights or insults. It will be easier to let things go.

- Be kind and forgiving to yourself.

Anger Prevention

Preventing anger and learning how to handle minor frustrations in your life are the best ways to manage your anger in more challenging situations.

- Begin by making sure you have sufficient rest and nourishment.

- Learn and practice meditation, yoga, or deep-breathing skills to reduce your baseline stress.

- Get at least light to moderate exercise and fresh air every day, even if you only commit to taking ten minutes of your lunch break to walk outside.

- Do a random act of kindness for a stranger.

- Make time for hobbies and fun.

- Understand the nature of your fight-flight response.

Putting These Skills into Practice

How to remain calm when you find yourself in the heat of the moment:

- Practice the pause tool in everyday situations to make it easier to use when your adrenaline is racing and your temper is rising.
- Take deep breaths. Breathe in for a count of four, hold for a count of five, and release for a count of six. You can do this as many times as it takes.
- Burn off the extra energy productively: Take a walk, do some push-ups, or run up the stairs.
- Tighten and then release your muscles, focusing on the energy draining from them as you release them. For example, clench your fists for a count of five, slowly release the tension in your hands for a count of six, and then consciously feel the lightness in your hands/muscles for a count of seven.

Addressing and Coping with Someone Else's Angry Outburst

Sometimes you are on the receiving end of someone else's irritation, hostility, sarcasm, or the like. When this happens to you:

- Prioritize your physical and emotional safety.
- Practice setting boundaries with your family members. Use your tagline to end or take a break from a conflict.
- If you are in a setting like work, school, or business, use the agree-and-limit technique or a grounding exercise to reduce the intensity and volume of the conflict.

If the angry person is a client, customer, coworker, or child, and the intensity of the anger is manageable, I have found the following steps to be very productive:

- Give the other individual your full attention.
- Take reasonable accountability. For example, say "There has been a mistake made here, and I want to help resolve this problem."
- Allow the other individual a reasonable amount of time to vent their feelings.
- Ensure that they understand that you have heard what they're saying.

- Ask them what you can do to help resolve the situation. What is it specifically that they want you to do?

- Detach their anger from yourself. The individual is more likely mad about a behavior or an action, or something other than who you are.

Build and Maintain Healthy Boundaries

Boundaries are guidelines for others' behavior that we erect as figurative walls around ourselves to protect us from being hurt or harmed by others. In our relationships, this includes establishing and expressing how we want and expect others to treat us. Healthy boundaries allow for flexibility as a relationship grows and trust is built. Developing healthy boundaries begins with respecting and valuing yourself.

What are your current boundaries? Are they appropriate? Do you have walls around you set so high that no one gets close to you? Do you appear unapproachable? Do people fear you just because of your body language and appearance? Or are you at the other extreme, with no boundaries at all? Do people seem to take advantage of you? Can you say no to requests for your time and money? Are there threats to your physical and emotional health or sobriety?

More questions to ask yourself:

- Where do you currently draw the line?

- Do you understand how your walls affect your loved ones?

- Do you honor others' boundaries?

- Do you know what others' boundaries are?

- Do you know each family member's current level of perceived safety? For example, does your eight-year-old take cover when you walk into the room? Has your sixteen-year-old become your partner's protector?

- Have you physically or emotionally threatened others?

Tools:

- Acknowledge the boundaries that you have previously set for your friends, family, or coworkers to respect. For example:

  - I am entitled to lunch breaks at work.

- I will only work forty hours a week at my job.
- I will make time for myself at least one day a week.
- I will walk away from escalating arguments with my close friends and family until we are ready to proceed calmly.

- Practice boundaries with your family members by making small, attainable requests. For example, "Please call when you are going to be late." "Turn the lights off when you leave a room."
- Create and follow through with consequences.
- Communicate your needs to others in an appropriate manner.
- Learn to meet your own needs with self-care.
- Learn to say no. You don't always have to explain why you are saying no. "No" can be a complete sentence. If needed, you can use a phrase like "I would like to help right now, but I have too much going on to provide you with good service."
- When you are comfortable, move on to more difficult boundaries. For example, "I am not going to speak to you when you have been drinking." "I am not going to talk to you when you are yelling."

Learn to Manage Criticism

When constructive criticism is given in an understanding and compassionate manner, it is intended to teach or to help someone improve a task or skill. It is not meant or used to harm, belittle, or manipulate another person. But it is hard for many people to take criticism, even if it is constructively presented. So let's rename "constructive criticism" as "feedback," and let's see it as an opportunity to learn more about yourself and allow for a deeper connection with another person.

Tools:

- Begin with self-examination. How do you currently respond to constructive criticism? Do you become defensive, deflect, or withdraw?
- Redefine criticism. Constructive criticism is an ally, not an enemy. It can give you information and insight into another person's expectations of you, helping you improve and grow.

- When being criticized, ask for the speaker's intention for giving the feedback. If their intention is constructive, ask yourself, "What can I learn?" and "How can this be helpful to me?"
  - If needed, ask for clarification, understanding that the feedback may need to be better worded or presented.
  - Do not take the criticism personally or as a personal attack (consider the source). Constructive criticism is not about you as a person but about behavior, action, or the quality of your work.
- If the criticism hits a sore point or a sensitive area, don't pretend it is not painful. Whenever applicable, explain to the other individual that these comments are triggering old wounds and that you will need to take some time to separate your emotional reaction from the constructive feedback.
- Practice healthy responses to criticism:
  - Pause before you respond, to ensure you are not *reacting* to the feedback. For example, you can stall for time by saying, "Let me think about that," or "You may be right; can I have time to consider what you said?"
  - Thank the person for the information.
  - Show your engagement and willingness to listen by maintaining eye contact and giving the speaker your full attention.
  - Attempt to control your own defensive responses.
  - Seek clarification of the criticism; ensure you understand the other person's point.
  - Restate their point. For example, "You are saying that it hurts you when I don't introduce you to my new friends," or "I hear you saying you get angry when I don't ask how your day was."
  - Do not make excuses, explain, or justify unless requested.
  - Ask what they would like to see change in the future.
  - State how you will try to change, and ask for a follow-up meeting to discuss your efforts and progress. Try not to make promises that you cannot keep.

Remember, most criticism is not an attack. But unless you have a lot of practice hearing direct feedback, even constructive criticism can sting.

Destructive Criticism

Most of us will experience destructive criticism, dirty fighting, unfounded accusations, and being confronted with painful truths about our past behaviors and actions from time to time. Managing this type of criticism is as crucial as managing constructive feedback.

If the intent seems destructive or given with bad intent:

- Control your defensiveness, and listen with an open mind.
- Thank them for their feedback, and tell them you need time to think about what they have shared.
- Use the agree-and-limit tool to keep the conversation brief.
- Do not meekly accept unjust or unfounded criticism. A better response could be, "I hear you, and I will give that some thought."
- Minimize encounters with harmful people.

Remember that your loved ones may have pent-up frustrations over your past behaviors. Many of these can be resolved when you complete a sincere apology or make an amends with them.

Balance

It is tremendously important for your recovery and your physical health to maintain routines and balance in your personal life and your relationship reconciliations. Spend time on your life's social, emotional, physical, and spiritual aspects. Family recovery needs balance, just as personal recovery does.

- **Diet, nutrition, and sleep**—I firmly believe that a reasonable level of good physical health is required for good mental health. One's basic needs of shelter, food, and safety must be met before we can address our more complex recovery needs.
- **Improve or increase exercise and physical fitness**—Create some endorphins naturally. Better yet, include your family members in

these activities. By attaining a natural high with another person, you both will associate those good feelings with spending time with that person.

- **Recreation with family**—Play and have fun with your family members. Recovery will not be easy if we are intense and dramatic all the time. Most people with "a little time in the rooms" know this. We learn to laugh with and at ourselves. It takes the sting out of painful experiences and provides welcome relief in tough times. Many don't know how to play and have fun without addiction. We can't imagine how we will ever have fun again without our addiction. To start learning how, include your family members in activities that you all will enjoy. It can be as simple as playing a board game, playing kickball in the street, or going to the park.

- **Learning something new with family**—Learning new things with another person is good for your relationship, as it demonstrates that you are making efforts to make positive changes. Studies show that developing new skills is also helpful for improving memory, mood, and motivation. Consider trying something your partner is interested in that you have not been supportive of.

- **Complete a project with a family member**—The point is that you work together and see something through from inception to completion. This could be building a puzzle, planting a small garden, or bathing the dog.

- **Spirituality/religion**—Do you practice a particular faith? Has your spiritual/religious experience had a good or bad impact on you? How important are these factors to you and your family members?

- **Goals and values**—Take time to examine your goals and values and to learn what values your family members or partner holds. Be honest with yourself and each other; there are no right or wrong answers. Are your values wealth and fame? Raising your children? Education and discipline? Are these similar to or different from your loved ones' priorities? The goal is not to change each other's opinions but simply to understand them.

Improve Your Self-Perception; Forgive Yourself

Self-perception is how you view yourself. For most of us, our self-perception developed from the feedback we received from others: our parents, caregivers, teachers, and other significant authority figures. We probably did not consciously choose to accept others' negative perceptions of us, but they became ingrained into our psyche over time. This developed into our own inner voice. If the messages are harmful, some people call this a critical inner parent; it follows us around, constantly addressing how we perceive everything that happens to us.

When you perceive yourself in an unhealthy way, you may get stuck in negative thinking patterns, lowering your expectations of yourself and your ability to change. For example, you may see the worst in yourself and think you are unworthy or unlovable. But when you perceive yourself in a healthy way, you can better handle challenges, assess your talents, and be more willing to work on your weaknesses, take responsibility for your actions, and believe that you can make positive changes.

Improving your self-perception and redefining yourself take time. This process begins with changing the "story" you believe about yourself—challenging and changing negative thoughts, and understanding where these thoughts originated. Next, look at the most critical circumstances that have shaped who you are, and reflect on how these situations made you feel about yourself. Then take time to change the meaning behind each of these circumstances. Finally, when the voice of your inner critic seeps through, suppress it and replace it with a mantra or positive affirmation of who you are or who you choose to become.

My family moved around a lot when I was young. The positive outcome of this was that I learned to be friendly, I made friends easily, I could read people, and I could adapt easily to new situations. The negative side was that I began to choose not to get too settled in any one place because I believed we would only move again, so I was hesitant to develop close friendships. I tried to fit in wherever we moved, but my friendships were superficial, and I strived to be likable so I could gain acceptance quickly. This is part of the reason why I developed people-pleasing habits. I told myself "I must be who you want me to be" to be accepted and liked.

Tools:

- Write down your self-critical thoughts, opinions, and beliefs.

- Examine the source of these beliefs. Did you have a critical or abusive parent? Did you have a harsh and judgmental teacher or spiritual advisor?

- Challenge these thoughts. Negate them. Replace them with an opposing affirmation. For example, when I was growing up, I was told that girls could marry a rich man as easily as a poor man. The messages I heard were that I should value men for the money they make, I could rely on a husband for my financial well-being, and wealth was based on how much money one made. I replaced those messages with these: "Wealth has nothing to do with money." "Marriage is a partnership between two people." "I am responsible for my peace and happiness."

- Acknowledge and list your strengths, and create affirmations out of these strengths.

- Decide who you would like to be. What traits or characteristics would you like to work on? Find a role model or mentor to follow.

- Behave and act as the person you would like to be. Speak your mantra or positive affirmation to yourself, no matter how awkward it feels.

- Be kind and patient with yourself.

- Celebrate your successes.

- Volunteer, do service work, or perform random acts of kindness in moderation.

There are many additional resources on the web to aid in this process. As you improve your self-concept, you will begin to acknowledge that you are responsible for your positive results, actions, and success. As you improve your self-image, it will affect how others perceive you.

Re-create Your Current Relationships

The temptation to enter into new romantic relationships once you are in sobriety and are meeting others struggling with similar issues is problematic.

Developing new friendships with other sober peers is essential; building a support network of friends with similar issues is excellent. This helps support your sobriety. Still, *it is dangerous to enter into any new romantic relationships.* When you meet and are attracted to a new person, your brain releases dopamine, increases serotonin levels, and produces oxytocin. This can cause you to experience a relationship high—euphoric feelings that are not as strong as the high you experienced when using alcohol or drugs, but similar. You must remember that you will carry the problems of your old relationships into any new relationship. Instead of taking the risks of entering a new relationship, why not put effort into your old relationships? Your old relationships may currently have a lot of struggles and conflicts, but they also hold many positive memories and experiences. The relationships with your family and those who depend on you cannot and should not be discarded easily.

Recovery is not just a time to rebuild your life; it's also a time to rebuild and repair your previous relationships—especially relationships with those who have not given up on you and who are still emotionally invested in you and your children. Don't discard these people; take this opportunity to re-create those relationships.

Tools:

- Treat the relationship like it is new again. Put in the same effort and energy now as you did at the beginning of the relationship. When you approach your family members, make sure to put your best foot forward.

- As you are becoming a different person in sobriety, share your new self with your partner. Present this as a positive change—something to be excited about and grateful for.

- Give the other people in your life the same respect and the opportunity to put their own best foot forward, and be patient with them while they are getting to that point.

- Remember that we often are more forgiving of the quirks and idiosyncrasies of our friends than of our family members. Offer your current relationship the same grace and patience that you give to others.

- Approach the old relationship as if it were new again. Enjoy the early stages of a relationship. Build new memories and experiences.

- Keep what is still working and strong about the relationship, and acknowledge and expand upon it.

- Don't try to bury your past until you have made amends for it. Actively explore and find a resolution to unresolved hurts and disappointments. (We will discuss this topic further in chapter 6, "Making Amends.")

- Approach things that have not worked in the past as an opportunity to learn what to do and what not to do.

- Spend quality time together, face to face, whenever possible. Share your good news, accomplishments, and thoughts. Do not brag about your successes. Show, don't tell, your loved ones how well you are doing.

- Acknowledge your family members' and friends' achievements and positive changes. Give them sincere praise.

- Perform random acts of kindness for your loved ones. Even a short phone call or text can go a long way when it is impossible to do this in person.

- Take time to ask them about their dreams, goals, and hopes.

- Create little positive surprises, such as coming home early or leaving a note in their lunchbox. Let them know you are thinking about them throughout your day.

- Be consistent in your actions and words.

- Follow through on promises you make. Acknowledge when you fail to fulfill the contract or commitment.

- Give direct compliments to them, and do it in front of other people when you can.

- Learn your family member's love language, and keep in mind that this language is not just meant for romance; you can also use it to show appreciation, admiration, and respect.

- Keep track of birthdays, anniversaries, and other important dates.

- Try something new together that you will both (or all) likely succeed at or enjoy. This will allow you to be more vulnerable in other areas.
- Take note of and acknowledge your partner's good news, celebrate their successes with them, and stand by their side when they're facing challenges.
- Post a "gratitude list" of things your partner does that you're grateful for—including the reasons why you are grateful for them—where they can see it.
- Above all, honor the boundaries they have set with you.

Throughout all of this, remember that the goals are to nurture, build on what works, and become consistent in your words and actions. There will be a great deal of trial and error. You will make mistakes along the way. But this does not mean you have failed; it only means that you have ruled out one action or tool that does not work.

Summary

The information and tools in this chapter are meant to provide a starting point to create forward motion and positive momentum. Some of the ideas presented in this chapter may already be in your toolbox of skills; some may be more challenging to attempt at this point in your recovery. Regardless, please assess your strengths and skills, try new things, and approach this part of your recovery openly and willingly. It is important to remember that setbacks, mistakes, and even failures are essential to this process. They are all learning opportunities. As Thomas Edison said, "I have not failed 10,000 times—I've successfully found 10,000 ways that will not work." Facing your mistakes and learning new ways of improving your relationships will help you build resilience, positively impacting other areas of your life and recovery. Be kind to yourself during the hard times. Seek not to be perfect but to take imperfect action instead of no action at all. Take time to look back and see how far you have come, and above all, take time for self-care. Understand that this is not a linear process; each relationship is unique and will be healed at its own pace. Do not compare your relationships to one another. Seek out additional resources and information, and get professional help when warranted.

6

Making Amends

My biggest mistake in making amends to my family was postponing it. I used perfectionism as an excuse. I thought I had it to get it right. I wanted it to happen at the perfect moment on a perfect day, and be deeply moving. I envisioned taking their hands in mine, locking our eyes, baring my soul, and begging for forgiveness. After that, we would both burst into tears, and there would be understanding, love, and forgiveness. We would mend our relationship and never have to bring up my ugly past again. Then we would live happily ever after.

This was a fantasy. Although I had good intentions, the longer I thought about completing my amends, the more fear I created. I made many surface-level apologies, believing these apologies would suffice in the short term. In truth, these apologies held very little weight. My family didn't believe in me or trust me. I had lied too often and had made so many unfulfilled promises during my active alcoholism that they no longer trusted my words. This is not to say that I was not making amends to *anyone*; I started even before I left treatment. I began with simple amends, which I found less painful and risky. I continued to make amends to my boss, my friends, and my coworkers, thinking that this would keep my therapist and sponsor off my back. Still, these amends were valuable because they empowered me to take on the harder amends.

The absolute toughest amends to make were those to my children. I procrastinated making amends to each of my children because I feared rejection. I felt overwhelmed by my sense of shame. There were emotional injuries to my children that I did not want to look at, much less confess to causing them. I feared I might learn of unknown actions I had committed while in a blackout from drinking. I did not want to face their pain, and I had no idea how much work it would take to obtain their forgiveness. I sat in my excuses and justifications, while my procrastination only worsened their pain.

These amends became a burden to carry. They began to haunt me, and a new sense of guilt arose. These feelings followed me around until I finally started chipping away at the amends. Today, I can see the folly of my ways, and the pain of waiting to do them was much greater than the pain of actually making the amends.

How an Apology Is Different from an Amends

An apology is the expression of regret for actions. In contrast, an amends requires an effort to acknowledge and compensate for any losses or damage you have caused and to correct the harm you've done. An apology is essential and can repair minor injustices. It is an excellent first step—a sign to your family that you are trying to be a better person and you have some insight into their pain, not just your own.

But an apology doesn't always bring closure. The betrayals and hurts we inflict during active addiction require more effort than an apology. They require an amends, which entails a recognition of your responsibility for your actions. It includes a willingness to make up for the wrongdoing or compensate the other person for their loss. It is meant to assure your loved ones that you are doing everything in your power not to continue the destructive behaviors. Amends are essential to begin rebuilding the relationship and restoring trust.

Benefits of Making Amends

In an ideal world, many benefits arise from completing amends, both for you and for the person on the receiving end. It is an opportunity to clear away some of the damage, initiate the healing process for both parties, and create a new foundation for a relationship. Benefits for the individual making the amends include the following:

- It will help you gain insight into your behaviors and understand them more.

- It can release some of the toxic guilt and shame that block your ability to open your heart to an improved relationship or a new relationship in the future.

- Hearing what the recipient has to say in response to your amends can reinforce your desire to stay clean or sober.

- Making thorough amends will allow you to release some of the burdens of living with regret and remorse, which could be a barrier to peace and contentment or a stumbling block to your sobriety.

- Making this effort will demonstrate to yourself and others that you are taking action to fix a problem.

- Lastly, when you make amends, you move one step closer to no longer regretting the past and to using your past to work for you rather than against you.

Benefits for the recipient of the amends:

- It allows the other person to know they have been heard and understood.

- If you have gaslit them in the past, it reassures them that you take responsibility for making them feel crazy or responsible for your illness and behaviors.

- It can reassure them that you are willing to do the work to remain sober and to continue working on the relationship.

- It will help them create healthy boundaries.

- It offers the potential for both of you to find resolution or closure.

Where to Begin

This process consists of implementing the eighth and ninth steps of the twelve steps of AA.[1] They provide an excellent guide for making thorough amends, and they have worked for me and for countless others. There are many ways to make suitable amends; below I'll discuss my recipe for amends that, if done well, may provide closure regarding the injustices between you and your loved ones.

Step Eight

The eighth step states, "We made a list of all persons we had harmed and became willing to make amends to them all." In the first part of step eight, we list all the people we have harmed. In my practice, this must be a thorough list, including everyone from your partner to your mail carrier. This may also include relatives who are no longer living or have no contact with you. You have to list them all and write out the harm that you committed to each person. Remember, the goal is to unburden yourself of the shame you hold; the process of writing down everyone you harmed and how you harmed them is an excellent first step to coming to terms with this shame.

Step eight specifies that you must become "willing" to do this work. That requires being *sincere* in your desire to right your wrongs. It involves adopting the right attitude, asking yourself if you are ready to make amends, and determining whether you are capable of making proper amends.

Questions to ask yourself:

- How much time do you have in recovery?
- Sometimes growth is painful; are you willing to experience a little pain for the possibility of reward?
- Do you have a solid foundation of recovery skills?
- Do you have a sponsor or therapist who will support you before and after completing your amends?
- Are you thinking clearly again? Has your brain fog cleared?
- Can you listen to another person talking without reacting or responding (explaining, justifying, denying, or arguing)?
- How much insight into your behavior do you have?
- What is your primary motivation for completing your amends? Are you doing this for yourself or for the recipient?
- What do you hope to gain from this experience?
- Are you willing to be accountable and take responsibility for your actions?

I am not saying you have to be fully, completely ready to make amends before you do it, but the more insight, preparation, and sincerity you can bring to bear, the better the outcome will be. The goal is to be as thorough as possible so healing can occur for both parties and you will not have to make amends again. There will be people for whom it will be wise to postpone making amends, either because you are not ready or they are not available because of boundaries they have imposed. In these cases, you will still add them to your list and do the written work as best you can. If necessary, you can let them know you intend to make a thorough amends but want to wait until a later time. Ask them what they need from you now, and seek to fulfill their short-term needs.

Step Nine

The ninth step states, "We made direct amends to such people wherever possible, except when to do so would injure them or others." In keeping with the idea of making "direct amends," I recommend that you complete your amends in person as often as possible because it can make the experience and the results more meaningful. However, if this is not possible because of legal or personal boundaries, then a phone call or letter is better than not making amends at all. If the recipient is a friend or family member no longer living, or if it is a business or institution such as an employer, school, or store, there are still ways to make proper amends, which we will discuss shortly.

I recommend starting with the easiest amends first because it will allow you to practice sharing and listening. It helps build you an amends "muscle" and enables you to toughen up, and it may even give you a sense of achievement or pride in your efforts.

The second part of the ninth step, "except when to do so would injure them or others," can easily be misused as a loophole. One could use this phrase to justify the conclusion that revisiting a painful topic or event in your life could be too painful for the one receiving amends. For example, let's say your partner caught you having an affair. When that happened, you ended the affair, apologized, and hoped it would never have to be brought up again. But if your partner has unresolved feelings or unanswered questions, you will have to address them again.

However, there still may be situations where making amends is not a good idea because it would harm someone, such as in the affair example mentioned above. You may need to apologize to the individual you cheated with but not to their partner or spouse if they still don't know about the affair.

> **NOTE** People who have had affairs without getting caught often wonder whether they should confess the affair to their spouse or partner. If this is you, remember that you cannot buy your peace of mind at the expense of others. If your spouse or partner has no idea about your affair, I discourage disclosing it.
>
> Here are some additional instances when you should not do an in-person amends:
>
> - You should not attempt amends with anyone who refuses to see you. By honoring their boundaries, you are completing a small portion of your amends to them. You can finish your amends in other ways.
> - Do not put yourself in danger. Do not put yourself at risk for any threats to you physically or emotionally; do not set yourself up for further abuse.
> - You should not seek to make amends in person to anyone you've harmed physically or mentally unless a therapist or objective third party is also present.
>
> There are many creative ways of completing amends in the above situations, which we will discuss later. When you're unsure if you can or should complete amends with an individual, seek advice from a sponsor, therapist, or objective peer.

A word of warning: not all amends you make will be well received. Some people may have harsh reactions to your efforts. Some people will not believe you are sincere. Sometimes you may have to give such people more time and revisit the amends with them later. This does not mean that you don't have to make amends to them; it means you must find another way to right the wrongs you have done.

Here is a simplified version of my recipe for amends:

1. Write out your list of individuals (or institutions) you have harmed.
2. Specify what you did to harm each individual.

3. Review your list with your sponsor, therapist, or an objective peer; then edit your list based on the feedback you receive.

4. Meditate or pray about it.

5. Meet with one person at a time. Plan ahead, and ask the person to whom you will make amends if you can meet with them at a time when you both can do this. Meet on neutral territory.

6. Discuss each incident of harm. Share your remorse and regret without the expectation of a positive response. Be authentic. Do not attempt to explain or justify the action or behavior unless the other person specifically asks you to do so.

7. Listen, empathize, acknowledge, and honor their response, whether good or bad. Do not attempt to minimize or diminish their response.

8. Ask what you can do to make it right, and thank them for their time, even if you did not get the outcome you hoped for. (In some cases, the mere fact that they showed up may mean something positive.)

9. Review with your sponsor, therapist, or friend.

This is often a difficult and painful process. You must come prepared and willing. You do not want to have to repeat this process with the same person. That would bring additional pain to them as well as yourself. I believe that when you have made a sincere and thorough attempt to correct or repair the damage you created, you are less likely to have to revisit your mistakes.

Now let's examine in detail how to make thorough amends to empower you and your loved one—an amends that will enable you to release some of the baggage you carry into your sobriety and relationships. A thorough amends, performed well, may result in enough closure that the issue, mistake, or error will not have to be addressed again.

My Recipe for Making Amends

Step Eight

1. Write down the following items:

   • Make a list of the people you have harmed.

- Write how you have hurt each of them, and be specific for each one; don't write "ditto" or "same."

- Write about how you have become willing to make amends. What barriers, concerns, and fears about making amends do you still hold or have yet to overcome?

- Are you willing to take the necessary actions to correct the wrongs you have committed? If the amends is a financial restitution, can you afford to make this amends? If needed, can you suggest an alternative form of restitution, such as time, actions, or effort?

- Write why you are willing to make this repair. What do you have to gain? What is your motivation?

2. Review this work with your sponsor, therapist, or objective peer.

3. Edit if necessary.

4. Write the list out again, and share it with your sponsor or objective peer.

5. Pray for the individual to whom you will make amends.

6. Meditate, pray, or contemplate all potential outcomes.

7. Know that if you have done the work well, the outcome for you will be good regardless of the response you receive because you can release toxic guilt and shame.

8. Remember that this process is also uncomfortable for the recipient.

9. Rehearse or practice making amends, paying close attention to your opening statements.

Step Nine

1. If possible, make the amends in person. Briefly explain why you want to meet, and ask if they would be receptive to meeting.

- Be patient about setting an appointment with them. Honor any boundaries that they set. Honoring their boundaries would be an example of "becoming willing" and taking small steps, which demonstrates your growth or potential for growth.

2. Meet on neutral territory. This can even be in the presence of your therapist, coach, or sponsor.

3. Begin with a positive attitude.

4. State the mistakes you made, harms you committed, and so on, and express your remorse or guilt without the expectation of a positive response.

5. Avoid using the words "you" and "we." State as much as you can in first person: I did, I am, I made. Using the words "you" or "we" tends to cause defensiveness in the listener. If you must use these words, make sure you do so in a positive statement.

6. Ask whether or not they recall any additional actions or incidents you may not remember. Acknowledge that you may not remember all of the harm you have done because of memory loss or blackout, and ask them if there is anything you have missed. Reassure them that anything you don't remember is important to you and that you will take accountability for it.

7. Acknowledge what they say, listen to their response, and empathize with their thoughts and feelings about the situation.

   - Repeat and name the specific mistakes (e.g., lying, stealing, etc.) that you heard them say so that they know you heard what they said.

   - Do not attempt to explain, justify, or minimize their point of view or opinion.

   - Do not use the word "but." If you do, it will negate everything you said until that point.

8. Ask them what they want you to do to make it right.

9. Take responsibility for your actions, behaviors, and deeds. Do your best not to become defensive.

10. Tell them what you will do differently next time. For example: "The next time you ask me to _____, I will _____."

11. Be authentic. Do not fake any emotions.

12. Do not play the victim. That is, do not attempt to explain yourself by blaming your actions on your frailty or weakness.

13. Listen well, and make eye contact as best you can.

14. Ask what you can do to receive their forgiveness, understanding that forgiveness is not about forgetting or excusing wrongs.

15. Be accepting, and recognize that forgiveness may not come at this time. This exercise is meant as an opportunity to move forward in this relationship and provide some relief from your shame and self-punishment.

16. Honor their response, good or bad. You must allow the person harmed the freedom to respond, even if the response is angry, sad, or unforgiving.

17. You do not have to take any physical, emotional, or mental abuse. If this arises, ask for a time-out so you can continue later.

NOTE The person to whom you are making amends may respond with anything from immediate forgiveness to outright refusal to believe what you are saying. No matter how they respond, you *must* accept their response. This is not a time to explain or justify your behaviors, activities, or mistakes. How the other person responds is up to them.

In situations where there is a likelihood of an abusive response, I recommend including your therapist, counselor, sponsor, or religious advisor in the meeting.

---

18. Review this experience with your sponsor or counselor.

19. Thank your higher power for giving you the courage and strength to do your part.

20. Find the positive in the situation, and share your experience, strength, and hope with others without compromising the anonymity of the other people involved.

21. Forgive yourself.

22. In this process, you may learn of some injustices done to you. This is an opportunity to forgive the other person for their actions or any harm they've caused.

23. If unexpected issues of grief or anger arise from this experience, share them with your sponsor, therapist, or an objective friend.

Roadblocks you might encounter:

- When there is a threat of violence or abuse, do not attempt to make an amends in person. For these people, as well as for those who are no longer in your life because of death, estrangement, or imprisonment, do your best to continue to make amends to them in other ways, such as:

  - You may decide to pray for them.

  - You can release the resentments you hold toward them.

  - You can write a letter to them. If it is not wise to actually mail the letter, you can attach the letter to a balloon and release it, or you can burn it, essentially delivering it to them spiritually.

  - You can visit their grave, leave flowers, or speak to them.

  - You can make something positive out of the loss or mistake by speaking or sharing about your experience, turning it into a teaching moment for others.

  - You can contribute or volunteer your time to a charity that either you or they support.

  - You can pay it forward to someone else by reaching out to someone in need.

- The other person may not be willing to hear or receive the amends.

  There may be people in your lives who will never acknowledge your amends, no matter how thoroughly you make them. In these cases, you do not have to repeat the effort more than once. The act of amends is primarily for your benefit and your healing. You cannot control the other person' reaction.

- Your loved one cannot stop bringing up your old mistakes after you have made a thorough amends.

There are varying opinions on how to address this problem. Some people will say that you must endure and suffer until the other person gets it out of their system, but I believe you do not have to make the amends more than once. Instead, I encourage you to use the agree-and-limit technique: you agree that you have harmed them, but then gently remind them that you have made amends, and set the boundary that they cannot continue to use this particular misdeed against you. Remind them that you are working on building trust and that you understand that they are hurt. Limit the conversation.

- They respond in a hostile manner.

  If this happens, do not react or become defensive. They are entitled to their feelings, but they do not have the right to be verbally aggressive or abusive. If you feel threatened, stop the conversation and ask to return to it later when both of you can be calm, or seek to complete the amends in the presence of a therapist, coach, or sponsor.

- You or your partner recall additional harms and mistakes that happened during active addiction.

  New events may trigger old memories of unfortunate events, which may need to be addressed. Consider this an opportunity to provide closure on a sad or hurtful event from your past. Working through these challenges will demonstrate your growth and offer you another chance to move closer to your loved one.

- You have procrastinated or avoided completing your amends.

  I encourage you to make amends as soon as possible. If your memory is still clouded or the pain is too great, at least try to chip away at the amends, expressing the desire and willingness to revisit the issue and listen to your loved one's grievances as they get triggered.

For example, when I was in active addiction, I would often lose my temper in the evenings and get upset about something small: the mess in the house, the late notice I had been given about a school project, or the like. I would start whining and complaining, and then I would order the kids around. I was sometimes loud and often emotionally abusive. I had forgotten about this tendency until one night several years later when I was in a bad mood, frustrated with myself and my messy home. I began to bark orders at one of my sons, demanding (rather than asking) him to help me clean up.

He froze. I was perplexed until he shared with me that he was flashing back to one of those times when I had been hurtful and abusive. By the grace of my higher power, I was able to stop my rant, calm down, and acknowledge what he was saying. I, too, flashed back to those evenings, and a wave of guilt washed over me. We were both reexperiencing heartbreak and pain. Again by the grace of my higher power, the words came out of my mouth without my thinking, and they went something like this:

"Oh, I love you, and I am so sorry. I remember those nights too. I treated you horribly and projected my internal anger onto you. You were not responsible for my frustration and anger. I will do my best to be more aware of my tone of voice and personal feelings and try not to do this again."

The conversation only lasted a few more minutes, but in the end, we hugged, and he forgave me. This was a gift—an opportunity for me to heal one of his wounds that I had caused, and an opportunity for our relationship to become closer.

My recipe for a "chip away" amends:

1. The moment arises, as in the example above.

2. Pause, gather your thoughts, and rehearse (as quickly as possible) what you need to say.

3. Acknowledge and take accountability for your mistake, while making eye contact and being emotionally present.

4. Listen to their response, acknowledge their feelings, and affirm that their memory and feelings are valid.

5. Ask what you can do to make it right.

6. Listen to their request, and follow through on it.

7. Thank your higher power for giving you this moment.

Making a Living Amends

At its most fundamental level, "living amends" means you are clean, sober, and in recovery. You are not abusing substances, and you are working to maintain your physical and mental health. It does not necessarily mean that you are or have to be a perfect person or that you have it all together. It means you are still working toward changing and evolving from the person you used to be in active disease, to become a better person. A living amends demonstrates consistency; it creates a new normal and reassures those who may be skeptical about your sobriety. A living amends is a way for you to make an amends to someone who is no longer in your life.

Summary

Making amends is essential to rebuilding relationships with your friends and family members. The goal is to bring resolution and repair to the relationship the *first time* you complete an amends step with another individual. You cannot take shortcuts on this step. Making a serious amends requires planning and forethought in order to be sincere and authentic. It requires picking the right time for both parties involved, presenting yourself humbly, and being willing to make changes in yourself and your behaviors. It is complex and painful, but you don't have to let it be overwhelming. It does not always have to be done immediately, but some action must be initiated for the relationship to survive, let alone to thrive.

Sometimes the opportunity to make an amends comes up naturally. Let us grasp these moments and take advantage of the opportunity. Remember that you may need to revisit this particular individual or indiscretion. I still make mistakes, but I do my best to make on-the-spot amends immediately or when I have seen the error of my ways. Sometimes it takes me hours or days to fully understand the mistakes I have made. My friends and family have become used to this and are no longer afraid to tell me when I have erred, made a mistake, or hurt them. They are less fearful of my reactions. We are all still improving our ability to manage differences and resolve conflicts, and I would like to think that I am continuing to make a living amends to all my loved ones.

7

Getting to Work

Any athlete will tell you that only a small part of their success comes from talent. Their achievements have come through hard work, patience, mental exercise, persistence, and never giving up. They might tell you that some of their training is tedious, monotonous, and boring; or they might say that some of their training is fun or that they enjoy certain aspects of their workout routine. Many athletes also use therapeutic tools like therapy, meditation, mindfulness, or visualization to enhance their training and workouts. Some listen to inspirational stories and guided meditations, or they may watch motivational or inspiring movies, reports, or speeches.

All athletes use a variety of tools to achieve success. I propose that the same approach is beneficial in your efforts to improve your familial relationships. It begins with adopting a positive outlook on working toward healing, improving, and growing these relationships. Some of the work will be fun, like spending quality time with your loved ones; and some parts will be difficult, like facing your mistakes and taking responsibility for your actions. But the outcome will contribute to the healing of your relationships.

Strengthening the Foundation

First you will need to strengthen your foundation, which begins with ensuring that you and your family have your basic needs met: food, shelter, and clothing. At the same time, you must make sure you have a plan for staying sober or maintaining your recovery. Next, you must care for yourself physically, eat a balanced diet, and get adequate rest and play. Remember the HALT acronym we discussed before: hungry, angry, lonely, and tired. HALT is a useful tool because it reminds you to be aware that whenever you are hungry, angry, lonely, or tired, you are more vulnerable to triggers, emotional fluctuations, and exaggerated reactions to life's daily problems. For most of you, rebuilding relationships may mean attending meetings or therapy sessions, or involvement in a treatment program; but it also means that you have to provide emotional and physical support to your loved ones to meet their needs and yours, and staying aware of HALT can help you with that.

The second step in strengthening your foundation is to develop and implement a game plan. You have already begun to do this by examining yourself and learning the new skills shared in the earlier chapters of this book. Revisit these areas often; repetition is crucial to replacing old habits with new, healthier ones. Build on this game plan by adopting a good attitude, which includes willingness and a hopeful or positive outlook. Depending on your situation, this may seem like an impossible task. I personally felt this way when I was about five months sober. My family would have little to do with me; phone calls were limited, I lived in a halfway house two hundred miles away from them, and they had little desire to come and see me.

At this point, I began to acknowledge that I had been making little effort to engage with my family. With some introspection, I saw that I had replaced my nuclear family with my recovery family. I had to reevaluate the foundation I had created in recovery, and I had to acknowledge my family's needs as well as my own. After seeking information and support from the older, wiser members of my AA community, I realized my errors. I sank into a depression. My situation seemed bleak, but again I reached out to trusted members of my AA community who had been through similar experiences. I adopted a more positive attitude after hearing their stories. I came to believe that if it worked for them, then it could work for me too.

Overcoming Self-Doubt and Negative Self-Talk

Another critical component of the foundation is developing and maintaining self-compassion. This means giving yourself grace and forgiveness when you make mistakes or fall back into old habits. It is natural for you to experience setbacks; it's simply part of the learning process. These setbacks do not have to be mistakes if you learn from them. Instead, they can become valuable tools or motivators to help you in your growth process.

If you struggle with self-doubt, being able to forgive yourself, or even being kind to yourself, here are two approaches I like to recommend to my sponsees and clients:

- Use the SNAP tool: stop, notice, ask, and pivot.

    - **Stop** the thinking or runaway thoughts.

    - **Notice** what you are saying to yourself or how you are reacting. Notice what is happening inside your body and in your environment.

    - **Ask** yourself: Is this true? Are my thoughts based on fact or fiction? Am I being called a name or accused of something I did not do? Is this how I want to react in this situation?

    - **Pivot** by changing your thinking or behavior. Take a time-out, say affirmations to yourself, and do what it takes to break the momentum of self-doubt or negative self-talk.

    - Make every effort to speak to yourself as if speaking to a dear friend. Would you talk to a loved one condescendingly? Would you make fun of them if they made a mistake? Or would you be understanding and try to lift their spirits or help them see the positive in every situation?

- You might offer a friend or loved one compassion and understanding. You may hug them or give them a shoulder to cry on. You would refute the negative self-talk or self-doubt by reminding them of their good qualities and assets. You should do the same for yourself.

Build on Your Self-Compassion

Practicing self-compassion also means acknowledging your efforts and successes. Any reasonable effort deserves recognition, regardless of the outcome.

Another phrase often heard in twelve-step groups is "progress, not perfection." Acknowledge that the goal is to make progress because seeking perfection is not reasonable. Maintaining your course counts as progress. The phrase also reminds us that results may not come immediately, and the changes you're making may not feel normal. Changes may feel awkward or even uncomfortable.

I believe strongly in the final component of the foundation: have a coach, therapist, sponsor, mentor, and/or other support system who can help you through this complex and confusing time. These people should be someone you respect who can tell you when you need constructive feedback. Having a support network can also help motivate, inspire, or redirect you when you lose focus. It will aid you in this process and will accelerate your growth immensely.

Therapeutic Work Options

Many of you began your recovery journey in a twelve-step program, while others got here through inpatient or outpatient treatment programs for addiction. Most of the information and tools introduced in these settings are about staying sober, but many of these skills can also be applied to improving our relationships. However, healing your relationships may often require additional help. This may come from individual, group, or family therapy; it may take working with a life coach, sponsor, or mentor; or it may involve taking advantage of support groups and educational classes offered through community resources, houses of worship, schools, and mental health centers.

I will use the term *therapeutic work* to refer to resources that will help you understand your struggles and yourself more deeply. If you do engage in therapeutic work, remember that you can still benefit from the support of other resources. For instance, this book is probably not the only resource you need to help you repair your relationships, but if you combine it with family therapy and participation in a group, your growth will accelerate.

Professional Help vs. Self-Help

What is the difference between professional help and self-help? The first and most significant difference is the cost and accessibility of treatment. Only some people have the resources to pay for private help. When seeking private help, take your time. There may be free or sliding-scale practitioners in your area.

The most significant benefit of professional therapy is that you will receive targeted attention and may receive quicker results.

Professional help is designed to meet your needs. The focus is on you, your relationships, or your family. It is private and confidential. Your therapist cannot discuss your case with anyone else without your permission (the only exception being threats of physical harm to oneself or others), which may help you to share personal things you would not share while doing self-help work. This unburdening of feelings and emotions will in itself be therapeutic. Some therapists will explore the reasons for your thoughts, feelings, and actions, to help you gain understanding and insight into yourself.

Signs that you could benefit from individual therapy include:

- Your current level of discomfort and dysfunction is impairing your ability to perform the activities of daily living, such as eating, sleeping, or going to school or work.

- You have been struggling with a particular problem for an extended period of time.

- You have not been able to overcome your issues or relieve your suffering through self-help options.

- You generally feel anxious or overwhelmed by everything.

- You are not able to turn off your thoughts.

- You are sleeping, eating, or exercising significantly more or less than usual.

- You have lost interest in activities that you used to enjoy.

- You feel hopeless, or you have reached a point where you just don't know what to do anymore.

- You have thoughts of hurting yourself or others.

Signs that you could benefit from marriage or family therapy include:

- You have reached an impasse where no one is willing to compromise.

- There has been physical violence or threats of violence.

- There has been emotional abuse.

- Infidelity has occurred, or trust has been broken in any significant manner.
- There are significant levels of dysfunction in one or more of the following areas: communication, anger management, conflict resolution, financial issues, intimacy issues, or parenting.
- There are unresolved conflicts with extended family members, in-laws, stepchildren, or ex-partners.

Therapists vs. Life Coaches and Recovery Coaches

It is important to note the differences between therapists, on the one hand, and life coaches or recovery coaches on the other.

- A therapist will focus on mental health issues and emotional healing. They are licensed to address mental illness and mental health, and they often explore how past experiences or trauma affect a client's mental health in the present.
- A life coach will focus most on the present and will help clients develop and achieve professional, personal, or overall wellness goals. They can help you build healthy habits and uncover current obstacles to well-being.
- A recovery coach focuses on helping you manage people, places, and things that may lead to relapse. Their work is directed toward helping their clients maintain sobriety; they may help their clients set goals, recognize triggers that lead to relapse, and better understand the principles of addiction.

Life coaches and recovery coaches will also aid you in defining your needs, help you identify additional resources for support, and direct you to these resources. The majority of therapists have extensive educational and professional training. All professional therapists, including psychologists, licensed professional counselors, social workers, licensed marriage and family counselors, and licensed clinical drug abuse counselors, must maintain professional licenses, adhere to a code of ethics, and provide documentation of continuing education to practice professionally. In contrast, the accreditation, licensing, education, and experience requirements for life coaches and recovery coaches vary from state to state.

Finding Professional Help

The key is to determine what kind of support is right for you. Professional therapy or coaching is an investment in your physical and mental health. It is a good investment if you work with a qualified individual. Because there are many types of therapists and therapeutic approaches, I firmly believe that it is essential to work with a therapist who specializes in your specific needs and has experience with addiction, trauma, posttraumatic stress disorder (PTSD), issues that are common among adult children of alcoholics, and your specific mental health issues.

Furthermore, I believe you should invest time in finding a good therapist or coach. A therapist or coach who is a bad fit can do more harm than good. To find a therapist, life coach, or recovery coach, begin by asking your trusted friends and community for references. You can also check with a local treatment facility, ask your family physician, or ask community leaders for recommendations. You can also use online resources such as Psychology Today, which offers a tool for finding therapists. Once you have a few names of people to call, take time to interview them, and remember that you do not have to commit to the first therapist or coach you find. You want to ensure that you can build a therapeutic relationship with them. A good coach or therapist will be happy to answer your questions. Some of your questions may be:

- What is your specialty? (Relevant specialties would include addiction, anxiety, depression, and OCD, among others.)

- What are your qualifications? Can you prescribe medications? Do you refer to or accept referrals from psychiatrists or physicians who can prescribe medications?

- Do you primarily see clients individually, in groups, or in families? How long do sessions usually last? Do you see clients after five p.m. or on weekends?

- What is the setting for appointments? Are there options for phone or video appointments?

- How many years of experience do you have?

- What is your availability? What happens if I have a crisis and want to speak to you at a time other than my scheduled appointment?

- What does your typical session look like? How long do the sessions typically last? How often would you see me or my family, and for how long?

- Do you assign homework?

- How much do you charge? Do you take insurance? Is there a sliding fee scale? Do you accept credit cards?

- What school of thought or therapeutic philosophy do you follow? (Examples include CBT, family systems, behavioral therapy, Freudian psychoanalytic therapy, humanistic therapy, holistic therapy, and emotionally focused therapy.)

- Do you use any specific therapeutic tools to enhance the therapeutic experience, such as EMDR (eye movement desensitization and reprocessing), guided meditation or imagery, art or music therapy, play therapy, or neurofeedback?

- What are your strengths and limitations as a counselor?

- Have you been in therapy yourself? Do you seek peer support or consultation from other professionals?

- Do you create a treatment plan or treatment goals for our work? What happens if I do not improve?

- Have you seen other clients like me? Have you been successful with them?

Please note that your relationship with your therapist or coach is much like any other, and it will build over time. Signs that a therapist/coach is a good fit for you include the following:

- You feel respected, seen, and heard.

- You feel accepted and not judged.

- Your boundaries are honored.

- You feel a sense of connection.

- Your therapist or coach takes time to answer your questions.

- Your therapist or coach defines their boundaries clearly and concisely.

- Your therapist or coach helps you develop a treatment plan or methodology that you perceive as feasible.

- Your therapist or coach will help you find your own answers instead of providing them for you.
- Your therapist or coach will ask for feedback from you.

Self-Help Options

Many of you are using self-help strategies without even realizing it. Social media, television, news programs, and workplace training offer self-help skills and self-soothing tools. In this book I define self-help as a strategy or technique one can use to improve one's mental and emotional health. A benefit of self-help is that it is entirely private, information on it is abundant and accessible, and you can work or study at your own pace. Self-help strategies are effective for many people in overcoming issues of low motivation, self-esteem, procrastination, time management, behavior modification, and minor levels of anxiety and depression. However, the effectiveness of self-help is based upon self-discipline and your ability to look objectively at yourself to understand the core of your problems.

Support Groups

Support groups allow access to community support, feedback, and advice from others. In these groups, you can realize you do not have to face your problems alone. These groups can help you gain some of the objectivity and perspective you need to correctly identify your concerns and find alternative ways to address them. Support groups come in many different shapes and sizes, including twelve-step programs, LGBTQ support groups, family, study groups, bridge clubs, sports teams, and book clubs. To get the most out of your self-help groups, I encourage you to ask questions, participate in discussions, recommend discussion topic ideas, and attend meetings regularly. Focus on positive answers and suggestions in the groups, and notice the strength and hope in others' experiences. Don't be afraid to disclose your challenges; there will likely be someone in the group who has gone through a similar experience and can share what worked and didn't work for them. Many of these groups also provide an opportunity for fun, such as picnics, barbecues, movie nights, and museum visits, especially around the holidays.

It is important to note that each twelve-step group will have its own distinct personality and group of core members. For instance, at the clubhouse in my community, there are a variety of recovery-focused meetings held daily and weekly, and each meeting offers something different. The 6:30 a.m. daily meeting is composed mainly of professionals trying to attend a meeting before work. The lunchtime meeting is a mixture of retirees and stay-at-home parents, and the six p.m. meeting is popular among people on their way home from work. The content of the discussions reflects the experiences of the members. You might have to try several different groups before you find a meeting where you feel you have met your tribe of people—a place where you feel at home and can relate to the other members.

There are support groups that can benefit your loved ones too. You should support their attendance at meetings that are independent of your own so they can get the help and support they need.

Work with a Sponsor or Mentor

Twelve-step programs like AA or NA encourage you to get a sponsor. This is a person who has significant time and experience in sobriety. Sponsors can offer you one-to-one support, answer questions, share their personal experiences, advise you on how to work the steps, and help hold you accountable in your program. This individual is not a therapist or a coach; a wise sponsor will know when to refer you to professional help. But they often are more available and accessible than your coach or therapist. The relationship can be informal and friendly, or it can be more of a teacher-student relationship. Picking a sponsor or mentor is an important task. Seek out healthy individuals who have experienced issues similar to the ones you are facing. A good sponsor is someone who can be objective and is not afraid to give you constructive criticism when necessary. Many people begin with a temporary sponsor to get them started in the program until they find someone they feel more connected with.

Faith Communities and Spiritual Groups

This type of support may include scriptural studies, talking to a clergyperson or spiritual advisor, or taking classes to expand your beliefs. In researching this topic, I found that almost every type of spiritual practice offered some type of support group for mental health issues. This information can be readily found on the internet.

Volunteer Work or Service Work with Others

Research has shown that people who volunteer with others report better physical and mental health, higher life satisfaction, greater social well-being, and less depression than those who do not participate in volunteer activities.[1] Although volunteer service does not particularly stand out as an avenue for self-help, I am a huge proponent of getting involved with service groups or volunteering for a cause you believe in. Volunteer and service work confers many benefits:

- It repairs or builds self-esteem. Helping others without expecting to get something in return enables you to practice putting others' needs before your own.

- It builds self-confidence and gives you a sense of purpose.

- It allows you to put your problems into perspective and removes your feelings of isolation, difference, or brokenness. It is hard to feel sorry for yourself when you see others in challenging situations.

- By helping even one person, you are making a positive impact on your community.

- Service work fills time and combats boredom. It also offers an opportunity to laugh and have fun with others.

- When you do volunteer work, you're building trust and respect among your community, your close friends, and your family members.

When Professional Help Is Essential

Professional help is advisable in these situations:

- If you want to hurt yourself or someone else.

  Do not be ashamed of these thoughts and feelings. You are not alone; these thoughts are common in early sobriety. But keeping this information to yourself is not going to help. You will overcome depression much quicker with the help of others.

- When your attempts at self-help have failed, and you need more clarity or objectivity to understand the nature of your issues.

- When you and a loved one have reached a prolonged stalemate or plateau and no longer see forward movement in your relationship.

- When your anxiety or compulsive behaviors keep you in a constant state of fight or flight, you continuously feel on edge, or you have persistent worry, nervousness, or fear.

- When your stress or anxiety interferes with regular daily activities.

- When you feel you or someone else is in acute danger. In this situation, do not hesitate to call the police or a hotline for additional help.

- When you or a loved one is seeing or hearing things that are not there (hallucinations or delusions). This may be caused by a chemical imbalance best treated with medications and psychiatry.

I emphasize that there is no shame in getting professional help. On the contrary, as with most successful athletes, coaching and guidance can accelerate your growth and be a tool to reveal the best in yourself, your loved ones, and your relationships. We must normalize addressing our mental health issues just as vigorously as we address our physical health needs.

Work Skills for Recovery

Why do I have to explain how to do the work involved in recovery? Well, most of us spent the last days or weeks of our active addiction putting all of our energy into our addiction—chasing the bottle or the drugs. We let our family members down as well as ourselves; we became unreliable; we made promises and plans that we failed to follow through on; we missed birthdays, sporting events, social occasions, and sometimes even holidays.

The new work you're facing now begins with showing up and having a positive attitude. The next step is to be prepared for the work. Then the work continues by showing up regularly, implementing change, and reinforcing positive new behaviors. Along the way, you evaluate your results and return to the drawing board as often as you need to in order to solve your problems.

Then you either implement a new plan or repeat what worked so often that it becomes a new good habit. Along the way, you offer kindness to yourself and your partner, and you maintain the work. You might celebrate success, but once you have achieved one goal, you move on to the next one. This is what it takes to do the work. It is much easier said than done.

When you think about it, making any life change requires showing up and doing the work. To take a more mundane example, when I send my child to school to learn Spanish, they will attend a Spanish class. I expect them to learn some Spanish from this class. I know that for this to be accomplished, not only do they have to be present; they also have to pay attention. They have to complete the classroom exercises and then finish any homework. They will have to practice basic skills for a long time before they can successfully read, write, and speak the Spanish language. While my child is doing their part, I am also counting on the teacher to prepare to teach my child. I expect them to have knowledge and understanding of the Spanish language, and to have the requisite teaching skills. I expect the teacher to make plans for each lesson. My child and the teacher will work together to accomplish mutual goals. Now, my child might be able to learn Spanish independently, but with the teacher's guidance, their own hard work in completing the assignments, my support, and the class participation of their peers, they will reach this goal much faster, with a much better command of Spanish.

Show Up with Your Homework Completed

The phrase "show up" may seem a little harsh, but most of us were not reliable during active addiction. You must try to follow through on your obligations to your partners and attend classes and therapy appointments. The next step, completing your "homework," may be hard for some; it takes not just an open mind and a willingness to learn but also a little preparation. Most therapists, coaches, and sponsors will assign homework. This may entail completing writing exercises or practicing the skills and tools you learned in therapy. Being diligent about completing your homework will allow you to reinforce new skills or habits that will enhance your time in therapy. You will save time, energy, and money if you do your homework. If you are working on a twelve-step program, you may already be practicing the homework tasks of journaling, meditating, and completing inventories.

Start with Small, Reasonable Goals

Set reasonable goals that can be achieved, to ensure that you'll see progress and to give you a sense of hope and accomplishment—especially if the tasks in front of you seem insurmountable. Life coach Katie Van Orden de Assis recommends setting small goals that are, for all practical purposes, impossible not to achieve.[2] For example, suppose that the overall goal is to resolve conflicts in a manner that is satisfactory to both partners in a relationship. In that case, your first small goal might be to have both individuals sitting silently in the same room. No speaking, no overt body language; just sitting in the same room. You recognize and acknowledge the success of this goal before moving on to the next one, which might be for each individual to write down what they like about themselves (not the other person) on paper. Then each person could write about their current skills for addressing conflict. This continues with manageable goals until more challenging issues can be addressed. By the time you have reached the more challenging tasks, you have built a mountain of success stories to carry you through the more challenging task of resolving any conflict.

Take Action and Review the Results

Do your homework. Attempt the prescribed exercises, even if they seem overly simple or emotionally painful. Therapeutic change does not come solely from attending meetings or going to an appointment. To be successful in therapy, recovery, or relationship repair, you must commit to implementing tools and taking steps to change. Some skills are going to work for you, and others may not. Thus, when you implement a new tool or skill that doesn't work, you have not failed; you have only ruled out one technique and have come one step closer to finding the right solution. This is why you need to come with an open and willing attitude.

Have Empathy for Yourself and Others

I recently enjoyed seeing some of my granddaughter's first steps. I felt an overwhelming sense of joy at her accomplishment. Seeing her walk three steps to her mother's waiting arms, I felt exhilarated. It took her many attempts to do this; she had failures and tears along the way, but not once did we shame her or make her feel bad for not walking. We were sure she would eventually master the balance and coordination to walk. We understood that she must overcome fear and give up on taking the easier route of crawling where she wanted to go. We offered her empathy and encouragement, and we supported her efforts. We must also do this for ourselves and our relationship partners. Seek to view problems from another's perspective. Seek to understand your loved one's feelings. Offer kindness to yourself and to them when you make errors.

Repetition and Commitment

When I am learning a new skill or task at work, I repeat it at least three times before I set the expectation of having learned or mastered the skill. For me, the use of technology in my job always seems to be changing. I struggle with this. Thus, I give myself grace the first three or four times I have to ask for help. You may take days, weeks, or months to master a new behavior or relationship skill. Several research studies have shown that it may take thirty to ninety days of repeated effort to break an old habit or form a new one. Repetition is essential to learning.

Forward progress must be nurtured and maintained. It is like building a muscle; if you increase your strength by working out at the gym for several months and then quit exercising, you cannot expect to maintain your newly acquired strength forever. You must apply effort to keep those muscles strong. In recovery, it's easy to get off track and to slide into old behaviors. It's easy to forget the consequences of past behavior. You might experience periods where you plateau; this is common, and it does not mean your efforts are not working. Sometimes progress is being made without any external indication of it.

There is no magical finish line to reach when improving your relationships. I propose that you never complete the tasks you begin here. You will not always have to work so hard, but the work in relationships never ends. Accepting this makes it easier to do the work. As mentioned, I encourage you to break big goals into smaller ones. This will keep your energy focused on the positive. Climbing to the top of a mountain begins with taking the first step.

Focus on Changing Yourself, Not Others

Don't waste your energy on self-defeating thoughts or trying to justify a lack of effort to achieve your goals with statements like "This will never work for me," "You don't understand my situation," or any sentence that begins with "Yes, but . . ." Focus on changing yourself, not the other person. You can only change your own thoughts, feelings, and reactions to any given situation, not someone else's. We may hope for an improvement in a relationship and a change in another's reactions or behaviors, but we cannot control anyone but ourselves. You need to save your energy for real work that matters: the work on yourself. The effort you put into yourself will improve all of your relationships.

Measuring Progress

Our culture likes to measure things; we keep scores, compare ourselves to others, and even rank ourselves. For some, this fuels fear of failure and feelings of inadequacy by directing them to value their contributions less than the contributions of others. I am asking you to use this as a healthy tool in moderation—a tool for acknowledging the positive growth you are achieving in your relationships, recognizing improvement no matter how slight, and keeping you motivated to continue doing the work even when it is difficult to see significant growth.

Let's begin by revisiting the problem-solving steps presented in chapter 5. The first step is problem definition, followed by brainstorming—creating as many ideas for a solution as possible. Then you select one idea for a solution and implement the corresponding action, behavior, or change. Within a reasonable time, you pause and assess to see if the effort worked. If it did, practice this skill until it becomes a habit. If not, return to the drawing board and start again.

Acknowledging and tracking progress may not seem like a tool that will improve your interpersonal and relationship skills, but the point is to become aware, be mindful, acknowledge growth, track what works, and determine what can be improved for more remarkable change. This can be helpful when you do not see a significant change in a relationship, progress is slow, or your efforts are working in some of your relationships and not others. For example, my relationships with each of my children progressed at different paces. My relationship with my middle son improved the quickest. He was the most open to moving toward repairing the relationship. Part of our progress came about because he had written me an "impact letter" while I was in treatment. This is a therapeutic tool that involves an individual writing to you about some or all of the ways that your addiction has affected them. Although reading it aloud in front of my peers in treatment was bone-crushingly painful, I believe it forced me to address in great detail the wounds I had created within him. It also allowed him to safely confront me about the pain he felt because of my actions during active addiction. This honesty and vulnerability opened the door to healing.

At first our progress was slow, but a significant change occurred when he asked me to take him to visit several colleges the summer before his senior year in high school. This would require a three-day car trip, two nights in a hotel, tours of three colleges, and hours alone in the car together. This was about one year into my sobriety. I cannot describe how excited I was when he asked me to do this. First, I recognized it as a massive leap of faith for him. Then I realized it was somewhat of a test: an opportunity to make living amends and demonstrate some of the skills I had learned in sobriety. I made some mistakes at first—I talked too much, slurped on candy, and asked too many annoying questions—but the fantastic thing that happened was that he felt comfortable speaking up and asking me not to do these things. He wasn't scared of my reaction anymore.

I also did some things right: I stayed sober, honored his boundaries, listened to his thoughts without interrupting or giving my opinion, stopped talking about myself, and remained in the moment. I tried to meet him where he was, not pushing my agenda or expectations on him. Our relationship progressed. It was initially superficial, but it helped lay a foundation for future growth. We visited more colleges after that first trip, and the conversations became more profound and more meaningful on each one.

Keeping track of your efforts and acknowledging progress, no matter how small, is crucial to maintaining positive momentum for continuing the work of rebuilding relationships. There are many ways to do this, including journaling, charting, goal-setting, doing step work, writing gratitude lists, and taking morning and evening inventories.

- **Journaling:** Journaling comes naturally to some; for others it takes a little practice and repetition. However, regular journaling offers many possible benefits, such as promoting creativity, enhancing your ability to gather insight into your behavior, and providing an outlet for the daily stressors that come your way when you do not have a roommate, friend, or spouse to vent these feelings to.

- **Charting/worksheets:** My sponsor is a teacher; she loves printed worksheets and has used them to give me many assignments over the years. In early sobriety, I had a binder of all the handouts, assignments, and notes I had taken to review and reflect on topics as needed. Charting also allows you to mark your progress, providing positive reinforcement.

- **Posting your goals where you can see them:** When I was in high school, my swim coach recommended that we post our goals on notes around our homes, lockers, and vehicles to remind ourselves of them constantly. I still do this today.

- **Gratitude lists:** Taking time to write out lists of the things you are grateful for every day is an excellent habit for combating negative thinking and self-talk. Just the act of writing out in longhand the things you are grateful for slows down any compulsive or runaway thoughts.

Honestly Evaluate Your Starting Point

It is time to take a hard look at your starting point. If you have linearly worked through this book, you will have already assessed the health of your relationships.

> **NOTE** It does not matter what level your relationship is currently at, regardless of whether it has several positive traits or is nonexistent. Take a hard look at where the relationship is today and in the recent past. This is your starting point from which to move forward.

Understand That Sometimes Progress Hurts

Some growth comes with pain, just as beginning a new workout routine is often accompanied by sore muscles. Not all pain is terrible. I challenge you to walk through the pain and to feel the hurt. You will survive, and pushing through it will make you stronger. Each crisis that you survive will build your self-confidence. You will learn to tolerate change and discomfort. Your sobriety depends on this, as you will encounter many painful changes in sobriety: challenges, deaths, and heartbreak.

Sometimes Plateauing Is Right Where You Need to Be

- You will encounter periods where little to no growth can be visibly seen or measured. This can be a good thing, temporarily giving you time to rest the relationship muscle. It can allow you to display your ability to be consistent and reliable. In addition, it could provide your loved one time to catch up to where you are in recovery.

- Remember that just recognizing you are stagnant or have taken a step backward demonstrates that you have grown. Developing self-awareness and insight is crucial to healing yourself and improving your relationships.

- When a plateau creates a restlessness within you, or when you feel dread or pain increasing, ask yourself these questions:

  - Do I need to redefine or reassess the problem?
  - Do I need to return to the basics? (You can always benefit from working on the fundamentals.)
  - Am I assessing the situation correctly?
  - Do I need to seek the help of a professional?

Turn a Setback into a Strength; Understand That There Will Be Tests

I propose that setbacks are not a bad thing. I usually hate it when people say, "There are no mistakes if you turn them into lessons." I recoil at these words, but I will eat them right now. Mistakes *can* be lessons. Setbacks can prove to be fruitful. If the setback is significant, seek objective feedback from a friend, sponsor, or therapist, and ask yourself the following questions:

- Are you overlooking small, simple demonstrations of progress?
- Are you confusing normal rites of passage in adolescence for acts of rebellion or apathy? For example, I allowed my feelings to be hurt when I forgot that most sixteen-year-old boys prefer to drive home from their sporting events with their friends rather than with their mothers.

Take Time to Acknowledge Growth and Improvement

In my experience, each child's healing and progress came at different times. I experienced many frustrations in my efforts to heal relationships with my kids. There were highs and lows, periods of great forward movement, and a few backslides. Sometimes an example of growth could be easily missed or overlooked. It is important to look for and acknowledge these signs of improvement, no matter how small, because this process can be very challenging.

I admit that I got discouraged at times and worried that I might never have authentic relationships with all four of my kids. The youngest was the most reluctant to reengage. I wondered: Would he ever forgive me? Would he ever open up to me? Would he ever yell at me or scream at me? Show any emotion at all? There were times when I would have preferred anger over apathy. I share this because I want you to know I had to accept his reluctance to trust me. I could not force a relationship with him. Instead, I had to continue to work on myself, maintain my sobriety, be patient and hopeful. With time, this paid off, and about three years into my sobriety, my youngest child (then about sixteen years old) asked if he could have friends over to the house for a Super Bowl party. I did not miss this sign of progress. I was thrilled that he wanted his friends in our home. For me, it meant that he felt safe and secure enough in my behavior that he could risk having his friends over to our home.

Maintenance

Repairing relationships will get easier, and it will continue to be beneficial to you, your friends, and your family. There is no end point or final goal because life presents new challenges and new experiences. These are opportunities to create more profound and more lasting relationships. To maintain the health and/or positive momentum of your recovery:

- **Make receiving feedback or constructive criticism a normal part of your day.**

  In early sobriety, I ran almost all of my bigger decisions past my sponsor, peers, or therapist. In part, I did this because I realized I did not know what normal behavior was, and I needed guidance. I also did this because I needed encouragement to move forward through difficult situations. When I lacked hope or experienced frustration at not seeing positive results from my efforts, I was able to draw on the experiences of others. With practice, this feedback enabled me to stop being overly sensitive and helped me learn to accept constructive criticism from others.

- **Have some fun, take breaks, laugh, and find joy.**

Taking breaks and allocating some time for play are essential for maintaining your energy for the work in front of you. Your body requires rest. Having fun as a family offers a contrast to difficult times. It promotes family bonds, reduces tension and stress, and introduces laughter and joy, which children need for healthy emotional development. Studies show that children who have regular playtimes have better interpersonal skills, problem-solving skills, creativity, and regulation of their emotions.

- **Never stop learning.**

Continue to be a seeker of information and knowledge. Do research on topics that interest you. This type of study does not have to be related to your sobriety or mental health, either. By learning new things, you are keeping your mind healthy, encouraging the growth of new brain cells, and challenging your neural pathways to rebuild and repair themselves. Learning new things may also ease social anxiety, as you will gain new topics to discuss. Learning a new skill may reduce tension and stress if it simplifies your daily routines. For example, I feared using an electric drill when repairing or assembling furniture in my home. Once I learned how to use a drill, I cut the time to assemble a bookcase in half. As you learn, ask yourself, "How can I apply this in my life? How can I use this to help myself or help others?"

- **Be creative, and practice mindfulness.**

Take an art class, and draw or color in a book with your child. Make up imaginary stories and tell them to your kids. Becoming more creative may help you break through a plateau or a stagnant relationship level. It will also help fight against black-and-white thinking, which can lead to negative self-talk, limiting your potential to pay attention to the present moment without judgment or evaluation.

- **Share what you know (experience, strength, and hope) through service work.**

Service work and volunteering have become my best go-to fix for dealing with my depression, anxiety, and self-pity. Volunteering allows me to take the focus off myself and my problems. It also helps me to put my problems into a healthier perspective, counteracting my tendency to dramatize or catastrophize my situation.

Dedicating your time to a volunteer cause also allows you to make new friends, demonstrate your altruism to your family, and polish your social skills, possibly helping to ease any anxiety you may feel around others.

- **Be realistic when it comes to time expectations connected to goals.**

Most of us look for instant results of our efforts. My friends in sales know better; they tell me that they typically don't expect to see results of their actions for up to three months. New habits take months to become second nature. When dealing with human emotions, it will take months to see real, long-lasting results. You must not expect immediate results. However, I don't want you to ignore or diminish the value of simple, minor improvements like a smile, or a conversation that expands to more than yes-or-no questions and answers, because such events *do* matter. Instead, just set the expectation that it will take time.

- **Maintain a positive attitude.**

Become hopeful, not hopeless. Whenever possible, look on the bright side. Become a person others want to be around because of your cheerful disposition. Make this change in your behavior, and you will find that other positive people, places, and things will be attracted to you.

For some of us, this behavior is hard work because we have been so programmed or habituated to being negative. Be kind to yourself, and give yourself time to make this change.

- **When in doubt, just do the next right thing.**

  Situations will arise where you will be left on your own to decide, take action, or respond to a question—and your mind goes blank, and you aren't sure what to do. As mentioned earlier in this book, I and countless others have learned that in these situations it's best to just do the next right thing. There are different ways to interpret and use this principle in your life, but I use it in two ways:

  - I use it to ask myself what the *right* thing to do is. What would my sponsor or therapist say was the right decision?
  - I use it to stay in the present. What is the right decision right *now*?

Summary

You do not have to consider "work" as something negative or a burdensome chore that you have to do. You're acquiring new skills, and there is a learning curve involved. Learning any skill takes effort, trial and error, practice, and patience before you are rewarded with the results. Just as my granddaughter learned to walk or you learned to ride a bicycle, it took some work to experience the freedom of walking or riding a bike.

Don't quit, maintain a healthy diet, get enough sleep, keep emotions in check, remember your HALT, and redefine the word "work." The key here is to balance hard work with fun work. Don't push yourself too hard when you are hungry, angry, lonely, or tired. Take breaks, give rewards, and enjoy the process.

Helpful Resources

There are many different resources that you can use to build your relationship muscle strength. Libraries, bookstores, and the internet have endless options for self-help books, blogs, video channels, and the like. Some of my favorites include the Big Books and twelve-step books of AA, NA, Al-Anon, and Adult Children of Alcoholics; *The Happiness Advantage* by Shawn Achor; *The Seven Spiritual Laws of Success* by Deepak Chopra; and *The Four Agreements* by Don Miguel Ruiz. Additional resources include podcasts, documentaries, and information from your local community and religious institutions.

8

Challenges

Your Attitude

You will have relationships where, despite making a sincere effort, you do not see progress. You may be losing hope and thinking of giving up. You will likely ask yourself, "Where do I go from here?" Self-examination is the best place to start. Begin by examining your attitude. Are you setting yourself up for failure because of your fears or through negative self-talk? Are you anticipating a negative outcome? Have you set your goals too high? Success lies in believing that positive results are possible. You cannot change other people; you can only control your thoughts and actions. This book directs you to work on yourself, learn new insights and tools, and increase your empathy and emotional intelligence. It is meant to help you improve your ability to understand your family's feelings. Just because you don't see measurable progress, that doesn't mean your efforts have gone to waste. Sometimes a seed lies dormant for years until just the right amounts of sun, wind, and rain combine to create an environment where the seed can germinate, take root, and grow into a beautiful plant. Likewise, changes within your friends and family may occur that you cannot see or measure.

We all will experience roadblocks that can feel insurmountable on our paths to family unification. These dynamics may take extra patience and may involve challenges such as time and distance away from your family; divorce or separation; financial, legal, and health problems; incarceration; and different levels of progress in each family member's personal growth due to the intensity of treatment. Do not be discouraged. Some problems will be more complex than others, but that does not mean you should abandon your relationship work.

Physical Distance

You may be physically separated from your family because your treatment facility is in another city or state, or because of the facility's limitations on visits and phone use. Alternatively, your family may have established boundaries for emotional and physical safety. Despite your separation, there are still actions you can take and mistakes to avoid. In early recovery, I spent almost eighteen months living away from my hometown and my family. I did not attempt to explain my absence to my family, which was my primary mistake. I expected them to understand that I was following treatment advice, but I never helped them to see why these were the rules or how they would help. In truth, I avoided the confrontation that might ensue if I spoke directly to them about my absence. I didn't want any of them to try to talk me out of it, and I didn't want to hear about their hurt or disappointment either. I hoped they somehow knew I was doing what was best for all of us. But to them, it looked like I was continuing to be selfish and doing what I wanted despite their needs and wishes. They believed I was still inaccessible, regardless of my reasons or rationales. I failed to see the difference between what was best for my sobriety and what was a reasonable request to ask of my family.

Knowing What, How, and When to Explain

Take time to explain the separation to your family, no matter the reason. Get your peers, therapist, or sponsor to help you practice what to say and how to say it, and to determine when is the best time. If you cannot tell them in person or by phone, write it in a letter. Tell them you recognize their hardships in this situation, and explain that you are following treatment recommendations. Share your longer-term goals, hopes, and intentions. For example: "One of the reasons I cannot return home now is that I need more time to build my foundation of recovery skills, and I need to distance myself from the temptations of access to my drug of choice." Or, "Living in a sober home will remove me from the things that trigger me." Within those parameters, keep your loved ones as involved as possible. Write letters, make calls, and encourage them to come to visiting hours and family therapy meetings.

One benefit of physical distance is that it can ease the everyday tensions and stressors in relationships. Remember that your family may be grateful for their time away from you. It may offer them peace of mind, calm, or relief from conflict and fighting. They may believe that while you are in treatment or incarcerated, you are physically safe from an overdose, accident, or injury. Some may not want you to come home or will not allow you to return home after treatment. Consider all of this sympathetically, and understand that it may even be a positive sign of their growth; they are now able to establish their boundaries. The healthier they become, the less they will enable your addiction. In honoring their boundaries, you are demonstrating your growth to them. Manage your feelings of rejection with the help of supportive peers, a therapist, or a sponsor.

Challenge: Intensity or Strength of Treatment

A person in early recovery is likely to undergo more treatment than their friends and family members, which can create a common obstacle to family reunification that is often overlooked. If you are in treatment or participating in a twelve-step program and achieving milestones, you will consistently receive therapy, information, and other forms of support, and you will receive them in greater amounts than your family members will likely receive at home. A person who is in an inpatient treatment program or an intensive outpatient program will likely be removed from some of the everyday stresses of daily living, such as paying the bills, getting the kids ready for school, and managing the household. Your family members will not have the same access to a therapeutic environment that you do, and they may also have to bear additional burdens created by your absence.

Each family member heals if they are willing and at their own pace. There is no one path to reconciliation. Family members will have different needs based on the roles they have taken on, such as hero/shero, scapegoat, lost child, or mascot. The ages, developmental stages, and maturity levels of your loved ones all affect their responses and their ability to adapt to the changes you are making. That's why it's a mistake to lump all your children together in one counseling experience. This practice doesn't account for their specific individual needs. Also, keep in mind that your extended family members such as parents and grandparents may receive little to no therapeutic intervention during this time.

Tool: Empathy and Grace

Be patient and understanding with your loved ones, and grant them the same grace and empathy you hope they will give you. It is easy to prioritize your recovery needs or your family's recovery needs, but your recovery will be enhanced if they are also working on their personal growth.

By being a role model, you can encourage them to do their own work. Reassure them that you know their mental and physical health is important and that you want to support them. Be as kind to them as you would be to a new patient entering your treatment program or a new individual attending their first twelve-step meeting.

Challenge: Divorce/Separation

You cannot force reconciliation, and if your partner has requested a separation or has begun divorce proceedings, remember that your relationship with your romantic partner is likely the one that has suffered the most pain and strife. Your partner's reaction to your sobriety can range from being in a honeymoon period where they are living in the pink clouds of hopefulness, to the opposite response of filing for divorce and refusing to see you. Your partner may cycle through a full range of emotions: they may be supportive and loving in one moment, then angry and hostile in the next. Be prepared for this roller-coaster ride, and do not seek solace in the affection and romantic attention of another.

Tool: Patience and Compassion

Be compassionate, and practice the skills of patience, such as pausing, not reacting, and the other tools discussed earlier in this book. Take joy in the good moments, acknowledge them, and express gratitude for this moment of grace. Understand that your loved ones' feelings are more about your disease than they are about you as a person. Do whatever it takes to be civil to your partner. Save your conflicts for counseling or court. Pick your battles; do not bicker over the small things. Offer praise for their self-work. Offer compassion and empathy when they are struggling with their personal growth.

If relevant, reassure your kids that they are not the reason for the conflict, separation, or divorce. Encourage your kids to join a support group that explicitly addresses the issues that affect the children of alcoholics and addicts. Being with other children going through the same experiences can help with feelings of isolation, fear, and anger. Do not keep secrets from them. Be as honest as possible, but don't disclose information they are too young to understand.

Can divorce or separation ever be beneficial to children? Children should not be exposed to constant fighting and turmoil, especially if there has been physical, emotional, or mental abuse or threats of abuse. They should not be exposed to unfair fighting, gaslighting, or other behavior that teaches children dysfunctional ways of managing conflict. I believe that well-managed divorce and separation can be beneficial to children. They can see their parents set physical and emotional boundaries that offer structure and safety that may not have been present before recovery. They may learn healthier communication skills as parents learn to communicate effectively. It may be easier for children to experience quality time with their parents when they live in two different households. Children are more likely to be empathetic and resilient when they live in healthy environments and witness their parents improving their lives.

Challenge: Legal Problems

Legal problems can include incarceration, restraining orders, removal of children into the care of child protective services, court-supervised visits, and the consequences of driving under the influence, public intoxication, or other crimes. There may be instances when legal consequences depend on how well the patient responds to treatment. This may create anticipatory stress from not knowing what might happen.

Tool: Get Assistance as Soon as Possible

Legal issues must be dealt with, not avoided. If legal problems arise, get legal assistance as soon as possible. Procrastinating or avoiding the problem will not resolve it and may worsen it. If you need a lawyer and cannot pay for legal counsel, the court will appoint you a lawyer. If you are dissatisfied with your counsel, seek information from the courthouse, legal aid societies, and your state or county bar association for additional assistance. Legal aid societies are nonprofit organizations that provide free legal services to low-income people. If the issue is related to child custody, you may have an independent court-appointed lawyer or representative who works on behalf of the child, not the parents or guardians.

If your legal problems have involved a child of yours being removed from your home, your child has probably been assigned a social worker or attorney who will advocate on behalf of the child's best interest to a family court judge. The first step in this situation is to cooperate with this professional and then gather as much information as possible from your lawyer, social worker, or case manager. Do not be afraid to ask questions, write down the answers, take notes, and make a plan. In addition, you must be concise. These professionals have limited time to manage your case, so use your time well. The next step is to abide by whatever requirements and recommendations you have been given. Do not resist, or try to explain or justify noncompliance with these requirements. Invest your time and energy into cooperating with legal and social program requests, not fighting them.

Challenge: Financial Struggles

Financial problems are among the most common issues in marriages and relationships. They may be a significant source of stress and can include such problems as unemployment, unpaid bills, mounting debt, loss of utilities, loss or foreclosure on your home, tax issues, and bankruptcy.

Tool: Face Debt, and Don't Procrastinate

Face your debt head-on. Do not procrastinate. Begin by ensuring that you and your family have housing, food, safety, and sobriety. Once the basic needs are met, gather as much information as possible. Collect and organize your bills, tax liens, bank statements, pawn slips, promissory notes, records of loans to family and friends, and so on. Identify sources of income. Pay your essential bills (housing, food, and shelter) first.

Make two lists. The first is a prioritized ranking of your bills. What are the most important bills to pay first? For instance, you could make small payments on your medical bills, which are usually interest-free, to have money to pay your electricity bill. Second, make a list of bills that do not need more than a minimum payment. Then rank them from smallest to largest, to begin paying off one creditor at a time. Seek conservative advice and professional guidance on addressing your financial problems from experts, and avoid your local pawn shop or quick-loan establishments if possible. Ask your peers, friends, and counselors for referrals and recommendations.

Challenge: Physical Health and Impairment

This may include dementia, brain fog, physical recovery from an injury sustained during active addiction, temporary acute illness, or permanent disability. The first step is to find the correct medical diagnosis and care. This may require a second opinion. You must always be honest with your physician about your addiction. Seek medical care from physicians who understand addiction. You do not want them to prescribe medication that can be addictive or medical interventions that could trigger your addiction.

Tool: Gather Information from Your Physician or Another Qualified Source

If you are struggling with chronic pain or illness, it is easy to feel overwhelmed or depressed. It's crucial to gather as much information as possible from your physician or another reliable source. Find support groups for your specific diagnosis or area of need. Speaking to someone with a similar condition can relieve some feelings of helplessness and isolation. Offer support and encouragement to others within this support group. Helping others will take your focus off yourself and may distract you from some of your symptoms. Focus on what you can do about your condition rather than what you cannot control. Stay organized, and create a file with a record of your symptoms, emotional experiences, and feelings. Create a list of questions you have for your next doctor's appointment. Investigate other resources like biofeedback, meditation, yoga, and mindfulness. Define your circle of support and the people you can safely vent or share your feelings with. Take this opportunity to note what is important to you, how you define yourself, and how you can turn this limitation into something good. Lastly, don't forget to set some goals, exercise, and enjoy the things you can participate in.

Challenge: Relapse

You cannot rebuild an authentic relationship with your family and friends until you demonstrate and maintain sobriety. But relapse is common with our illness, and if you do experience relapse, begin with honesty and humility. Do not be discouraged or engage in negative self-talk or self-shaming behavior. Take responsibility for your drinking or drug use. Do not blame other people or other circumstances for your relapse. Tell your friends and family what you will do to resume sobriety. What will you change? For example, will you attend ninety meetings in ninety days, return to a detox program, or increase your level of counseling or outpatient services? Ask for help, and face the relapse squarely. It is essential to examine and understand what led up to it. Identify—but do not blame—the triggers or situations that led to your relapse.

Tool: Learn from Relapse

The key is to learn from this experience and avoid the situations or triggers that led you down this road. Identify your weaknesses, and ask for help in these areas. Suppose your relapse was a reaction to receiving bad news. In that case, you can seek help from your sponsor, group, or therapist to explore healthy coping mechanisms for dealing with feelings of loss or grief. Build a set of coping mechanisms for dealing with similar situations in the future. Or if your relapse resulted from prolonged temptation, perhaps you constantly drive past your old favorite liquor store on your way home from work, and you are tired in the evenings and find the temptation too difficult to resist. Find a new route home, and change your behavior to avoid temptation.

Your relationships with your family and friends will suffer from your relapse. It is better to meet this fact directly. Don't deny it happened; this will only lead to more distrust. Instead, focus your energy on listening to their concerns, allowing them to have their feelings, and telling them your plan to combat relapse. You must experience the consequences of your relapse in your relationship for you to move forward. If you have to change your routines, do it. If your family asks you for greater transparency, oblige them. If your family makes requests that are not unreasonable, cooperating with them will build trust, and it will demonstrate humility and an effort to change and accept help.

Challenge: Living with an Alcoholic or Addict

There is no denying that living with an alcoholic is challenging. Ask any veteran member of Al-Anon or your family members about their experience as the family member of an alcoholic or addict. If you must live with a person in active addiction, I urge you to seek support, information, and guidance from Al-Anon, your sponsor, your peers, and professionals when possible. You will find others who share your feelings and frustrations; you will see that you are not alone. You will learn that you are not to blame for their use and that you cannot control or cure them, and you will learn how not to enable them, among other things.

Tool: Boundaries

Self-awareness is the first key to maintaining sobriety. Can you keep your sobriety while someone else in your home is abusing alcohol or drugs? Physical and emotional boundaries must be set and enforced. Do you have the ability or opportunity to put physical distance between you and an active addict if you share a home? Can you put emotional distance between you and the active addict?

Challenge: Concerns about an Addicted or Alcoholic Child

Trying to cope with a son's or daughter's alcohol abuse or addiction is one of the most difficult challenges in life, whether you are sober or not. When it comes to our children, our ability to be objective goes out the window. Our sense of urgency to fix them can sometimes be overwhelming. When we combine this with our guilt from being an addict, we create a tangled mess that is difficult to sort out.

Tool: Take Care of Yourself, Then Your Child

You must put your own oxygen mask on first. This means you must remain sober and take care of yourself. By staying sober, trying to improve your life, and dealing with your problems, you will demonstrate that maintaining sobriety is the first step to addressing life's problems. Next, seek support from your peers, counselor, or twelve-step groups. Finally, begin to set limits and boundaries. Tough love is a tool that does not come easily to most parents. Start small, set restrictions that you can live with and rules you can enforce, and then move onto boundaries that embody the principles of tough love.

Challenge: Dual Diagnosis

It is not uncommon for people suffering from a substance use disorder to have a dual diagnosis, meaning that they also suffer from another type of mental illness. Depression, anxiety, OCD, personality disorders, and PTSD are common co-occurring diagnoses. Often it is hard to tell which came first—the addiction or the mental illness. This may mean that treatment initially focuses on addressing the mental health issue in order to stabilize the patient so they can be receptive to addiction treatment.

Tool: Release the Stigma

First, let's remove the stigma attached to mental illness. Scientific research is proving that many mental illnesses are a result of chemical imbalance in the brain. There is no shame or embarrassment in having a mental health diagnosis. Next, seeking medical care from physicians who understand addiction is essential for proper care and management. Finally, find support groups in your area or create one that addresses addiction complicated by mental health illness. Be self-aware and honest with your sponsor and peers. You will find that there are many people out there who have similar struggles. You can be a resource to them and help yourself along the way.

Challenge: Traits of Codependency or of Adult Children of Alcoholics

Codependency is a learned behavior that can be passed down from generation to generation. It is not clearly defined as a mental health illness. Instead, most mental health professionals describe codependency as an emotional and behavioral condition that affects an individual's ability to have healthy, mutually satisfying relationships. It is sometimes known as a "relationship addiction" because codependent people often form or maintain one-sided, emotionally destructive, and abusive relationships in which they give more than they receive. Common codependency traits, which are frequently displayed by adult children of alcoholics (ACA), include trying to control the behaviors of others, making ourselves physically and mentally ill because of isolation, being people-pleasers, being afraid of abandonment, having a fear of authority figures, being avoidant of criticism, being unable to stand up for oneself, feeling addicted to excitement, confusing love and pity, stuffing down feelings, judging oneself harshly, being hyperresponsible, and playing the victim.

There is an increasing amount of research showing that the impact of growing up in a family with a chronic health issue, addiction, or mental health issue can impair our ability to deal with stress and anxiety and affect our self-esteem and relationships. We discussed codependency and the family disease model in chapter 2, and it bears repeating that these traits demonstrate how the issues in our family of origin can affect our current relationships with our families and friends.

Tool: Identify Common ACA Traits

The first step is to become aware of common ACA traits and explore which traits you identify as your own. Addressing and treating your ACA traits and their long-term effects on you will greatly help your overall contentment and support your relapse-prevention efforts. The unresolved experiences of dysfunctional childhoods cause many relapses. I propose that you should have a firm foundation of recovery skills and a strong support system before you explore childhood abuse issues. Understanding your ACA traits will help you empathize with your spouse/partner and children. The goal is not to try to fix them but to acknowledge that you played a part in creating these behaviors in them. The goal is for you to be empathetic and understanding with them as they move through their recovery process. You will not judge them; you will support their growth and the time they spend on their recovery.

Challenge: Crisis

Here I will define a "crisis" as any situation involving an impending change, an emotionally stressful event, or a point where a decisive action must be taken quickly. In a story or drama, this is the point when a conflict reaches its highest tension and must be resolved. It may involve intense feelings, danger, or the threat of doom. Your definition of a crisis may be different from the one given here. Crisis management can vary dramatically from one person to the next. Some people thrive on crisis; their lives do not feel ordinary unless everything is dramatic. If people like that are not in a chaotic situation, they may create drama or perceive that they thrive in high-intensity conditions. Conversely, some people avoid drama and crisis as much as possible. Such people run from crisis and do not tolerate conflict of any kind; or, when it does occur, they freeze and can't think straight. Most of us have traits from both of these sets of characteristics.

Tool: Managing Crisis

Let's review our body's primitive response to crisis or danger. Initially, our fight-flight-freeze-fawn response is triggered, and the body responds with a wave of stress and physiological changes. An adrenaline response of a rapid heart rate, increased blood pressure, and a reduced perception of pain may result in your senses of sight, sound, and smell being heightened, blurred, or highly focused on one thing. You may spring into action without thinking, or you may become frozen, unable to move or react. The frozen or fearful response may limit your ability to think and speak clearly, so your emotions and affect appear to shut down. This response is instinctual and difficult to control at the height of the experience.

The first step in learning to manage your response to a crisis is to become aware of your body's natural reactions. Review a past situation where you felt a moderate level of distress, such as when your child comes home from school and says they have to bring brownies to school the following day, or your boss says, "I need to speak with you before you leave work today."

> **NOTE** When performing this exercise, do not pick traumatic events that may trigger unresolved issues.

The next step is to examine your behavioral and verbal responses. Did you lash out? Did you react or freeze? Did you become tongue-tied? Did you become immediately fearful or engage in doomsday thinking? What did you like or dislike about your response? What would you like to do differently next time? What is a reasonable expectation of change? Do not judge your responses; simply observe and acknowledge them.

Let's take the above example of your child coming home from school and saying they need to bring brownies to school the following morning. Depending on the stressors and experiences of the day, your response might vary from delight to frustration or anger. What were your verbal responses to your child? Did you raise your voice or get angry? What did you tell yourself at that moment? Did you embrace the idea of baking brownies? Did you exaggerate or catastrophize the process of making brownies or engage in negative self-talk? What were your behaviors? After you respond to these questions, take some time to think about your answers. Imagine how you could manage this situation the next time. What would you like to do, feel, and experience differently? Finally, use your new knowledge to rehearse or walk through a situation like the one above.

Tool: Decision-Making in a Crisis

Whenever possible, do not make any significant decisions when you are in a crisis or a heightened emotional state. However, there will be times when you will be forced to do so. The first step is to acknowledge your physical response. Take time to pause, breathe, and clear your mind. Turn your attention to your breathing and heart rate. Fight every instinct to react; wait until you can pause and think clearly, and the adrenaline has begun to wear off. If necessary, use a centering skill. For example, focus on a calming word, take deep breaths, or try the five-five-six method: breathe through your nose for five seconds, hold for five seconds, and blow out through your mouth for six seconds. Another activity you can do to give your body and mind a chance to get in sync with each other is known as the five-four-three-two-one centering activity. To do this activity, notice five things you see around you; acknowledge four things you can touch; notice three things you can hear; and acknowledge two things you can smell and one thing you can taste.

Remember to honor your boundaries. For example, if someone is pressuring you to make a decision or take action, tell them you need time to collect your thoughts; or you can say, "Let me think about that," and then take a few moments to assess the situation accurately. You are essentially stalling for time in a manner that honors your boundaries while communicating to the other person that you are not avoiding the situation. Then revisit your physical self, and when you are ready, review the question or situation and ask yourself, "How significant is this threat? How quickly must I make a response? What action is *essential* at this exact moment? What tactics can I use to make a good decision?"

Here are some phrases you can use to ask for more time:

- "Sorry, I need a minute, I am not quite ready."
- "I need to think about this."
- "May I have a few moments to gather my thoughts?"
- "I am still deciding."
- "I am unsure what to do."
- "How quickly do you need an answer?"
- "I am trying to think of another option."
- "You might be right."
- "Can you clarify [the options, my choice, this information] for me?"
- "Can you repeat the question?"

While you are working on a solution or answer, do not leave your loved ones or family members in the dark, believing you are avoiding the situation or procrastinating. Be firm, and let them know you will address this situation again at a later time. Be sure to give updates that demonstrate that you intend to return to the subject.

Challenge: Runaway Thoughts

Racing or runaway thoughts can be destructive and can disrupt our ability to cope with difficulties or crises. When your mind is in overdrive, it is difficult to focus on anything else. You may get stuck focusing on the worst-case scenarios, which can lead to a feeling of helplessness. Avoid getting caught in a negative self-talk loop, such as: "This is the worst thing that could have happened." "I wonder what they are thinking about me." "I can't believe I said that." "I don't know what to do." "Why can't someone help me?" "I wish I could have said something different." These are the kinds of thoughts that distract us from staying in the present and seeking productive solutions to our problems.

Tool: Managing Cyclical Thinking

Again, the first key is awareness and acknowledgment that you are experiencing racing thoughts that are counterproductive. First, normalize your breathing and take care of your physiological response. Then bring your attention to the present and the racing thoughts themselves. Lean into them for a moment and feel the pain that is associated with them. Then follow these steps:

- Ask yourself what you are feeling. Is it helplessness, fear, dread, lack of control, depression, or something else?

- Listen to what you are saying, and ask yourself, "Is this true?" or "What part of this is true, and what part of it can I control?"

- Recognizing what you have control over and what you can't control will help you stay in the present.

- Letting go of what you cannot control and not taking responsibility for it will remove some of the pressure you put on yourself.

Deep breathing in combination with soothing statements, affirmations, or mantras can help block negative thoughts. For example, take a negative statement and follow it with an affirming statement about yourself or your abilities, like the following:

- I release this stress and affirm that I am a strong and capable individual.

- I release the feelings of helplessness and affirm that I have overcome many similar situations.

- My past does not predict my future.

- Only I can control what I think, how I react, and what I say.

- I release the burden of overresponsibility and affirm that I will only take on what I can manage right now.

Tool: Preventive Measures and Stress Management

Follow these measures to prevent cyclical thinking and enhance your stress management and relationship skills, so you can prepare yourself for the unexpected events that will come your way.

- Recognize your basic instincts: fight, flight, freeze, or fawn. Respect them and honor them. These are your body's instinctual responses designed to help you survive.
- Work on your life-management skills when you are not stressed.
- Remember that you do not have to experience significant problems to seek therapy, counseling, or coaching.
- Take advantage of classes in stress management or anger management offered in your community.
- Identify and understand crisis-triggering events specific to your past experiences.
- Learn how to use tools like guided imagery. There are many resources for this online, such as YouTube videos and podcasts.
- Get regular exercise. Exercise has been shown to decrease stress hormones, including adrenaline and cortisol, increase endorphins, and promote better sleep.
- Practice yoga, mindfulness, and meditation, including breathing and calming techniques.
- Attract positivity into your life.
- Adopt a practice of being happy, looking for joyful experiences, and expressing gratitude whenever possible.
- Ask your peers to keep you accountable and help you be aware when you engage in resistive thinking, runaway thoughts, or negative self-talk.
- Volunteer and get involved in service work.
- Build a social-support network of friends, peers, and/or coworkers. Social support can minimize your psychological and physiological reactions to perceived threats. It provides a sense of safety and protection, which makes you feel less fearful.

If you find yourself in a constant state of fight or flight, continuously feeling uptight, stuck in persistent fear or nervousness, unable to go about your normal activities of daily living, or anxious about nonthreatening situations, I encourage you to consult with a mental health professional. They can help you determine the underlying cause of these feelings and help assess the best coping skills and most effective strategies for your situation.

Deal-Breakers

I am discussing deal-breakers in a separate section of this chapter because I think it is important to go beyond the basics of setting boundaries. We all need to identify what our deal-breakers are. Some of us have had our boundaries stepped on or ignored so many times that we are not sure what we should or should not accept from our loved ones.

Abuse

Do not put yourself or your children in harm's way. Never expose yourself or your children to any physical, mental, or emotional abuse. For some relationships, you do not have to have in-person contact to heal them. In best-case scenarios, you can use a video conferencing platform like Skype or Zoom to have counseling sessions in order to provide closure or to address legal or financial issues. However, the best type of healing that comes from living in a relationship where abuse was present may be:

- Having no relationship at all.
- Learning how to *let go* of destructive relationships.
- Learning how to grieve destructive relationships.
- Learning how to break the pattern of attracting toxic people into your life.

If you have been the perpetrator of abuse, you must not attempt to repair this relationship alone. You must follow the guidelines and restrictions of all legal orders related to your case. You must honor all of your family members' boundaries. The best action to take in these cases is to cooperate with all recommendations of the court, your therapist, or child protective services.

Breaking the Law

Under no circumstance should you violate any morals or ethics, or break any laws, in an attempt to rebuild a relationship with a family member. This includes, but is not limited to, defying court orders, telling white lies, lying by omission, and bending the rules. When you're not sure whether a course of action runs afoul of these stipulations, consider the long-term consequences of the action. Seek advice from your sponsor, therapist, or coach. When you are unsure, always pick the most conservative answer, which is usually "no."

Summary

We will all experience challenges on our paths to family unification. There will be obstacles and events you cannot control, and surprises will occur. The keys to surviving these challenges are prevention, preparation, and practice. The common denominators of *emotionally growing* through these challenges, crises, and deal-breakers are sobriety, self-care, and self-compassion. Take an occasional break from these problems. Rest, sleep, eat, and play. Do not be afraid to talk aloud about your struggles in your support groups. You are not the first person to go through situations like yours. Learn from other people's experiences, strengths, and hopes. There may be another person who needs to hear what you are saying, and they may need to know that they are not alone. By sharing your experience, you are extending hope to them. Surround yourself with wisdom of the old-timers. Take small steps, forgive, and focus on what you can do instead of what you can't. Most of the time, just the act of maintaining and working on your recovery will dramatically reduce the stressful and chaotic events of your life. As you gain time and skill in your recovery, you will be better able to manage all of life's unexpected events.

9

Healing and Acceptance

ealing is often painful. For example, a few years ago I broke my leg. The initial injury was excruciating. I was treated and released from the emergency room with an appointment to see an orthopedic specialist. There I learned that my injury was going to require additional surgery, as well as physical therapy, to get it to heal correctly so I could regain full use of my leg and ankle. This also meant that my mobility was going to be drastically altered. I was not allowed to put any weight on my leg for the first six weeks of recovery. I would need a wheelchair, a walker, and eventually crutches. I was not going to be able to drive. I was going to have to ask for help and rely upon others. Progress would be slow, but I had to follow the doctor's and physical therapist's advice for the ankle and leg to heal correctly.

The healing process for yourself and your relationships will require similar efforts. It will require work in the form of learning and using new tools. It may involve mandatory classes or therapy. Your improvement will depend greatly on how good you are at asking for help and how willing you are to participate in either self-help or therapy. Change may take time, and you may not see results in the short term. But for you to recover and repair your relationships, you will have to take the advice and heed the wisdom you're given.

Physical Healing

There will be physical healing of your body, which could include detox, withdrawals, cravings, postacute withdrawal symptoms (PAWS), and mental confusion. PAWS may occur days, weeks, or months after the acute phase of detox. Some people may experience days of feeling relatively healthy, followed by a return of moderate physical symptoms such as nausea, muscle aches, sleeplessness, and fatigue, or they may experience mood swings, anxiety, and irritability.[1]

Healing may also mean coming to terms with new physical limitations if you have done permanent harm to yourself. Some of you may have lost a limb due to driving while impaired and having a motor vehicle accident. Others may have permanent brain damage from having an overdose that resulted in oxygen deprivation to the brain, or shrinkage of brain tissue from prolonged alcohol use.[2]

Mental and Emotional Healing

You may have dulled your emotions during your active addiction, so when your feelings come back, they hurt exponentially worse because you can no longer numb the pain with mood-altering substances or behaviors. Or perhaps your feelings and reactions have been flattened or deflated by years of avoiding your emotions. When I was first in recovery, I found it hard to cry because I had been denying my feelings for a long time.

If your intake of alcohol or drugs was high, you may have a reduced mental capacity, which may make it challenging to learn and understand new things and make good decisions. Healing in these areas may simply be about giving yourself time and exercising patience; or you may require therapy, programs, and medical help to experience the ups and downs of everyday life.

Spiritual Healing

Healing our spiritual nature can be an excellent tool for self-forgiveness. This includes coming to terms with things you have done or experienced that were contrary to your morals and values. Spiritual healing, accepting forgiveness from others, and turning your mistakes into lessons are important parts of recovery.

Spirituality can take many forms; thus, healing in this area can also take many routes. You may choose to return to a faith or doctrine you practiced before, or you may seek a new practice or belief that feels more comfortable for you. However, even for those who are agnostic or atheist, practicing the first three steps of any twelve-step program sets the foundation for a spiritual healing process. Agnostics and atheists can simply replace the word "God" with "higher power" and then choose who or what to make your higher power, such as your support group, the universe, or nature.

However, if you have experienced religious or spiritual abuse, which can take physical, verbal, emotional, mental, or financial forms, or if your friends or family members may have used their religious doctrine to justify their abuse, control, or manipulation of you or others, I encourage you to seek professional intervention and therapy.[3]

Healing Our Social Selves

There may also be healing that needs to take place in your social life. You may need to apologize and make amends to friends you have harmed. You may also need to cut ties, whether temporarily or permanently, with friends who are in active addiction and even friends you used to drink or use with. Ask for help from others, and admit that these struggles are easier addressed with support, whether from a group, an individual, or a higher power. You may need to make new friends and learn how to celebrate, socialize, or have fun without the use of drugs or alcohol.

How to Begin Healing

Honor Your Feelings

Feel your feelings as best you can. Please go through them, not around them. Sometimes you can manage the pain and slow the waves' momentum, but you cannot stop them from coming. Be fearless, use your tools, and get support from your peers, sponsors, and therapists. Don't try to go through this alone. Don't avoid or deny your feelings. If necessary, compartmentalize your feelings if they seem too great to endure. Bite off a small piece at a time, work on that piece, and then move on to the next one. Pause if you have to, catch your breath, pat yourself on the back, and believe that healing will come.

> **NOTE** I believe emotional pain, like grief, can be cumulative. What you don't address will build on itself and contribute to the risk of relapse.

Affirm Your Feelings

It's okay not to be okay. It is human to feel sadness, grief, and anger. Ask yourself the following questions: Are you trying to be perfect? Do you want to control your feelings like you control other aspects of your life? Do you fear being exposed or vulnerable when you express your feelings? Take time to honor your experiences and emotions. Keep in mind that you are trying to modify the negative *behaviors*, such as yelling and cursing, not the negative feelings and emotions.

Do the Work

Do something differently when it comes to acting on your feelings. Practicing a twelve-step program is a part of doing the work. The steps provide guidance and a structure for healing. The fourth and fifth steps are designed to help you acknowledge and release feelings of guilt, shame, regret, and embarrassment and to promote healing your relationship with yourself.

There are many other types of approaches you can take to do the work:

- Examine what secondary gains you might obtain by staying in the pain. Allow yourself to experience your feelings and the pain. Then affirm yourself for allowing these feelings.
- Address healing as a topic in your individual, family, and group therapy or twelve-step group.
- Take care of yourself physically, eat nutritious food, get plenty of rest, and strive for balance daily.
- Remove yourself from drama, like gossip at work, even if it seems simple.

- Meditate and practice your spirituality.

- Stop replaying negative thoughts, behaviors, and actions in your mind.

- Practice the tools you have learned. Use skills like SNAP and ask, "Is this negative thought true?"

- Forgive others. Fighting the system, staying angry, and remaining resentful take a lot of psychic energy. Release the burden of holding grudges. Practice gratitude and grace.

- Rewrite your story, and imagine what a happily-ever-after looks like. This may include daydreaming or asking yourself, "How is this going to work?"

- Perform random acts of kindness and service work. In early sobriety, I was in AA with a new mom who had to bring her baby with her to meetings. She was tired, so everyone in our AA group took turns holding her child. Giving her a break allowed her to rest and engage more fully in the meeting, and it made all of us who helped her feel needed. Being of service to others can help you feel more connected to a community and help develop your empathy skills.

Acknowledge Plateaus

Your path to repairing relationships will not be linear. You will experience highs, lows, setbacks, and plateaus, all of which are a normal part of any personal change or growth.

When you find yourself feeling stuck, I recommend the following:

- Return to your affirmations; be kind and compassionate to yourself.

- Reframe how you see your current experience. Focus on how you've grown or how far you have come. Do not look at how far you have yet to go.

- Challenge your inner critic—the negative voice in your mind that fuels shame. Instead of ignoring this voice, take time to refute what it is saying to you by citing evidence to the contrary.

- Begin some "inner child" work. This work is based on the belief that many of us possess a wounded inner child who did not get what they

needed as they grew up. This model states that we were all born inno-
cent and pure, full of curiosity and potential. However, some of our
basic needs went unmet, and we carry those wounds into adulthood,
which often leads to self-sabotaging behaviors. Listening to this
wounded child, exploring their experience, and providing reassurance
that you will take care of them in the present may help you resume
your forward progress in your healing journey.

- Acknowledge that your family members also have a wounded inner
  child who needs care and reassurance.

Have Fun, Celebrate, and Take Breaks

It is important to take breaks from intensive work. Incorporating rest and play
into your schedule can help you better manage stress and conflict, be more
resilient in the face of setbacks, and be more compassionate to others.

Here are some examples of ways to relax or have fun:

- Get a massage.
- Play recreationally, avoiding being overly competitive.
- Draw, paint, color, or play a musical instrument.
- Watch a funny or inspiring movie.
- Compliment yourself and others.
- Try out a new recipe.
- Call an old friend or family member.
- Read a book.

Moving Forward

Sometimes it is hard to let go. Staying in the problem can feel comfortable
because the toxicity is familiar. For me it was hard to break the habit of self-
pity. People with addictions commonly identify as a victim. You must be willing to walk away from the security of these feelings, embrace your agency, and
move forward.

Healing may also require effort and the desire to move forward in life and
away from resentments, past hurts, and damage that you have done or that

has been done to you. This does not necessarily mean forgiving the person who abused or neglected you, but it does mean no longer allowing the anger, pain, or wound to affect the quality of your life today. For some, it may be helpful to forgive people. However, I acknowledge this is a very controversial topic and should be undertaken with the guidance of a therapist, sponsor, or coach.

For example, being vulnerable was a part of my healing process. I had become so accustomed to people leaving me unexpectedly due to death, relocation, or simply leaving without explanation that I let very few people get close to me. My fear of abandonment drove this behavior. I had to resolve my grief and trust issues in order to stop using this defense mechanism.

Family Healing

The guidelines for family healing are similar to the steps described above. It is essential to acknowledge that you cannot control other people's thoughts, feelings, and actions. You can't do their work for them. You cannot expect them to trust, love, or forgive you. You can, however, reinforce a culture of healing by respecting each individual's experience with your addiction and recovery and by supporting their choice to find a path to reconciliation—or not. Here's how:

- Focus on learning, not blaming.
- Let go of timelines and expectations.
- Keep your communication open. Focus on your listening ability. Encourage your family members to express themselves in healthy, productive ways.
- Listening, rather than giving advice or looking for solutions, may be what your family members are looking for when they express feelings about a problem or concern to you.
- Remain hopeful.
- Model positive communication by showing honesty and trustworthiness in your words and actions.
- Honor the boundaries set between you and your loved ones.
- Practice patience while your family observes your actions or words. They want to make sure you are being consistent.

- Balance your program schedule with family time. You must be responsive and aware of your commitment to your program, but you must also be intentional about not spending more time with your recovery community than with your family.

- You are not your family's life coach, sponsor, or therapist. Your role in the family is to provide support and patience while your family members find their inner peace.

- Don't make promises. It may be hard for your family members to believe or trust you.

Trust, truth, and compassion are the foundations for uniting a family. Remember to be there for each other. Validate that your loved ones' experiences are real. Many of us spent a lot of time denying what was evident: "No, I am not drinking." "Everything's fine." "I will be there for you."

As a parent, be willing to allow your child to find support from a therapist, teacher, school counselor, family friend, or trusted family member. Please don't allow yourself to be threatened by your child building healthy relationships with others; on the contrary, you should encourage it. It may allow your child to trust adults and mend their wounds so that one day they will be able to open up to you.

When Relationships Don't Heal? Detachment and Acceptance

When it comes to addiction, we use the term *detachment* in several ways. For the most part, family members are encouraged to *detach from us* when we are in active addiction. Programs like Al-Anon and Nar-Anon teach about *detaching with love*. Detachment could be described as distancing oneself from an individual or group so that the other's choices and behaviors stop affecting you painfully.

Can all relationships be healed? No, and you cannot control this fact. You are ultimately powerless over your loved ones' reactions to your efforts. The only thing you can truly change is yourself.

In early recovery, a friend of mine was distraught when her spouse told her he was leaving her without making any effort to reconcile, support her recovery, or participate in counseling. He announced that he would only communicate with her through his lawyer. He shut the door on their relationship and has never reopened it. This was a painful experience for my friend, but he set a boundary, and she had no choice but to honor it. To heal, she had to put her time and energy into grieving it.

All relationships can experience growth and healing if all parties are willing participants. But what do you do when a family member does not want to go through the work and pain that healing requires? How do you manage relationships that have been broken due to physical or emotional distance? How do you heal relationships you have terminated because they are the people you used with or drank with? Should you try to heal those relationships at all? And what can you do when your loved one has passed away? The steps to detaching with love are surrender, acceptance, grieving, and closure.

Surrender

Pause; stop trying to fix what you cannot. Let go of bargaining. You cannot control distance, death, and the will of other people. You can still do the work you need to do in order to heal for yourself. Work with your sponsor, peers, or therapist to do your part in healing or finding closure. Giving yourself the space to feel and process your emotions is integral to detaching safely when necessary. Practice self-compassion, and create the space and distance you need to heal.

Acceptance

Give the relationship to God, the universe, or whatever you consider your higher power. Be objective about the relationship, be truthful to yourself, take baby steps, and celebrate reaching your goals, no matter how small. Stop romanticizing the relationship and be honest about both the good elements and the harmful ones. Work the AA steps one through three.

Grieving

Seek support from people who understand what you are going through. If you feel comfortable, present your relationship as a topic for discussion in a meeting. Use the grieving process to aid in letting it go.

In Cases of Abuse or Danger of Abuse

The type of healing that comes from recovering from a relationship of abuse may need to happen without further contact with your abuser. Learning to heal and let go of destructive relationships may mean accepting that, when it comes to an abusive person, *no relationship* is better than a threatening or unhealthy relationship. Thus, healing may come in the form of your ability to refrain from putting yourself in dangerous situations or around abusive people.

Closure

You may say, "But I need closure," or "How can I get closure if they won't see me, if I can't talk to them, or if they won't acknowledge me?" Closure is not about what *they* do; it is about what *you* do and how you feel. It is about coming to peace with your actions and knowing you have done your best at this particular moment. The serenity prayer advises us to accept the things that we cannot change. This prayer reminds us that we cannot change others, and we can only change ourselves. This process may take weeks or months, but don't give up. Hang onto hope. The final step is to let go of control and allow your higher power to do some of the work.

10

Don't Fight the System

I n twelve-step programs, we recommend you give up the fight against mood-altering substances or behaviors. In AA, we describe this as *surrender*, and we promote it as a positive action to improve physical and mental health or an effort to give up our battle against things we cannot control or change. Choosing to surrender typically doesn't come easy, but when we view surrender as an act of acceptance or a sign of good faith, it takes some of the pain out of letting go. You don't want to fight so hard that you miss out on noticing the beauty around you.

Deciding to surrender and then surviving the experience of letting go is empowering. When you let go of the struggle against surrender, you open yourself up to the opportunity for reasonable changes to happen in your life. In backpacking, when hikers have to surrender—when they have to scale back their goals for the hike because conditions have intervened to make those goals unrealistic—it's called a *tactical retreat*. A seasoned hiker will understand that practicing a tactical retreat signifies strength and wisdom. This indicates that their mental and emotional health is more potent than their desire to push beyond our limits. There have been times when I have set my hiking goals and expectations too high for my physical ability. Sometimes I've tried to keep up with others and hike at their pace, even though it was too fast; at other times I've underestimated the obstacles I would encounter. When I plan my route, I hope all the conditions will be favorable; but hiking, like life, can be unpredictable, and sometimes you can be slowed down by the elements or by overestimating your strength and ability. When weather, wildlife, or more personal elements have interrupted my hike, I have pitched camp alone in a less-than-ideal camping spot, or I have decided to return to a previous shelter to wait for more suitable conditions. This is a tactical retreat, but it does not mean I have given up. If I were to push on, I would be more likely to injure myself due to weariness or clumsiness. In the past, I have even had to ask a fellow hiker for help or call a shuttle driver to help me get off the trail.

The point is that although my progress may be slowed or maybe even reversed for a while, I will ultimately reach my destination. Like a hiker making a tactical retreat, sometimes a person in addiction recovery decides to surrender if a delay becomes necessary to avoid risks and harm.

When Life Isn't Fair

There will be obstacles in your journey to family and relationship reconciliation that will seem impossible to overcome. Things will seem to happen *to* you rather than *for* you. There will be injustices and times when it seems as if life is just not fair. Those times will be frustrating, and those trials will test your resolve to rebuild your relationships. It may be hard to continue making efforts when you see no concrete benefits. You could feel as though nothing will ever work, and you may want to quit or give up—or, worse yet, your exasperations could threaten your sobriety and your physical and mental health. I ask you to see these moments as tactical retreats and opportunities to rest and regroup instead of thinking of them as failures. Remember that choosing a tactical retreat signifies emotional and mental health. When you delay immediate gratification for a better long-term outcome, you're exhibiting growth and maturity.

For many, accepting setbacks, changing plans, or adopting new approaches can be challenging. You can get stuck on one path or used to one way of doing things, and you may fail to consider all the other options. But let me remind you that you have a limited amount of energy to address your daily physical, mental, and emotional challenges. Putting all your efforts into something that doesn't improve your quality of life will take away from the energy you have to spend on enrichment and enjoyment. For example, do you want to spend your energy arguing with your ex about how long a visit with your children will be?

Or do you want to invest your energy in experiencing and enjoying your time with your children?

You must pick your battles, know when to give in, and know when to stand your ground. Improving your ability to release the struggle begins with self-awareness. Start by asking yourself the following questions:

- Which do you value more: winning, compromise, or equity for all?
- How do you define the word "defeat?"
- When making decisions, are you a leader or a follower?
- Are you open to suggestions from others?
- Is your conflict resolution style collaborative or authoritative?
- Do you have a hard time admitting when you are wrong?
- Are you able to agree to disagree? Do you recognize that often there is more than one correct evaluation or resolution of a problem?
- Do you want to improve your relationships? If so, what lengths are you willing to go to?
- Are you truly committed to staying sober?
- Do you believe that giving up or surrendering can have positive outcomes?

How you answer these questions will provide insight into your ability to accept compromise or defeat in commonplace situations. Every day, we all face small opportunities to test our ability to surrender or give in to a situation or someone else's will. Some examples include obeying the speed limit, stopping for a stop sign, and allowing others to merge into traffic before you. Acknowledging that you are willing to surrender in these situations may help you surrender under more challenging conditions. Let's look at some possible obstacles:

- Legally defined boundaries regarding spousal, family, and child visitation
- Restraining orders
- The requirements your professional organization has placed upon you to maintain your professional license (for physicians, nurses, pharmacists, etc.)

- Incarceration, probation, and parole guidelines
- Mandatory drug screening
- Mandatory participation in therapeutic services (rehabilitation, anger management classes, family counseling, etc.)
- Providing restitution for damages, stolen items, etc.
- Paying your bills and fines

These limitations may be the most important boundaries you must comply with. Common reactions to restrictions include feeling stuck, defeated, or angry, or ruminating over negative self-talk and focusing on your perceived unfair treatment. These reactions can be tiring and a waste of your energy. I propose that what you focus on will predict the outcome. If you continue to perceive this situation as hopeless, you will not make any progress. With an attitude of willingness, these boundaries can be reframed. For instance, instead of considering these restrictions unfair and unfavorable, think of them as opportunities to display that you are now capable of honoring and obeying others' boundaries. This demonstrates how you are growing and changing for the better. Focus on the opportunity in each situation.

You can demonstrate strength through surrender and compliance. If you were in a situation where your children have been removed from your home and you cannot see them without supervision, you could react negatively by yelling, making threats, and ignoring the restrictions. You could lie to or mislead the courts, the supervisors, or your family about your alcohol, drug use, or other risky behaviors. You could isolate, drink, use, or waste away in self-pity or self-destruction, or you could waste a lot of time and energy contemplating how unfair the situation is.

Instead, you should work *with* the limitations, honor the visitation hours, show up when you are supposed to, and be on time and prepared. Cooperate with court-ordered parenting classes, anger management classes, therapy, aftercare, and twelve-step meetings. Be sincere and authentic in all your communication with your children if contact is allowed. Communicate and cooperate with the authorities via phone calls, letters, emails, or texts.

Use your time wisely; don't spend ninety minutes of your two-hour visitation time arguing with the other parent or the supervisors. Instead, replace these energy-draining activities with energy-building activities that promote your health and well-being and help build your relationships. Play, have fun, smile, laugh, and be grateful. You may not see immediate results, but you can feel good about your efforts. More noticeable changes will happen in time.

Reframing the Concept of Surrender

It takes work to make a seemingly impossible situation favorable to you. The next step in learning to survive the surrender is to reframe your concept of what it means to surrender.

The definitions of the verb *surrender* are as follows:

1. To cease resistance to an enemy or opponent and submit to their authority.

2. To yield to the power, control, or possession of another upon compulsion or demand.

3. To give up completely or agree to.[1]

To reframe our opinion of surrendering, I propose that you choose to believe that you are not helpless and that there can be honor in giving up the struggle. Let's add to the definition of surrender with the following affirmations, which imply that you are an active participant:

- To surrender is to let go of things that can't change or be changed.
- Surrendering allows me to step back with my dignity and maintain my honor.
- I relinquish the struggle to a power greater than myself, who has more wisdom than I do.
- I am choosing to cease fighting and give up the chaos.
- I redirect my energy to a *good cause* rather than a *losing battle*.
- I concede that the benefits that a third party (children, job, coworkers, etc.) experiences exceed the loss I experience.
- To surrender is to resign voluntarily for the betterment of the whole.
- I demonstrate strength and personal growth in ceasing to engage in struggle.

Steps of Surrendering

Identify and Evaluate the Parameters of the Surrender

The next step in surviving the surrender is identifying precisely what you are surrendering to or complying with: requirements, restrictions, legal restraints, what you are allowed and encouraged to do, and so on. Be specific; do not admonish anyone involved, overgeneralize the problem, or catastrophize what you are giving up. For example, just because your car has been repossessed, that does not mean your world will end. It means you are going to have a more difficult time arranging transportation. It is an inconvenience. But if you are behind on your car payments and have not made any effort to contact the loan holder, you must face the consequences of your lack of action.

What are the specific rules, guidelines, and boundaries of any legal matter that you must surrender to? Ensure you have a complete and thorough understanding of what you are allowed to do and what you are not allowed to do. In addition, what are you being *required* to do? If you have broken a boundary or failed to complete a task, you cannot use the excuse "I did not know" or "I did not understand" to remove your responsibility. Let's say your caseworker asks you to attend a parenting class every Monday night, and you miss a session on Memorial Day because you did not check to see if your class would be canceled that day; you just assumed that it would be. You cannot excuse your absence based on your faulty assumption. You must own your mistake.

Clearly define what you are agreeing and conceding to. If your child has been placed into foster care, find out whether you are permanently losing all your parental rights, or whether this restriction is temporary. Is there a plan in place for your child to be returned to you? Do you have to participate in rehabilitation, therapy, or classes to earn visitation rights? Consistently review any legal documentation, and maintain contact with your lawyer or caseworker, especially if you have difficulties understanding the legal proceedings.

Does the situation you are complying with have the potential to change or improve? If so, what do you have to do to promote positive change? What are the consequences of noncompliance with the recommendations? Will you lose your professional license? Will you be incarcerated? Will you lose custody of your children? Don't avoid looking at the consequences of your actions and noncompliance; these can be powerful motivators to encourage you to push through difficult struggles.

The following questions are meant to be thought-provoking and to encourage you to find deeper meaning in the act of surrendering.

- **What is my motivation for continuing the fight?**

  For not giving in? Is it to be right, to win in this conflict? Is it an authentic need, or is it driven by pride or ego?

- **What could I learn from this experience?**

  Might I learn humility, patience, communication skills, and willingness to ask for help? What do I have to gain from this experience? For example, participating in marital counseling with your spouse or partner could benefit your relationship with your partner and improve your relationship with your children by demonstrating respect and love for their other parent. Improving your communication skills will benefit you in social and work relationships. The lessons you learn in therapy may allow you to work through and address inner wounds and triggers. It may help you become more understanding and empathetic in all situations.

- **What will the consequences of making this decision to surrender or comply be in ten minutes, ten months, and ten years?**

  What may seem like the most excruciating sacrifice today may be just a stepping stone on your path to bigger and better things. For instance, before I left my rehabilitation program, I was advised to go to a halfway house for the next six to nine months. My initial reaction was resistance. I had already been away from home for twelve weeks; I had missed my son's sixteenth birthday, helping him get his driver's license, and endless school events and sporting activities. My thoughts and feelings were very conflicted. I agreed that I needed more therapy to deal with my issues and more time to build a stronger foundation of sobriety skills, but I worried about continuing to miss out on my kids' lives.

Applying the ten-ten-ten rule to my situation as I faced this decision, very little would have changed in the next ten minutes. The worst-case scenario was that I might disappoint my kids and family when I informed them of this decision. I was going to have to address my feelings of guilt and shame about this action. The consequences of my decision in ten months looked a lot more promising. I would have a stronger support network so that my sobriety skills would likely be better able to handle the stressors in my life and the triggers I would encounter that might lead me to drink or use. I would have time to deal with some of my deeper wounds and issues that I had masked by using alcohol and had avoided all my life. The potential negative side of being away for ten months included missing out on school, holidays, and family events. It would make participating in family counseling difficult because I would still live two hundred miles away from home.

The consequences of this decision for my life (and my family's lives) in ten years looked very promising. Ideally, I would have continued sobriety and would have sufficient skills to manage all the challenges and troubles in my life. The memories of my being gone from my family's life for a year out would be overshadowed by the new, happy, joyful experiences we could have in those ten years. Most importantly, I would have the love, respect, and trust of my children by modeling a healthy lifestyle and striving to be the best mother I could be and be the best version of myself. They would see me overcome obstacles and learn how to build healthy relationships. They would know that it is human to make mistakes, and it can be empowering to take responsibility for those mistakes and clean up after them. They could see how delayed gratification is worth the short-term sacrifice and how you can overcome almost any obstacle.

Take Action and Choose to Comply

Once you thoroughly understand your situation, you can comply and surrender, or you can continue the struggle. This is a choice. You have a choice, no matter how unlikely that may seem; no matter how many roadblocks are placed in front of you. It may seem as though surrendering means not taking action.

But I propose that surrender is still a verb, an action, a behavior, a decision. It can be an active choice you consciously make, or an unconscious choice when you choose no action.

Making this decision does not come lightly. There are situations where you have no choice but to surrender, which may include but are not limited to:

- When you are in a verbally, physically, or emotionally abusive relationship. In these circumstances, you should walk away.

- When the environment is unhealthy because of alcohol or addictions in the home, and your sobriety is threatened.

- When your ethics, values, self-respect, or self-worth are compromised.

- When asked to do so, e.g., when a loved one says they want or need time or when someone asks you to back off.

- Before you break the law.

- To avoid further punishment. For example, if you have made sincere amends for stealing money from a parent, and they constantly remind you of this mistake and are unwilling to forgive you for it, let it go.

Specific Tools for Surviving the Surrender

The very act of giving in and surrendering can be a painful process. It could quickly stir up unresolved issues, grief, and other triggers, leading to relapse, depression, or anxiety. Here are some tools you can use in these situations to enhance your overall physical and mental health:

- Get sufficient rest, food, and exercise. Be sure not to be too HALT (hungry, angry, lonely, or tired).

- Practice affirmations. Each time you find yourself wallowing in self-pity, sitting in self-doubt, or speaking negatively to yourself, try replacing the negative self-talk with affirmations. Here are a few:

  - I accept the things that are beyond my control.

  - In choosing to concede, I demonstrate my strength.

  - Regardless of the outcome, I will be taken care of.

- Anything I give my attention will flourish and grow.
- My situation doesn't hurt me; my expectations do.
- What I do today can improve all my tomorrows.
- By surrendering, I demonstrate courage and faith.
- By surrendering, I demonstrate growth and acceptance.
- It's okay to be right where I am.
- Progress, not perfection.

- Redirect your energy. Use your extra energy for positive distractions like exercise, yard or household work, and service to others.

- Stop concentrating on the obstacle; this only gives it more weight. Focus on what is working right, and think creatively about the positive actions you can take. For instance, instead of focusing on the fact that you are only allowed a two-hour visitation period with your children, think about what activities you can do with them during that time. Plan out and research activities you can do together. Go to the dollar store and buy cheap puzzles, coloring books, games, or balls. Remember, your children want your time and attention more than they want gifts and text messages.

- Ask for help. Learn from others' experiences, and ask them what worked for them. Ask them how they made it through the hard times and what their relationships are like now.

- Before you go into an unpleasant meeting or situation, role-play with a friend, therapist, coach, or sponsor. Don't avoid thinking or preparing for the difficult questions your family might ask.

- "Play the tape out." This means thinking ahead to the likely consequences of your actions. For example, let's say you have taken your son to a baseball game, which has gone into extra innings. If you stay until the end of the game, you will be late in returning your son to his mother, which would violate your agreement with his mother. You could make excuses or justify staying to watch the game by saying, "Our team is winning, and it would be a shame to miss out on the end." But if you play the tape out and look at the bigger picture to see the consequences of your actions, you might resist the temptation to stay or decide to consult with the child's mother.

- Surround yourself with people who will lift you up, not feed into your fears and anger. Take time to reflect on how far you have already come. Share your progress with a peer or in a meeting. Ask others to share their success stories with you.

- Recognize that your anger may be a mask for your fear and grief. Seek support for these masked emotions.

- Meditate, pray, and trust your higher power. Focus on the positive. The more you focus on happy, joyful, positive things, the more positivity you will attract. Watch comedies on TV or in movies, and avoid the nightly news. Listen to success stories and happy endings on social media.

- Keep track of your progress, no matter how small. Set your goals small. Have faith that change is occurring even though you cannot see it.

- Express gratitude. Write or list what you are grateful for every morning and evening.

- Get some moderate exercise; walk, sing, dance, join a yoga class, or simply get out in nature and expose yourself to the sun.

- Help someone else or volunteer. When I could not speak to my children, I reached out to every family member who came to a twelve-step meeting to support their family members. I thanked them for coming and told them it meant a lot to people like me who were alienated from their families.

- Remind yourself that by choosing joy and releasing the struggle, you will have more time and energy for living.

- Visualize forward momentum. Wonder aloud what good could come out of this for you. Imagine what your future looks like. Look for the lesson in how this can benefit other venues of your life.

- Trust the process. Recognize that what seems negative is often the best thing that could have happened.

This process can be harrowing. It can stir up unexpected feelings and contradict old, ingrained thought patterns telling us we must take action. Letting go of something you are used to taking total control over can be physically exhausting. Breaking old habits or just resisting old behaviors sometimes requires more energy than doing the behavior itself.

Summary

Your pain is real, but it won't last forever. The phrase "let go and let God" is commonly used in twelve-step programs. Of course, this is much easier said than done. It takes patience, repetition, trust, and hope. Know that you can only change yourself; nothing else is guaranteed. So when the system seems to create a wall you can't climb, leave it be. Don't bang your head against it, don't throw rope on it and try to climb it, don't try to tear it down, don't try to dig a tunnel underneath it. Admit your powerlessness over the situation, listen to others, and trust that if it worked for them, it could work for you too. Do the work, keep the peace, and leave the results to your higher power. Recognize that there is much to be gained by letting go of the struggle and negative energy in your life, such as joy, peace, and calm, while having less conflict and more energy for the good things in your life. By practicing constructive habits and breaking negative, repetitive cycles, you can take pleasure in knowing that what is meant to happen will happen. If you still have an abundance of grief, anger, and resentment, you should seek professional help.

11

Grieving and Letting Go

Throughout our lifetimes, we will all experience loss due to such causes as death, divorce, illness, and more. We usually recognize that these losses warrant grief. But more subtle or even positive changes in our lives—changing jobs, getting married, having a child, moving to a new house, getting a degree—can also generate feelings of loss. Unresolved grief is a burden we carry into all aspects of our lives. It is like a shadow that blocks the sunshine from even the happiest days. If we do not allow ourselves time to address our hurt, we may build walls around the wounds to protect us from the pain. Those walls can prevent us from being fully present in other aspects of our lives.

It is important to take time to identify your losses, understand your grieving process, learn healthier ways to adapt to loss and change, and allow yourself time to grieve. Learning how to respond to and support another person's grief is significant too. Coping with your loss or your partner's loss can significantly disrupt any relationship. But when this type of loss is combined with the losses generated by addiction and entering recovery, the weight of the challenges you face is amplified. This can impair your ability to address the problems in your relationships. In addition, you have likely lost connections with some friends and family because of your actions during active addiction. You will need to take time to grieve these losses as well. In their book *The Grief Recovery Handbook*, authors John W. James and Russell Friedman state that "unresolved grief experiences accumulate and carry over into each new experience of loss."[1] The pain you experience with each new loss stacks on top of old, unfinished grief. The weight of this grief and sadness directly affects one's capacity for happiness.

I believe that many people can benefit from dealing with grief in a therapeutic setting, but that is not what I am proposing here. Instead, I am asking you to pause and examine how your grief and grieving may affect your ability to reengage with your close friends and family members.

- Is your fear of loss holding you back from entirely giving yourself to your current or future relationships?
- Are you unable to develop new authentic attachments to others because of painful past experiences?
- Are you overreactive or overly sensitive to miscommunications?
- How do you manage your reactions to someone else's grief?

I also want you to examine and understand how your family members grieve, so you can be more compassionate and understanding toward them. You should resist trying to fix them or erase their pain. I am offering an introductory insight into understanding grief, normalizing it, and becoming more comfortable with grief and your own or someone else's loss. Some questions to ask yourself are: Do you know what to say or how to reach out when one of your colleagues or coworkers experiences the loss of a parent, sibling, spouse, or child? Do you approach them awkwardly, or do you avoid them altogether? Does their loss trigger your own experience with loss? Many of us were never taught how to cope with loss, change, or the deaths of friends and family. We were never allowed to grieve and had to guess how to support another person through their grief.

Identifying and Acknowledging Loss

It is important to identify the losses in your life, both in active addiction and in recovery, and how they affect your current relationships. During active addiction, most of us experience many losses related to our actions and behaviors, such as the loss of a job, money, possessions, friends, or family members, or even our freedom if we find ourselves incarcerated. Although entering recovery is considered a good thing, transitioning to a new sober lifestyle comes with grief and losses as you adapt. These losses may include:

- Losing your way of coping with the problems of your daily life. You no longer have access to your drug of choice or your favorite coping mechanism, so you must rely upon yourself and the healthy coping strategies you have learned to handle the stress and pain of your struggles.

- Losing the friends and acquaintances that you drank or used with.

- Losing the romanticized relationship you had with your drug of choice. It may seem odd that you would miss something that became so destructive in your life, but many people in recovery cling to the idea that their drug of choice brought them pleasure and peace.

- Losing your scapegoat—the drink, drug, or addictive behavior that allowed you to justify all your mistakes. How many times did you say, "But I did that when I was drinking/using" to explain away your misguided actions? Now you have to take ownership and responsibility for your past and present mistakes.

- Losing your identity. If you have been drinking or using since you were young, you may not even know who you are without substance use. Your identity may be wrapped up in your persona as a stoner, drug user, heavy drinker, or partier.

- Losing your sense of purpose. Addiction may have led to a job loss or unanticipated career change, so you may have also lost the security or identity attached to your profession (e.g., doctor, nurse, lawyer, minister, teacher).

- Losing social culture or social understanding. You may not know how to interact with others in social situations such as ball games, picnics, tailgates, and other recreational activities without using alcohol or drugs.

- Losing your habits and usual daily routines, however dysfunctional they may have been. You may have regrets about celebrations and experiences you lost out on due to your addiction, such as birthdays, holidays, funerals, or celebrations of life.

- Losing your health. You may experience temporary or permanent medical issues, including brain damage. For example, you may have damaged your liver to the point that you need a transplant; or your mobility might be temporarily or permanently damaged or limited due to an accident that happened during your active addiction, such as a drunk driving incident.

If you don't acknowledge these losses, they can impede your progress. Processing your losses is essential in your recovery. If you are working a twelve-step program, processing your losses is a part of reconciling your past so that you can move forward. The promises given for the ninth step in the Big Book of AA say that by doing the work, "we come to terms with our past, we are going to know a new freedom and a new happiness. We will not regret the past nor wish to shut the door on it. We will comprehend the word Serenity, and we will know peace. No matter how far down the scale we have gone, we will see how our experience can benefit others."[2]

What Are Grief and Grieving?

I define grief as emotional pain from experiencing a loss. It ranges from sadness to a sense of overwhelming loss and despair. Grieving is the act of emotionally responding to loss. Grief is a natural and normal part of life. It can manifest as physical pain, weight fluctuations, insomnia, numbness, detachment, shock, disbelief, or denial. The grieving process is how we come to terms with loss and the pain in our lives. It is how we integrate a loss into our lives, make sense of it, put it to work for us, and move on without allowing it to disrupt our day-to-day functions.

There is no one correct way of dealing with loss or grief. Some will have intense, outwardly expressed feelings of love, sadness, compassion, relief, anger, hate, or fear. Others may be unable to verbalize their emotions and are better at expressing themselves through journaling, music, art, or dance. Unhealthy reactions to grief vary from denial, resistance, and avoidance to depression and anxiety. This process can be painful, and it requires time and patience. There is no set length of time for grieving; it can last weeks, months, or years. There is no right or wrong way of dealing with your grief, but you should accept and recognize that you have the right to feel and experience it. There are no shortcuts.

There will be differences in how each family member grieves, even if they all experience the same loss. Each member must be allowed the opportunity to suffer in the manner in which they feel most comfortable. It can be an individual experience, or it can be a group experience. Some may seek comfort from their spouse, parent, or child. Some may prefer to grieve alone by finding solace in a hike, meditation, prayer, or other physical activity.

For many, our social, cultural, and spiritual backgrounds have taught us how to suffer and experience loss and change. Different cultures have different traditions and understandings about death, life after death, reincarnation, and rebirth. The bereavement process for some may include a celebration of one life ending so another can begin; for others, bereavement will be a more somber experience. No culture's grief norms are more valid than another's. The examples I share come from a North American and Christian context, the culture I am most familiar with.

Grief's Impact on Relationships

Unresolved grief from your past affects how you approach and deal with relationships in your present. Your ability to be vulnerable with another person, express love, and be authentic is primarily based on your past experiences and interactions within your family of origin. Any issues and wounds that have not been resolved may be carried into future relationships. Sometimes you repeat the behaviors associated with an old pain until you get closure. For example, a person who grew up in multiple foster homes may have difficulty establishing trust and deep bonds in their relationships as an adult. That person may also become controlling in their commitments and relationships to replace what they didn't receive in childhood; if they become a parent, they could become hyperfocused on their own children.

There are more extreme and more subtle examples, but we all are affected by our upbringing in one way or another. When grief affects romantic relationships in unexpected ways, partners are often confused about how an apparently little thing could set their partner off. Issues that seem minor or manageable to one person may trigger a deeper wound for another. Therefore, conflicts that might have been resolved with little intervention under different circumstances get scrambled up with painful past experiences. This experience can confuse and baffle both partners and distract them from solving the current issue at hand.

Mutual loss and its associated grief can affect relationships in both beneficial and destructive ways. When a family experiences a collective loss, they may be able to rely on each other and walk through the pain, supporting one another. Their bonds may strengthen, and their connections may grow, especially if the comfort is mutual and they take turns expressing and responding to each other's feelings and pain. Trust can build, and relationships can improve as patience, understanding, and supportive actions are demonstrated. When family members allow each other the space to express their grief in their own way without judgment or offering unsolicited solutions, the opportunity for growth can be significant.

Still, grief can divide couples or families if they don't know how to support their loved ones. Emotions often run high when difficult decisions have to be made, especially when people are emotionally and physically tired. Old wounds may reopen, and minor conflicts may seem more significant. Fear and sadness may be expressed through avoidance, anger, irritability, and controlling behaviors. You and your loved ones might have different feelings about the same loss; while one person may feel relieved, another may be overwhelmed with guilt. Words and actions may be misconstrued. You could mistake your family member's or close friend's need for solitude as withdrawal or rejection. If you don't feel that your loved ones' responses are meeting your emotional needs, feelings of isolation can arise within you. Many of us aren't sure what we need when we are grieving and are especially unable to express what we need from our partners. If you are struggling to communicate your needs, your loved ones may feel left out or helpless; they may not know how to respond to your feelings and behaviors.

We must learn to identify our feelings and directly ask our friends and family for what we need from them. We must also learn to become comfortable with our friends' or family members' grief and grieving processes. If you do not know how to help your friend or family member, ask them what you can do to help. It is a mistake to assume you know someone else's feelings because you have experienced a similar loss. Avoid saying "I know how you feel." You may have been through a similar loss, but your experience of coping with it may well have been different. We can empathize with someone else's grief, but we can never actually experience their grief ourselves. Instead, ask what you can do to help them through their loss. If you feel compelled to reflect on your experience, encourage them to speak about their feelings too. Say something like, "When this happened to me, I felt [say how you felt]. How are you feeling?" Everyone grieves differently, and some people find comfort in relating to others. Just make sure the conversation is a reasonable give-and-take that helps, not one that causes more harm.

You cannot take on the burden of grief for someone else. If you try, that only serves to prolong the other person's grieving process. There is a difference between being there for someone and trying to relieve them of their pain. You cannot hurry them through their experience. We cannot resolve their sorrow for them, no matter how distressing it is to see them suffering. Detach lovingly, and understand that their feelings are a sign of the work they are doing. If they withdraw from you, know that this behavior may reflect their need for time and space. Do not assume they are abandoning you. Try not to take their sorrow personally. It is hard to watch someone else experience pain. For example, if you are a parent, it is challenging to watch your children grieve over loss. When a beloved family pet dies, you may want to relieve your child of their grief, so you might react by running out and buying a new pet to replace the one that passed. This may distract the child from experiencing grief, but it also takes away the opportunity for your child to learn about grief, and it removes your opportunity to teach them about grief. It may show the child that sadness and loss can be fixed through avoidance and distraction. When loss and grief come up again, the child may try to displace the hurt by focusing on something new, such as a person, an object, or a feeling.

Other People's Individual Grief Issues When You Enter Recovery

When one person in a family enters recovery or leaves for treatment, each of the other family members will experience different types of changes and losses. Your teenager may have to take over some of your responsibilities around the home, helping their siblings get ready for school or carpooling, which will take away time from their friends, school activities, and hobbies. Your younger children may feel fear and sadness around your absence. Your spouse may feel relief that you are getting help, but they might also feel resentful that you left home or are spending a lot of time heavily engaged in your treatment. There will be a mixture of emotions ranging from uncertainty to hopefulness.

Common Myths and Mistakes of Grief and Grieving

Myth: "You can chase away the harsh feelings."

When we experience a loss, sometimes we're told, "Don't feel bad," or "Don't cry, you need to be strong." But this will not remove your grief; it only supports the idea that there are good and bad feelings. Feeling sorrow or sadness is not bad, and it does not mean you are weak. Your ability to be vulnerable is a sign of strength and evidence of your willingness to do the work needed to heal.

Myth: "Grief is a linear process. There are specific steps you must work through, in a certain order, to finish healing."

More often than not, the grief process is cyclical. There will be days when your grief seems more manageable, and there will be days when something triggers an old memory and you feel like you are falling apart. You may go through periods when you can talk about the loss without experiencing overwhelming feelings but then fall apart over minor inconveniences. After the death of my father, while I was avoiding grieving his loss, I was also trying to be strong for my mother. One day I was walking through a supermarket, unable to find my mother's favorite snack. I was frustrated, and a store employee noticed me struggling and approached. They asked, "Can I help you find something?" at which point I burst into tears. This woman's small offer of kindness somehow allowed me to begin getting in touch with my grief needs.

Myth: "The pain will ease with time. You will eventually get over it."

Time alone is not sufficient to relieve the pain of grief. Time may allow you to get out from under the weight of the initial grief, but your feelings will remain until you have integrated the loss into your life.

Myth: "You can grieve later; right now you must be strong for others."

When you model your grief for your family members, they will learn that these feelings are acceptable. Your friends and family will benefit from seeing you be vulnerable or seeing your softer side. I have heard many stories from children who came to know their fathers in a kinder and more empathetic manner after seeing them cry.

Myth: "It's best to grieve alone. Do not let others see your weakness. It is rude to be sad, and you shouldn't burden others."

Seeking support and sharing your grief with others affected by the same or similar experiences help many people process and move through their emotions. In addition, sharing your story may inspire someone struggling with their own grief.

Myth: "The pain will go away faster if you ignore it, distract yourself with work, engage in surface-level socializing, or get busy with a new project so you can move on."

Trying to avoid grieving only prolongs the grieving process. This way of coping can develop into other mental health concerns like anxiety, depression, insomnia, and addiction.

Myth: "Grieving for over a year is a sign of weakness." Or: "Grief is a long-term experience that should last more than a year."

Many therapists would say it is common to grieve for about a year over a significant loss in your life, but there is no set duration for the process. Grief does not have a concrete beginning or end. Do not apply a deadline to your grief or your processing of grief.

Myth: "To complete the grieving process, you must move on with your life, get back to work, or begin a new relationship."

You can continue to grieve while you return to life's normal routines. It may be helpful to gradually return to your hobbies, leisure activities, and social activities, but some things may never return to normal. There will be a new normal.

Myth: "Crying is the best way to express your grief. If you don't cry, you're not really grieving."

Many therapists, coaches, and counselors agree that crying can be a good way to express your grief, but it is not the only healthy way. Journaling, creating art, doing a physical activity, and expressing yourself through music and dance can all be ways to release your grief. People experience sadness in many ways. One person may need silence and solace to feel their sorrow, while someone else may need to yell or move their body to physically work out their emotions. Do what gives you relief.

Myth: "Grief is accompanied by depression."

Grief and depression share the standard features of sadness and withdrawal from everyday activities. Feeling depressed may be a symptom of grief. However, in grief, feelings generally come and go in waves; moments of sadness may be interrupted by pleasant memories of happy moments. In depression, on the other hand, the negative mood is pervasive and may not be tied to any specific loss or experience. Although people in both situations can benefit from professional help, resolving depression often requires long-term therapeutic interventions or medical treatment.

Myth: "I know how you feel, because I have experienced a similar loss."

Everyone's experience with grief is unique. There is an endless amount of varying factors that affect one's reaction to a loss.

Introductory Tools for Grieving and Supporting Others in Their Grief

Grieving, accepting your feelings of loss and sadness, and being there for others through their own grieving processes are all skills that need to be practiced and will improve with time. The overall goal is to accept the loss and integrate it into your life in a way that does not conflict with or impede your daily functioning. Perhaps you will even make sense of the loss, turning a painful experience into a source of purpose. For example, if you lose a loved one to a drunk-driving accident, you could become an advocate for safe and sober driving. Through your actions, you can model healthy ways of coping with grief for your close friends and family. Although you cannot do the work for them, you can create a safe atmosphere for them to share their feelings.

Some tools for grieving and supporting others in their grief are listed below:

- Don't take unsolicited advice to heart. If you are given an opinion you did not ask for, I recommend responding with "Thank you for that advice; I will give that some consideration" or "I appreciate that idea; thank you," and then move the conversation in a direction you feel comfortable with.

- Be aware of your self-talk. Do not tell yourself that you *should* feel any particular way or perform any specific activity. It is all right if you do not cry or feel sad. Do not identify your feelings as right or wrong, good or bad.

- Please recognize that you have experienced a loss, and name it. It can be the loss of a job, the loss of a marriage, or the loss of once-in-a-lifetime experiences, like walking your daughter down the aisle.

- Allow yourself to experience your loss and the accompanying feelings of sadness, frustration, anger, pain, and relief when you are ready to, and when you are in a safe environment or with a safe person. Cry, scream, dance, it doesn't matter what you do; just do whatever you must to truly experience your emotions. Do not dismiss or diminish the weight of the loss. Grief is not a competition. There may be times when you are more devastated by the death of a family pet than by other losses that are seemingly greater. No matter what, your feelings are valid.

- You can chip away at your grief if the feelings seem insurmountable. Break the grief into smaller components, or address the loss one aspect at a time. For instance, upon leaving treatment, you may face a realistic threat of divorce in addition to losing your job. You could postpone addressing your deeper feelings about losing your employment and instead put your energy into your marriage. The other issue will still be there, but addressing your losses one by one will help you avoid feeling overwhelmed and aid you in maintaining your sobriety.

- Anticipate and plan for events that may trigger feelings of grief. If you know that you are scheduled to attend the funeral of a coworker's parent, whom you did not know well, consider that this event could trigger your feelings about losing your own parent. Be gentle with yourself when feelings of grief arise, and be grateful for the progress you have made in your grief process.

- Expect the unexpected, especially reignition of feelings of grief. For example, I recently attended the wedding of a friend's child. This friend had moved away many years earlier. I unexpectedly cried throughout the wedding ceremony, not out of happiness for the couple but because it triggered my sadness around being apart from my friend and missing watching their child grow up.

- Accept that grief can trigger many different and unexpected emotions. Overwhelming feelings of sadness and regret may be familiar, but they may be accompanied by anger, relief, gratitude, or peace. You may not expect every feeling you will have, but there are no right or wrong feelings.

- When you are ready, return to your positive, regular habits, hobbies, and interests. You are allowed to seek out and find pleasure. Moments of joy, relief, and laughter are all part of the process.

- Seek direct support from people who care about you and your sobriety. Do not try to be stoic or walk through this pain alone. Do not isolate yourself for a prolonged period. The passage of time is important, but so is help from supportive people.

- When your spouse or other family members are also grieving the same loss, take turns being available and providing care for one another.

- If your family members reach out to their own sponsor, spiritual advisor, or therapist for support, do not feel rejected or resentful that they are seeking support or giving their time and attention to someone else.

- Understand that your family members may react to your mourning with discomfort. They may not be used to seeing you so vulnerable, especially if they consider you a pillar of strength to lean on. Give them time and space to adjust to this version of you, and express your needs to them when appropriate.

- Support yourself emotionally by taking care of yourself physically. Eat, sleep, and remain active so you are less likely to get angry, tired, or restless. If your family members or close friends seem agitated, consider that they may be hungry, tired, or restless as well, and be compassionate and patient with their grieving process.

- Plan for breaks from the pain and pressure by doing something fun, relaxing, or pleasurable, such as taking a nap, getting a massage, or going to the park or beach. Participate in this activity without feeling guilty for finding moments of happiness and joy.

- Allow yourself to revisit your grief from time to time. At this point in your process, you may remember something new that triggers more grief. You can take time to process these emotions, or you can shelve them until another time. Be sure to acknowledge improvements in your ability to manage your emotions.

  In 2017, I lost one of my closest friends. I was emotionally gutted over this loss because it triggered my unresolved grief from previous issues. I sought therapy for help navigating my grief, and I joined a support group that specifically focused on tools for addressing unresolved guilt. Still, every year on my annual backpacking trip, I check in with my grief for all my losses, past and present. I often speak aloud to my loved ones. I usually cry, or I might yell, and then I allow myself to feel blessed for having had these people or experiences in my life. I close these efforts by thinking about what each of my loved ones would say to me now. Each year, I cry less, I become more grateful, and I grow in my ability to accept my losses and process my feelings.

- Don't be afraid to tell people what you are going through while you are actively grieving. Those close to you will likely be less judgmental than you think they will be; but if they do judge you, it may be because they have unresolved grief or are uncomfortable with their own feelings.

- Don't be afraid to ask for help or support. Make a list of things you need assistance with so that when someone asks what they can do for you, you can respond with concrete answers such as "Would you mind picking up the kids from practice?" "Can you please pick up the dry cleaning?" "I would really appreciate your help with the yardwork." "If you could just sit with me in silence, that would be great."

- Remember that sometimes moving backward is still progress. There is no such thing as a worthless effort. Just because you cannot see a measurable difference today doesn't mean your efforts have gone to waste. Sometimes you must step back, rest, and review your progress. Resolution can come in waves of healing; it can move fast; or it can move forward inches at a time.

- Do not make significant decisions or substantially change your life in the first year of sobriety or after significant loss, death, or divorce. You are more vulnerable to reactivity and impulsivity during these periods. Most major decisions can wait.

- Tread lightly when entering into romantic relationships. Once you have done work to heal your past wounds, you will be in a better position to care for someone else romantically and be cared for by them. The rush of endorphins experienced from a new romantic relationship can quickly become a substitute for your previous addiction. Instead, invest your time and energy in building a relationship with yourself. If you are lonely, volunteer your time to others in need, go to meetings, take up a new hobby, or renew the relationships you already have with your family and friends. No one enters a relationship as a perfect person. At this time the best thing to do is to practice patience and wait until you are ready to handle all the emotions that come with romance.

- Remain hopeful. The pain will likely never fully disappear, but it will become more manageable. Don't give up on yourself, your family, or your friends who are grieving. Provide support and encouragement. Be as available as you can to listen to and discuss their feelings when they are ready.

- Consider receiving help from your place of worship, therapist, or community groups offering grief support.

Seek assistance from a mental health professional who specializes in grief and/or depression if you are experiencing a prolonged period of sadness or are not able to return to your everyday activities. If you don't know whether you or a loved one could benefit from seeing a therapist, take the conservative approach and reach out anyway.

Summary

My refusal to grieve the loss of my father was a catalyst for the escalation of my drinking and dysfunctional behaviors. In treatment, I worked through feelings of sadness, regret, and guilt over my father's death. I began to learn how to accept loss and change in my life. I then focused my efforts on building a solid foundation of sobriety. During this time, I tabled my grief until my friend's death triggered it. I had to seek therapeutic help to address my grief over my friend's death, old wounds, and other losses. I know that surrendering to the grieving process has helped me move forward. It kept me from allowing grief in my past to interfere with my present and my future. By allowing myself to be vulnerable and acknowledge and feel my past losses, I can better manage loss and change now. Most importantly, a loss does not threaten my sobriety.

This chapter is not meant to serve as a deep analysis of your grief. Instead, I have offered you some tools to help you focus on building self-awareness. I hope this section on grief provides you with some preliminary steps for facing loss and preventing suffering from interfering with your long-term efforts to rebuild your relationships and maintain your recovery.

Experiencing loss and grief is inevitable. When we suffer a loss, grieving is the process that enables us to move on with our lives. It does not have a well-defined beginning, middle, or end. You may feel like you have come to terms with your losses, only to have grief rear its ugly head at an unplanned time. Although experiencing grief and walking through the grieving process can be painful and triggering, it does not have to interfere with your relationships or daily functioning. The process will allow you to release much of the pain surrounding your loss. It may close a wound cleanly without allowing it to become infected and cause long-term scarring.

I will close with two of my favorite quotes about grieving. The first is from Dr. Phil: "The antidote to pain and grieving is people and companionship." The second is from Joel Osteen: "Grieve hard now so that a season of grieving does not become a lifetime of grieving."

12

Moving Forward from Here

When I began doing researching for and writing this book, my relationship with one of my children was still fragile. Even after many years of sobriety, our relationship was nowhere near where I wished it could be. My feelings about this affected my self-confidence as a social worker, a recovering alcoholic, and an author. I felt that because this relationship was not as good as I would have liked it to be, I might not be in a position to help other addicts in recovery or their close friends and families. I share these thoughts because I want to point out that despite my education, experience, and efforts, I could not create the change in my parent-child relationship that I wanted to see within the timeline I had imagined. For me, it has taken patience, persistence, and prayer.

These situations can be perplexing, but you must continue to do the work and leave the results to your higher power. Individuals and relationships evolve at their own pace, and many factors can complicate the process, accelerate the pace, or slow it down, including age, maturity, and life experiences. Some relationships need more time, distance, healthy boundaries, and new experiences that create positive memories. My relationship with the child I mentioned above improved as I wrote and edited this book, and I am happy to say that I have beautiful relationships with all my children today.

Relationships can also become stagnant if you take them for granted. You must give your relationships time and attention to encourage them to grow and improve. Relationships often involve people who come with different experiences and challenges that affect how they relate, even when they are in the same family or have a close friendship. With children, they grow, change, and mature into adults. If you are a parent, your relationship with your child must also change. Similarly, our siblings will marry and have their own families, our parents will age and become dependent upon us, and our close friends may move away. Family roles, friendships, and romantic relationships all change and evolve, so we all must be prepared to adapt.

There is no such thing as a fully healed or perfect relationship, so wounds may reopen occasionally. Difficult life events and challenges will occur. These challenges can enable a relationship to grow, or they can cause further damage, especially if there is unaddressed grief or trauma. There may be differing levels of sensitivity in your relationships, so you should be aware of your loved ones' wounds or tender spots.

Using the Tools, Asking for Help, and Practicing Humility

Addiction is a complicated disease; repairing your relationships is equally complex. There is no one specific method for improving your relationships with your family and close friends. This book has ideas and tools to assist you in rebuilding these relationships, but simply being aware of these tools is not enough. You must practice using the tools to determine what works best for you and your loved ones.

This principle was illustrated recently when I had to assemble a desk I'd bought from a big-box store. The desk came with directions and all the materials required to build it. But because I can be impatient and often rely on my experiences or how I have always done things in the past, I began to assemble the desk without paying close attention to the directions provided. I made a couple of mistakes along the way, and I had to disassemble some parts of the desk a couple of times. To correct my mistakes, I referred to the directions and started over. I ultimately got the desk assembled, but I wasted a lot of time by ignoring the directions. I also got frustrated with myself and the desk. Ultimately, I learned a valuable lesson about using information and resources for the next time I need to assemble a piece of furniture, or the next time I attempt anything new or challenging.

One of the traits I've had to overcome is my reluctance to ask for help. It is a stubborn character trait buried deep in my subconscious. I have known this about myself all my life, and I've even considered it a strength at various points. I thought that handling everything independently made me wise, and I thought people would perceive me as weak if I asked for help or admitted that I didn't know how to do something. In reality, many problems are solved more efficiently and quickly by a team rather than an individual. Most recovery programs are based on maintaining sobriety with community help. While it is admirable to be self-reliant, it is also commendable to be a consistent and reliable member of a community, family, or friendship.

Keep It Simple, and Avoid Making Significant Decisions and Changes

I feel so strongly about this point that it bears repeating. Adapting to sobriety and working on your recovery are big enough hurdles, so why add to your burdens by making significant changes like moving, selling a home, getting divorced, or entering a new relationship? Although sometimes significant changes cannot be postponed, most twelve-step programs recommend that you do not make any major changes in your life for the first year of sobriety. This applies to your relationships as well. If possible, give your current relationships time to heal, and allow your family members time to catch up with you in their healing or recovery process. Do not begin new romantic relationships, even if your current significant other has made it clear that they are not interested in repairing their relationship with you. Don't try to fill the void in your heart with a new relationship. Instead, take time to understand yourself. Take time to repair or build your relationships with your children, close friends, and family members. You have likely been physically or emotionally distant for a while, so show you care about them with your presence, attention, and actions.

Recovering vs. Recovered

There is a bit of controversy about whether one should describe their sobriety as "recovering" or "recovered." There is also a question about whether a person can recover from addiction to one substance while using another mood-altering substance they may not have been addicted to. I would be lying if I said I was comfortable with any of my clients or sponsees using any mood-altering substances that weren't prescribed by a doctor when they are trying to rebuild their relationships with their friends and family. However, I am still open to learning more about addiction's physical and physiological effects on the body and brain. There has been a lot of research on various treatments for trauma, such as MDMA, psychedelics (including microdosing), and ketamine. Under the supervision of a professional, these modes of treatment may be effective in addressing trauma as well as addiction. More information on these treatments is being published all the time. As for the semantics of *recovering* versus *recovered*, I take no side. I believe that I am still recovering from my substance use disorder and that it is in my best interest to continue working within a program of recovery to ensure my mental and physical health. I propose that the answer to this question is found in each of the hearts and minds of every person who has been touched by addiction.

Maintenance vs. Stagnation

Steps ten, eleven, and twelve of twelve-step programs address the ongoing tools recommended for continued sobriety and recovery.[1] These programs encourage you to continue to examine your actions, address and correct any harm done, expand your spiritual understanding, build a relationship with your higher power, and help others when possible.

Step 10: "Continue to take personal inventory, and when we were wrong, promptly admit it."

This step encourages you to continue to build on your ability to be humble, practice asking for help, apologize when you have made a mistake, and correct injustices you have committed. This includes taking inventory of how you talk to and treat yourself. Are you being kind and understanding? Do you forgive yourself for the mistakes you have made and continue to make? Are you checking to see if you are HALT (hungry, angry, lonely, or tired)? What are you doing to take care of yourself?

The second part of this step encourages you to make amends or apologize as quickly as possible when you make a mistake. The weight or gravity of a problem tends to grow when ignored or avoided. Resentments are less likely to build when you have taken accountability for your actions and words.

Step 11: "Sought through prayer and meditation to improve our conscious contact with God as we understood Him, praying only for knowledge of His will for us and the power to carry that out."

Take time through prayer or meditation to improve your relationship with your higher power or expand your spiritual understanding. Seek out knowledge of the greater good, and gather the strength to implement the lessons you learn. This requires you to continue building self-awareness, practicing humility, and releasing excessive pride and arrogance. You must remain willing to admit that you cannot control or manage everything in your life by yourself and that there are some things you cannot control.

Step 12: "Having had a spiritual awakening as the result of these Steps, we tried to carry this message to alcoholics and to practice these principles in all our affairs."

I believe there is no better way to rebuild self-esteem and fight depression than to volunteer some of your time and energy to help others. This does not mean neglecting yourself or taking time away from your friends and family. Remember that many of your acts of service can benefit your family members and close friends. Balancing your service work, social obligations, personal needs, and family needs is essential.

Beware of the Self-Fulfilling Prophecy

You will find what you look for, so examine your motives. You can always find enablers or people who will tell you what you want to hear. If you are looking for someone to support your desire to blame others and stay in victimhood, you can find them. If you don't take any accountability or exercise any agency around your addiction, you will remain in the same cycle of behaviors that keep you stuck and unproductive. However, if you take the time and energy to surround yourself with people who are willing to tell you the truth, challenge you, and help you overcome the obstacles in front of you, you will grow stronger, improve your chances of success, and reduce the time it takes to get there.

Our beliefs and self-talk about ourselves and our circumstances also influence the outcomes of our efforts. Setting the stage daily with a positive image of your future is essential. Begin with gratitude and create a self-fulfilling prophecy of the good that your day may bring. Instead of starting your day thinking "I wonder what problems will arise today," replace that thought with "I wonder what opportunities lie ahead." Look for the good in each day. What you focus your attention on will grow.

Setbacks

I once worked for a woman who rarely used the term *failure*. Instead, she would describe our mistakes as opportunities for change or growth. She identified problem areas and collaborated with her staff to resolve conflicts and overcome issues. This attitude enabled our team to approach her for help without fear. You are going to make mistakes, and some efforts will not prove to be fruitful. You will likely repeat the same mistakes until you have learned the deeper lesson behind them. Setbacks are inevitable, but the key is to maintain a positive attitude so that when an effort fails to garner the desired response, you do not have to see it as a failure; instead, you have ruled out one way of doing something that did not work for you.

Don't Give Up

Remember that not all progress can be measured or viewed. No matter how well you know someone, you cannot read their mind. There may be changes going on within them that will only emerge after a period of time. Your loved ones may need to see that you are abiding by the boundaries they, or the courts, have established. Occasionally, you may need to reduce your efforts to contact or connect with them. During this time, ensure that when you are in contact with your family or close friends, the time spent is high quality and productive.

In your free time, away from them, you can redirect your efforts toward your own self-improvement goals. Recognize the areas where you can see improvement or personal growth.

Maintain a Balance of Giving and Receiving

In early recovery, I had difficulty accepting praise and help from others. It is in my nature to be a giver, and asking for help is not easy for me. It is far easier for me to focus on helping others rather than myself. I had to learn how to accept compliments and positive feedback. This was an important step that enabled me to seek help from others. Allowing yourself to acknowledge your growth better enables you to release some of the guilt and shame about your actions and behaviors during active addiction.

On the other hand, if you have been a taker in the past, you may need to get into the habit of providing service to others. Start by performing random acts of kindness for others, praising the hard work of your peers, and being proud of someone else's success. Doing this casually will make it easier to give back to your family and close friends.

Questions for Future Growth When You Reach a Plateau

I do not agree with the statement "If you aren't moving forward, you are moving backward," which you occasionally hear at twelve-step meetings. I think periods of rest and introspection are essential parts of recovery. Here are some valuable questions to ask yourself during these times of reflection:

What is my relationship with a higher power, spirituality, or God as I understand them?

Do I trust my higher power? Do I believe that they have my best interest in mind? Do I think that good can come out of a bad situation? What lessons am I being offered the opportunity to learn? What would my higher power want me to do in this situation? What struggle have I not turned over to my higher power? What situation, person, or thing am I still trying to control? Can I let go of it, knowing that it is in the hands of my higher power?

Am I living in the present?

The following questions are excellent tools to keep you focused on the present rather than being caught up in the past or worried about the future:

- Am I putting my focus and intention on today?
- Have I let go of the past and stopped letting worry about the future distract me from enjoying the present?
- What thoughts or past experiences keep me from enjoying the present?
- Do I have regrets or resentments that need to be addressed?
- Am I refighting a battle I have previously resolved?
- Can I separate new challenges from experiences in the past?
- Am I projecting old wounds onto a current situation? Am I letting the past dictate my thoughts, feelings, or actions right now?
- Am I predicting the future, catastrophizing, or worrying about something that has not happened yet?
- Am I assuming the worst-case scenarios will come true instead of focusing on positive results that may occur?
- Should I enjoy the present moment more?

Am I making time for rest?

Do I recognize that rest is essential to healthy daily functioning? I ask myself this to ensure I have taken time to see the peace and joy in my life. I use it to remind myself that I cannot create without recreating. As a working mother, I can always find something that was left unfinished or could have been done better, whether it's the laundry, a child's homework, unpaid bills, or communication with extended family and friends. During active addiction, I relied on a glass of wine or a shot of vodka to help me push through my life's complex schedule. Multiple alcoholic drinks alleviated my desire to stay on that productivity train at all. It took practice to allow myself a rest period without feeling guilty for not having finished all my tasks and projects. We must learn to prioritize rest and see the benefit of incorporating relaxation into each day.

Do I recognize that there are some things I have yet to learn?

There are things I don't know, as well as things I don't know I don't know. Since many of us grew up in dysfunctional families, our idea of "normal" behavior may still be unhealthy. For example, my friend's mother once said that the yelling, screaming, and controlling behavior displayed by her ex-husband was not that bad, because he had never beaten her. She had normalized his verbal and emotional abuse because it was less severe than what she had witnessed between her parents. Take time to acknowledge, reinforce, and share the new coping strategies and healthier behaviors you are learning in your recovery with your circle.

I want to strengthen the earlier point that sometimes we see dysfunctional behaviors as normal until we know that they are *generational patterns of dysfunction* passed down to us. We, in turn, can pass them down to our children, friends, and families if we do not address and change them. Here are some affirmations to help you make that change:

- I cannot give what I do not know. So, I will learn to love and appreciate myself. I will work on building my self-confidence and self-worth.

- I can only teach you what I know. So, I will learn how to resolve conflicts fairly.

- I cannot guide you where I have not been. So, I will adopt healthy coping mechanisms. I will learn how to live a life without relying on substances or behaviors to numb the pain.

Once you have recognized and broken these cycles, reinforce your new behaviors by teaching them to your peers, community, family, or friends. You can turn a painful experience into a good one and release the guilt and shame you feel over your past actions.

Remember that you may still have residual effects from the alcohol, drug use, or detox process, which may impair your ability to think situations through clearly. If you're not sure what to do in a given situation, the first step is to take a moment to slow down and breathe. Then answer one or more of these questions before taking any action:

- Does this activity, action, or thought support me or hurt me?
- Are these actions aligned with my short- and long-term goals?
- What difference will this decision make in ten minutes, ten months, and ten years?
- What other options do I have?

Play the tape out: What would happen if . . .

As we discussed earlier, playing the tape out is when you take a moment to consider the chain reaction of cause and effect that would ensue if you pursue a given course of action. What are the best-case and worst-case scenarios? The most commonly heard example of this is: what would happen if I just had one drink?

What is my motivation?

What do you hope to gain from this thought or action? I like this question because I have fallen back on it many times when I am trying to decide whether to proceed with an option. I ask myself, "What is my intention?" Is it selfish? "What do you hope to gain from this action?" Is it power? Establishing a boundary? Making a point? Revenge? For example, imagine saying no to your ex-wife when she asks you to switch your visitation times for the upcoming weekend so she can go on a trip with her friends. Is your motivation for saying no reasonable? Have you already asked for time off from your job that you cannot reschedule? Or are you trying to make it difficult for your ex to go away with her friends for the weekend?

Not all of us have the opportunity or time to examine all our issues in depth, so in the short term, ask yourself: How healthy are these thoughts? Would I say these things to my child or best friend? Am I being overly harsh on myself? Or are these thoughts or actions getting in the way of my happiness, growth, or serenity?

The following three questions are designed to help you retain and use the new information you are learning and incorporate it into healthy daily habits:

How can I use this information, idea, or activity?

Take time to think about how you could use this new information. Reflect on how this tool may have helped you avoid conflict in the past, and imagine how this information can help you in the future. Recently I attended a speaker meeting, and I was charmed and intrigued by the speaker's story. She shared how she set healthy boundaries with a family member. One helpful tool I learned from her was to stop trying to defend or explain why you have said no to a request for time or a favor. All you have to say is "No, I can't." This keeps you from overexplaining and providing information that can be used to fuel a request on the other person's part. For example, if a coworker asks you to switch shifts with them for a time that is not convenient for you, instead of giving them a lengthy excuse or explanation, you could respond with, "I am sorry; I am not available to do that." This statement limits the amount of negotiation or effort the other person can make to try to persuade you to take their shift.

When will I use this?

Think of how you can use this information in daily practice. Specify with whom and when you will use it, and write it down so you can review it later. Most of us encounter many good ideas in sources as diverse as meetings, news outlets, and social media. Still, research demonstrates people will only remember up to 50 percent of the information they consume within an hour, and they will forget 80 percent within a month unless they try to immediately apply it to their lives. Thinking about how you will use this information in your daily life will significantly increase your odds of retaining useful tools you learn in recovery.

How can I use this to help others?

One of the best ways to retain information is to teach or share on a topic or subject you have recently learned about. By sharing your knowledge with others, you are reinforcing it in your mind. When I am preparing to give a lecture, conference presentation, or workshop, I try to use multiple resources to demonstrate the information I am presenting. When I give a class or workshop on a particular topic, I use visual aids and handouts to illustrate my points. In addition, I present each specific topic at least three times during the lecture. I begin by telling my audience what I hope their takeaway is, and then I present the information with an example or exercise that involves audience participation. I usually close my presentation by restating my significant points and asking the participants if they have any questions. I also ask the audience to provide examples of how they might use the information in their personal or professional lives.

These last questions are designed to instill a sense of pride in your accomplishments and to inspire hope that you will be able to manage any challenges in your future.

What obstacles have I overcome?

Take time to make a list of all the challenges you have worked through. Consider the times you felt anxious but took action and achieved positive results. These do not have to be enormous challenges; they can be as simple as attending your first twelve-step meeting or saying, "Hello, my name is _____, and I am an alcoholic" for the first time in a group support meeting. After acknowledging these accomplishments, take a moment to meditate on how far you have come.

What would I do if I were not afraid? What thing have I never tried because of fear of failure? What is stopping me from attempting it now?

Now that you have considered everything you have overcome and accomplished, take a moment to make a list of new experiences you would like to have, big and small. These can range from trying a dish you saw on a cooking show to flying in a hot-air balloon. Reflect on the first few (small) steps you can take to move you closer to this goal or activity.

What's next?

No one expects you to know, create, or achieve your life's purpose in the first year of your recovery, but can you begin to look at the bigger picture? Are you on your way to understanding what your purpose is? Consider what good you can contribute to others based on your strengths, skills, and experiences. Developing a sense of purpose can lead to overall satisfaction and general contentment. You can start by establishing what your "why," or your motivation, is. Why do you get up in the morning? Why do you go to work? Why are you attending meetings? What are the most important things to you? Then take time to recognize your natural talents and strengths, and look for new ways to use them for the greater good. As you continue exploring, healing, and building your self-esteem, you can expand upon these skills and create a meaningful life purpose.

Summary: A Message of Hope

Creating change, healing, and attaining success are not about the degrees you have, the initials after your name, or where you work. The most important tools are universally available. Hope, willingness, and honesty combined with a sincere desire to repair relationships are the foundational building blocks of relationship repair.

AFTERWORD

A Note from the Author's Children

Katie's story

At the worst of it, I was my mom's toughest critic. At the time of my mom's active addiction, as well as during her early recovery, my siblings and I were old enough to see and remember what life had been like before. The beautiful, near-perfect childhood we once had shattered, and we, too, were lost and broken.

All I wanted during this time was stability and guidance. I had reached a point in college when I needed to decide what to do, which path to take, and where to go next. My younger brothers were navigating graduating high school and entering high school. My older brother was settling into a new city. We were all at points in our lives when we could've benefited from a stable family. Instead, we had to mourn the stability we had, and still wanted, and navigate these life changes differently. We had to figure out how to live differently. Even thinking back to those times now, I feel sick to my stomach. But I'm proud that I made it. My brothers became *my everything*, and we leaned on each other. My mom will recall it as me stepping in as a mother figure, but in my memory, I leaned on them more than they leaned on me.

Running parallel to us trying to create our stability was my mom working the steps and staying sober; she, too, was broken. She also needed support. She wanted us to take her back in with open arms, but the support she required couldn't come from us. We had to put our own oxygen masks on first. We were still broken, even if she had jumped fully back in, doing everything exceptionally well. And in order not to hurt so much if it happened again, I kept my emotional walls with my mom up. Looking back, we were both fighting for our relationship, but we were both, at the beginning, focused on ourselves and our own pain instead of on each other. Most importantly, my mom didn't give up during that time. She stayed consistent; consistent in her daily effort to stay sober and to continue trying.

I am in awe of how hard my mom works, how much research she does, how dedicated she stays to continued learning and growth, how she prioritizes mental health, how amazing a mom she is, and how sweet a grandma. My mom has gone above and beyond. She's my role model and best friend. And I hope one day I'll have the opportunity to be as good of a mom as she is.

Matthew's Story

Relief. Confusion. Sadness. Happiness. Anger. These were some of the feelings I felt the day my mom left for rehab when I was a high school student. I never knew anyone whose parents went to rehab. "These things don't happen to families like ours"—a misinformed notion I had growing up in a small, suburban, Christian bubble. A million and a half thoughts raced through my head, but I wanted my old mom back above all else. This day began a long, long journey with many ups and downs. I thought it would be a couple of weeks, but it turned into almost a year of my mom being out of the house. When my mom returned, our relationship could almost be compared to a hospital patient in the ICU. While I held hope that things would get better, I worried that the damage would be too much or that things would never be as they were when I was young.

I saw her relationship with my siblings and dad go in different directions at different speeds. Each of my siblings has their own stories and experiences with my mom. We were all in different stages of life and at different maturity levels when my mom was in active addiction, so similarly, we took different amounts of time to redevelop our relationships with my mom. Although our relationship was awkward at first, what I could see from my mom was that she still loved me and my siblings and was putting so much effort into her recovery. She wanted to repair the damage she had caused. It was only fair that I put effort into our relationship too.

I think my three siblings and I can all agree that over the last eleven-plus years of her recovery, there have been a lot of ups and downs. There have been tears, heart-to-hearts, and discoveries of trauma that we didn't know. And also, so many more good memories that we have made. We have been lucky enough to experience many life events (weddings, graduations, grandkids, etc.) and vacations with our mom. But above all else, the one thing that remains constant throughout this entire journey is my mom's unwavering love and dedication to being the most loving and sober mom she can be. So, while my mom may not be the exact "old mom" I had as a young child, the one I had wished for during her addiction, she has become an even better mom and a better representation of how hard work and determination to be sober can pay off to win back your family.

A Note from All Four Children

This book has meant so much to our mom and us children. We are privileged to be witnesses to its creation. Seeing our mom's dream of helping others through the writing of this book play out right in front of us firsthand has been inspiring. We can only hope it will help a family or child in the same situation that we were in. Looking back, we wish we could have heard the perspective of someone with a similar situation to give us the hope that things would get better.

Above all else, we are so proud of our mom and her sobriety, hiking journey, love of life, and everything she has accomplished in the past eleven-plus years. Without her dedication to sobriety, this wouldn't be possible.

We sincerely hope this book can give hope to other families that things can get better. We have seen our mom create a vision and fulfill this dream. A dream that also took a lot of hard work. It has brought reality to the belief that dreams can be achieved with time and effort. Our mom is our role model, and we are so excited for her hard work to be shared with you. We hope it helps both those in recovery from mental health struggles as well as their loved ones. But most importantly, we hope that it gives you hope.

The trust came back with time, healing, learning, and our mom's consistent effort. And our relationship is better now than ever. Those days of struggle, which were years of struggle, now feel like a blip in time.

—Dennis, Katie, Matthew, and Michael

NOTES

Chapter 1: Introduction: I'm Sober, but My Family Is Destroyed. Now What?

1 Maslow, A. H. 1943. "A Theory of Human Motivation." *Psychological Review* 50: 370–96.

Chapter 2: The Disease Concept of Addiction

1 Samorini, G. 1992. "The Oldest Representations of Hallucinogenic Mushrooms in the World." *Integration* 2/3: 69–78. https://samorini.it/doc1/sam/sah_int.htm.

2 Britannica, s.v. "Mead," last updated May 20, 2024, https://www.britannica.com/topic/mead.

3 McGovern, P., J. Mindia, S. Batiuk, and D. Lordkipanidze. 2017. "Early Neolithic Wine of Georgia in the South Caucasus." *Proceedings of the National Academy of Sciences of the United States of America* 114, no. 48: E10309–E10318. doi.org/10.1073/pnas.1714728114.

4 Oxford Classical Dictionary, s.v. "alcoholism, Roman," by O'Brien, J. M., and B. Rickenbacker, March 7, 2016, https://oxfordre.com/classics/display/10.1093/acrefore/9780199381135.001.0001/acrefore-9780199381135-e-7331.

5 Mills, J., and P. Barton, eds. 2007. *Drugs and Empires: Essays in Modern Imperialism and Intoxication 1500–1930.* London: Palgrave Macmillan.

6 Cutler, A. 2007. "The Ashtray of History." *The Atlantic*, January. https://www.theatlantic.com/magazine/archive/2007/01/the-ashtray-of-history/305532/.

7 Winterson, J. 2019. "Vintage Wisdom: Jeanette Winterson on Wine." *The Guardian*, February 17. https://www.theguardian.com/food/2019/feb/17/jeanette-winterson-wine-lover-cellar-secrets.

8 *Britannica*, s.v. "Prohibition," last updated April 10, 2024, https://www.britannica.com/event/Prohibition-United-States-history-1920-1933.

9 *Britannica*, s.v. "War on Drugs," last updated May 27, 2024, https://www.britannica.com/topic/war-on-drugs.

10 Mann, B. 2021. "After 50 Years of the War on Drugs, 'What Good Is It Doing for Us?'" NPR, June 17. https://www.npr.org/2021/06/17/1006495476/after-50-years-of-the-war-on-drugs-what-good-is-it-doing-for-us.

11 Katcher, B. S. 1993. "Benjamin Rush's Educational Campaign against Hard Drinking." *American Journal of Public Health* 83, no. 2: 273–81. https://www.ncbi.nlm.nih.gov/pmc /articles/PMC1694575/.

12 *Alcoholics Anonymous Big Book.* 2002. 4th ed. New York: Alcoholics Anonymous World Services.

13 "Is Addiction Really a Disease?" 2020. IU Health. https://iuhealth.org/thrive/is -addiction-really-a-disease.

14 Jellinek, E. M. 2010. *The Disease Concept of Alcoholism.* Eastford, CT: Martino Fine Books.

15 "What Is the Definition of Addiction?" 2019. American Society of Addiction Medicine. https://www.asam.org/quality-care/definition-of-addiction.

16 "Understanding Alcohol Use Disorder." n.d. National Institute on Alcohol Abuse and Alcoholism. Accessed April 1, 2024. https://www.niaaa.nih.gov/publications/brochures -and-fact-sheets/understanding-alcohol-use-disorder.

17 American Psychiatric Association. 2022. *Diagnostic and Statistical Manual of Mental Disorders, Fifth Edition, Text Revision (DSM-5-TR).* Washington, DC: American Psychiatric Association Publishing.

18 Coyhis, D. and W. White. 2002. "Addiction and Recovery in Native America: Lost History, Enduring Lessons." *Counselor* 3, no. 5: 16–20. https://www.chestnut.org/resources /c046f0b2-ef0f-471d-b48e-13fe70d620cc/2002AddictionRecoveryinNativeAmerica.pdf.

19 Maxwell, M. A. n.d. "The Washingtonian Movement (Maxwell)." Silkworth.net. Accessed March 31, 2024. https://silkworth.net/wp-content/uploads/2020/12 /TheWashingtonianMovement_ReffrenceAndResource.pdf.

20 White, W. L. 2002. "Addiction Treatment in the United States: Early Pioneers and Institutions." *Addiction* 97, no. 9: 1087–92.

21 Anonymous. 1939. "Medicine: Keeley Cure." *Time*, September 25. https://time.com /archive/6761292/medicine-keeley-cure/.

22 "200 Years of Illinois: Home of the Keeley Cure - Illinois Press Blog." 2016. University of Illinois Press, June 10. https://www.press.uillinois.edu/wordpress/200-years-of -illinois-home-of-the-keeley-cure/.

23 Markel, H. 2010. "An Alcoholic's Savior: God, Belladonna or Both?" *The New York Times*, April 19.

24 McCarthy, K. (1984) "Psychotherapy and Religion: The Emmanuel Movement." *Journal of Religion and Health* 23, no. 2: 92–105.

25 *Alcoholics Anonymous*, 27.

26 Lean, G. 1985. *Frank Buchman: A Life.* London: Constable, 151–52.

27 Hermann, N., and E. Gorman. 1996. "Lifetime Alcohol Abuse in Institutionalized World War II Veterans." *American Journal of Geriatric Psychiatry* 4 (1): 39–45.

28 "Antabuse (Disulfiram) Treatment for Alcohol Use Disorder." 2023. Verywell Mind. https://www.verywellmind.com/antabuse-treatment-for-alcoholism-67506.

29 Kearney, T. E., and I. B. Anderson. 2000. "Use of Methadone." *Western Journal of Medicine* 172 (1): 43–46.

30 Payte, J. T. 1991. "A Brief History of Methadone in the Treatment of Opioid Dependence: A Personal Perspective." *Journal of Psychoactive Drugs* 23, no. 2: 103–7.

31 "Naloxone DrugFacts." 2022. National Institute on Drug Abuse. https://nida.nih.gov/publications/drugfacts/naloxone.

32 Aboujaoude, E., and W. O. Salame. 2016. "Naltrexone: A Pan-Addiction Treatment." *CNS Drugs* 30, no. 8: 719–33.

33 Garbutt, J. C., and A. M. Greenblatt. 2015. "Clinical and Biological Moderators of Response to Naltrexone in Alcohol Dependence: A Systematic Review of the Evidence." *Addiction* 109, no. 8: 1285–86. https://www.ncbi.nlm.nih.gov/pmc/articles/PMC4154559/.

34 "Buprenorphine." Substance Abuse and Mental Health Services Administration. Last updated March 28, 2024. https://www.samhsa.gov/medications-substance-use-disorders/medications-counseling-related-conditions/buprenorphine.

35 Fisher, G. L., and N. A. Roget. 2008. *Encyclopedia of Substance Abuse Prevention, Treatment, and Recovery.* Thousand Oaks, CA: Sage Publications.

36 Beronio, K., S. Glied, and R. Frank. 2014. "How the Affordable Care Act and Mental Health Parity and Addiction Equity Act Greatly Expand Coverage of Behavioral Health Care." *Journal of Behavioral Health Services Research* 41: 410–28. https://doi.org/10.1007/s11414-014-9412-0.

37 Congress.gov. 2010. "H.R.3590 - 111th Congress (2009-2010): Patient Protection and Affordable Care Act." March 23. https://www.congress.gov/bill/111th-congress/house-bill/3590.

38 Abraham, A. J., C. M. Andrews, C. M. Grogan, T. D'Aunno, K. N. Humphreys, H. A. Pollack, and P. D. Friedman. 2017. "The Affordable Care Act Transformation of Substance Use Disorder Treatment." *American Journal of Public Health* 107, no. 1: 21–32. https://www.ncbi.nlm.nih.gov/pmc/articles/PMC5308192/.

39 "The Neurobiology of Substance Use, Misuse, and Addiction." 2016. In Substance Abuse and Mental Health Services Administration, *Facing Addiction in America: The Surgeon General's Report on Alcohol, Drugs, and Health.* Washington, DC: SAMSHA. https://www.ncbi.nlm.nih.gov/books/NBK424849/.

40 "What Is Post-Acute Withdrawal Syndrome (PAWS)?" 2019. Hazelden Betty Ford. https://www.hazeldenbettyford.org/articles/post-acute-withdrawal-syndrome.

41 Ashton, H. 1991. "Protracted Withdrawal Syndromes from Benzodiazepines." National Library of Medicine. https://pubmed.ncbi.nlm.nih.gov/1675688/.

42 Viswarm, A., and P. Nagarajan. 2018. "Cognitive Functions among Recently Detoxified Patients with Alcohol Dependence and Their Association with Motivational State to Quit." *Indian Journal of Psychiatric Medicine* 40, no. 4: 310–14.

43 Wiginton, K. 2023. "Alcohol Use Disorder: What to Expect When You Quit Drinking." WebMD. https://www.webmd.com/mental-health/addiction/what-to-expect-when -you-quit-drinking.

44 Viswarm and Nagarajan, "Cognitive Functions."

45 Moos, R. H., and B. S. Moos. 2006. "Rates and Predictors of Relapse after Natural and Treated Remission from Alcohol Use Disorders." *Addiction* 101, no. 2: 212–22. https:// pubmed.ncbi.nlm.nih.gov/16445550/.

46 Sinha, R. 2011. "New Findings on Biological Factors Predicting Addiction Relapse Vulnerability." *Current Psychiatry Reports* 13, no. 5: 398–405. https://www.ncbi.nlm.nih.gov /pmc/articles/PMC3674771/.

47 Bergland, C. 2021. "Addiction and Recovery Rewire the Brain in Different Ways." *Psychology Today*. https://www.psychologytoday.com/us/blog/the-athletes-way/202102 /addiction-and-recovery-rewire-the-brain-in-different-ways.

48 Chioma, V. C. 2020. "Heroin Seeking and Extinction from Seeking Activate Matria Metalloproteinases at Synapses on Distinct Subpopulations of Accumbens Cells." *Biological Psychiatry* 89, no. 10: 947–58. https://doi.org/10.1016/j.biopsych.2020.12.004.

49 Goldstein, R. Z., and N. D. Volkow. 2011. "Dysfunction of the Prefrontal Cortex in Addiction: Neuroimaging Findings and Clinical Implications." *Nature Reviews Neuroscience* 12, no. 11: 652–69. doi.org/10.1038/nrn3119.

50 Felton, A. 2022. "Limbic System: What to Know." WebMD. https://www.webmd.com /brain/limbic-system-what-to-know.

51 Rodriguez de Fonseca, F., and M. Navarro. 2009. "Role of the Limbic System in Dependence on Drugs." *Annals of Medicine* 30, no. 4: 397–405. doi.org/10.3109/07853899809029940.

52 "How an Addicted Brain Works." 2022. Yale Medicine. https://www.yalemedicine.org /news/how-an-addicted-brain-works.

53 "Dopamine: What It Is, Function & Symptoms." 2022. Cleveland Clinic. https://my .clevelandclinic.org/health/articles/22581-dopamine.

54 Rissman, E. F., and W. J. Lynch. 2023. "Role of Hormones in Substance Use Disorders." *Neuroendocrinology* 113, no. 11: 1095–96. doi.org/10.1159/000533291.

55 Muller, C. P., and J. R. Homberg. 2015. "The Role of Serotonin in Drug Use and Addiction." *Behavioural Brain Research* 277: 146–92.

56 Pilozzi, A. 2021. "Roles of β-Endorphin in Stress, Behavior, Neuroinflammation, and Brain Energy Metabolism." *International Journal of Molecular Sciences* 22, no. 1: 338.

57 Heshmat, S. 2015. "Can You Be Addicted to Adrenaline?" *Psychology Today*. https://www .psychologytoday.com/us/blog/science-choice/201508/can-you-be-addicted-adrenaline.

58 "Neuroplasticity." n.d. *Psychology Today*. Accessed April 2, 2024. https://www
.psychologytoday.com/us/basics/neuroplasticity.

59 Vazey, E. M., C. R. den Hartog, and D. E. Moorman. 2020. "Central Noradrenergic
Interactions with Alcohol and Regulation of Alcohol-Related Behaviors." *Handbook of
Experimental Pharmacology* 248: 239–60.

60 Fernando Valenzuela, C. 1997. "Alcohol and Neurotransmitter Interactions." *Alcohol
Health and Research World* 21, no. 2: 144–48.

61 Taylor, M. 2022. "Acute Stress Response: Fight, Flight, Freeze, and Fawn." WebMD.
https://www.webmd.com/mental-health/what-does-fight-flight-freeze-fawn-mean.

62 Ressler, K. J. 2015. "Amygdala Activity, Fear, and Anxiety: Modulation by Stress." *Biological Psychiatry* 67, no. 12: 1117–19.

63 Martin, S. 2017. "How Addiction Impacts the Family: 6 Family Roles in a Dysfunctional or
Alcoholic Family." Psych Central. https://psychcentral.com/blog/imperfect/2017/05/how
-addiction-impacts-the-family-6-family-roles-in-a-dysfunctional-or-alcoholic-family.

64 Wretman, C. J. 2016. "Saving Satir: Contemporary Perspectives on the Change Process
Model." *Social Work* 61, no. 1: 61–68. https://doi.org/10.1093/sw/swv056.

65 Black, C. 2020. *It Will Never Happen to Me: Growing Up with Addiction as Youngsters, Adolescents, Adults*. Las Vegas, NV: Central Recovery Press.

66 Woititz, J. G. 1983. *Adult Children of Alcoholics*. Deerfield Beach, FL: Health Communications.

67 "Laundry List." n.d. Adult Children of Alcoholics. Accessed April 2, 2024. https://
adultchildren.org/literature/laundry-list/.

68 Beattie, M. 2022. *Codependent No More: How to Stop Controlling Others and Start Caring for
Yourself (Revised and Updated)*. New York: Spiegel and Grau.

Chapter 3: Assessment and Preparation

1 Luft, J. 1969. *Of Human Interaction*. N.p.: National Press Books.

2 Martin, S. 2017. "How Addiction Impacts the Family: 6 Family Roles in a Dysfunctional
or Alcoholic Family." Psych Central. https://psychcentral.com/blog/imperfect/2017/05
/how-addiction-impacts-the-family-6-family-roles-in-a-dysfunctional-or-alcoholic
-family#Common-Roles-in-Addicted-Families.

Chapter 4: Expectations, Myths, and Mistakes

1 Anderson, J. 2021. "The Effect of Spanking on the Brain." Harvard Graduate School of
Education. https://www.gse.harvard.edu/ideas/usable-knowledge/21/04/effect
-spanking-brain.

2 Van Orden de Assis, K. 2018. "How to Create Space for Your Priorities." Simplicity Rocks.
simplicityrocks.com/.

Chapter 5: New Skills and Tools for Building Relationships

1 Drigas, A. S. 2018. "A New Layered Model on Emotional Intelligence." *Behavioral Sciences* 8, no. 5: 45.

Chapter 6: Making Amends

1 Anonymous. 2001. *Alcoholics Anonymous*. Center City, MN: Hazelden Publishing.

Chapter 7: Getting to Work

1 Yeung, J. W. K., Z. Zhang, and T. Y. Kim. 2017. "Volunteering and Health Benefits in General Adults: Cumulative Effects and Forms." *BMC Public Health* 18, no. 8. doi.org/10.1186/s12889-017-4561-8.

2 Van Orden de Assis, K. 2018. "How to Create Space for Your Priorities." Simplicity Rocks. https://simplicityrocks.com.

Chapter 9: Healing and Acceptance

1 "What Is Post-Acute Withdrawal Syndrome (PAWS)?" 2019. Hazelden Betty Ford. https://www.hazeldenbettyford.org/articles/post-acute-withdrawal-syndrome.

2 Oscar-Berman, M. 2023. "Alcoholism and the Brain: An Overview." *Alcohol Research & Health* 27, no. 2: 125–33. https://www.ncbi.nlm.nih.gov/pmc/articles/PMC6668884/.

3 Heyl, J. C. 2023. "Religious Abuse: Spotting the Signs and How to Cope." Verywell Mind. http://www.verywellmind.com/what-is-religious-abuse-6259926.

Chapter 10: Don't Fight the System

1 *Merriam-Webster*. s.v. "surrender" (tr. v.). Accessed July 12, 2024, https://www.merriam-webster.com/dictionary/surrender.

Chapter 11: Grieving and Letting Go

1 James, J. W., and R. Friedman. 2009. *The Grief Recovery Handbook: The Action Program for Moving Beyond Death, Divorce, and Other Losses*. New York: HarperCollins.

2 Anonymous. 2001. *Alcoholics Anonymous*. Center City, MN: Hazelden Publishing.

Chapter 12: Moving Forward from Here

1 Anonymous. 2001. *Alcoholics Anonymous*. Center City, MN: Hazelden Publishing.

INDEX

ABOUT THE AUTHOR

PHOTO BY KATIE DOWD

Janice V. Johnson Dowd holds a BA from the University of Michigan and an MSSW from the University of Texas at Austin, where she worked as a teaching assistant and research assistant. Her master's thesis was titled "Alcoholism, PTSD, and the Vietnam Veteran." She has worked in employee assistance programs and inpatient and outpatient treatment settings. Dowd has been involved in community outreach, public speaking, and providing clinical services to patients. She has also been active in the twelve-step community in Texas, Alabama, and the Gulf Coast region. She is regularly asked to speak at workshops, conferences, and AA meetings on relapse, family recovery, and making amends. Dowd's work has recently been published in *AA Grapevine*, and she is a regular on podcasts that address addiction and recovery.

ABOUT NORTH ATLANTIC BOOKS

North Atlantic Books (NAB) is an independent, nonprofit publisher committed to a bold exploration of the relationships between mind, body, spirit, and nature. Founded in 1974, NAB aims to nurture a holistic view of the arts, sciences, humanities, and healing. To make a donation or to learn more about our books, authors, events, and newsletter, please visit www.northatlanticbooks.com.